JN044450

Japan's Economic Relations with Africa in a Historical Perspective

: A Study of the Pre-War Japanese Consular Reports

Japan's Economic Relations with Africa in a Historical Perspective

: A Study of the Pre-War Japanese Consular Reports

Katsuhiko Kitagawa

Kansai University Press

Kansai University Press
3-3-35 Yamate-cho, Suita-shi,
Osaka 564-8680, Japan.

First English edition published February 2020
Printed in Japan by Kyowa Printing Co., Ltd., Kyoto, Japan.

ISBN 978-4-87354-712-1 C3030

Published under the regulation of publication grants
for the achievement of research of the Kansai University

Contents

List of Map, Figure and Tables

Acknowledgements

This book has emerged at my narrow academic path, and in it I walked through a wide range of literature, issues and debates. Also this book owes much to many people who suggested me its course. Elements of this book have been presented in seminars and conferences within Japan and overseas countries. Chapter drafts and versions of argument were commented by many scholars. The research was informed by trips to several libraries and archives and conversations with a number of activists, academics, and bureaucrats who gave their generous emotion to me. I am most grateful and appreciative to those who walked this path with me. The deepest gratitude should go to Kansai University which makes it possible to publish this book in accordance with its regulation of Research Result Publication Subsidy.

List of Original Articles

This book is primarily written on the basis of those articles below. However, the contents of them are substantially rewritten and reorganized in order to publish this book.

1988, "A study of Japan's pre-War economic research on Africa: A preliminary Investigation" [Senzenki Nihon no Ahurika Keizai Jijo Chosa no Kenkyu : Sono Yobiteki Kosatsu] (in Japanese), Kansai University of Foreign Studies, *Kenkyu Ronshu*, 48, pp. 171-191.

1989, "A study of economic conditions in Africa in the pre-War period seen through Japanese consular reports : An analysis of 'The journal of commercial reports'". [Senzenki Nihon no Ryoji Hokoku ni mirareru Ahurika Keizai Jijo Chosa no Kenkyu : Gaimusho Tsushokyoku 'Tsusho Isan' o chushin ni site] (in Japanese), Kansai University of Foreign Studies, *Kenkyu Ronshu.* 50, pp. 303-320.

1989, "A study of economic conditions in Africa in the pre-War period seen through consular reports - An analysis of 'official commercial reports'" [Senzenki Nihon no Ryoji Hokoku ni mirareru Ahurika Keizai Jijo Chosa no Kenkyu : Gaimusho Tsuhokyoku 'Tsusho Koho' o chushin ni] (in Japanese), Japan Association for African Studies, *Ahurika Kenkyu (Journal of African Studies)*, 35, pp. 47-63.

1990, "Africa Exhibition : Pre-war Japan's interest in African market" [Ahurika Kokujo Tenrankai : Senzenki Nihon no Ahurika Shijo eno Kanshin] (in Japanese) African Society in Japan, *Gekkan Ahurika (Monthly Africa)*, 36-1, pp. 14-16.

1993, "Japan's trade with West Africa in the inter-war period : a study of Japanese consular reports" [Senzenki Nihon no tai Nishi Ahurika Boeki : Nihon Ryoji Hokoku o chushin ni shite] (in Japanese), *Economic Review of Kansai University*, 42-5, pp. 181-228.

1993, "Japan's economic relations with East Africa" [Nihon to Higashi Ahurika no Keizai Kankei], "Japan and West Africa" [Nihon to Nishi Ahurika] (in Japanese), in Okakura, Takashi and Kitagawa, Katsuhiko, *A history of Japan-Africa Exchange : from the Meiji Era until World War II [Nihon-Ahurika Koryu Shi : Meijiki kara Dainiji Sekai Taisen made]* (in Japanese). Dobunkan, pp. 97-136, 187-209.

1996, "Japan's Trade with South Africa in the Inter-War Depression" [Sekai Kyokoki ni okeru Nihon-Minami Ahurika Tsusho Kankeishi no Ichi Kosatsu] (in Japanese), *Economic Review of Kansai University*, 45-6, pp. 119-147.

1999, "Japanese trade with and business in South Africa in the inter-war period" [Senkanki ni okeru Nihon no Minami Ahurika Boeki to Kigyo Katsudo] (in Japanese) in Sugiyama, Shinya and Grove, Linda eds., *Commercial Network in Modern Asia [Kindai Asia no Ryutsu Netwak]*, Sobunsha, pp. 257-278.

2001, "Japan's Trade with East and South Africa in the Inter-War Period : A Study of Japanese Consular Reports", *Kansai University Review of Economic Studies*. No. 3, pp. 1-41.

2003, "Japanese Perspectives on Independence of African Countries in the Late 1950s and the Early 1960s", Tenri University, *Agora : Journal of International Center for Regional Studies,* No. 1, pp. 31-45.

2004, "Advance of Japanese Manufactured Goods to the Congo Basin in the 1930s" [1930 nendai no Kongo Bonchi ni okeru Nihonhin no Shinshutsu] (in Japanese), *Economic Review of Kansai University*, 54-1, pp. 123-142.

2013, "Retrospective and Prospects for Japanese Policy on Africa : Focusing on the Tokyo International Conference on African Development (TICAD) Process", *Kansai University Review of Economics*, No. 15, March, pp. 1-28.

2014, "The Relationship between Japan and South Africa before World War II", *Kansai University Review of Economics,* No. 16, March, pp. 31-57.

2015, "Japan's Trade with West Africa in the Inter-War Period : A Study of Japanese Consular Reports", *Kansai University Review of Economics,* No. 17, March, pp. 1~28.

2016, "Revision of the Congo Basin Treaty and Japan in the 1930s : Examining the Narratives of Consular Reports", *Economic Review of Kansai University,* 65-4, March, pp. 61-71.

Author Profile

Katsuhiko Kitagawa is Professor Emeritus of Kansai University, and was Professor of Economic History and African Studies. He took his BA and MA at Kansai University and his PhD at the Graduate University for Advanced Studies in Kanagawa. In 1999-2000 he was Academic Visitor at University of Kwa Zulu Natal working on South African economic and social history, and Japan's trade relations with South Africa in the Inter-War Period. He has written and edited several books on social and economic history in Sub-Saharan Africa, the history of the British Empire and contemporary African political economies. He was President of the Japan Society for African Studies (JAAS) 2006-2009 and the Japan Association of Private University Libraries (2009-2011).

At Kansai University he was Dean of the Faculty of Economics (2006-2008), and Dean of University Libraries (2009-2012). He has written and edited many books and articles in both Japanese and English, including *Contemporary African Economies : A Changing Continent under Globalization* (Co-editorship with Takahashi Motoki, Tokyo, African Development Bank, 2016), *History and Culture in Africa* (Co-authorship with Kusamitsu Toshio, Tokyo, Education Promotion Society for Open University, 2013), "Japanese Competition in the Congo Basin in the 1930s", in Latham, A.J.H. and Kawakatsu, Heita (eds), *Intra-Asian Trade and the World Market,* London, Abingdon : Routledge, 2006, "Japan's economic diplomacy in colonial Africa during the inter-war period", Latham, A.J.H. and Kawakatsu, Heita (eds), *Asia and the History of the International Economy : Essays in Memory of Peter Mathias*, London, Routledge, 2018.

Ch 1
Introduction

Africa's economic growth has been faster than the world average since 2000, showing relative buoyancy in a period of economic recession. Groundbreaking events have taken place in the Ethiopian capital Addis Ababa in recent times including the African Union's adoption of its *Agenda 2063*[1] and the Conference on Financing For Development. (AU, 2015) These new developments seem to symbolize what many term "Africa's Time". Turning to Japan, "Slow but for the long term" is the conventional interpretation of Japanese engagement in Africa. However, the inaugural Africa-Japan Business and Investment Forum took place in Addis Ababa in September 2015, and was recognized as a lead-up to TICAD VI[2], which took place in late August 2016 in Nairobi, Kenya. (Versi, 2016)

Today the center of the world economy is moving toward Asia, and this has had a profound effect on Africa. The rise of the East and South Asia in general and China and India in particular is closely connected to recent economic and political developments in Africa. African interest in Asian models and Asian interest in African resources and potential are leading to deeper ties between the two regions and the establishment of reciprocal relations. (Mazrui and Adem, 2013)

So this book is organized to enlarge and deepen the study of Africa-Asia relations by addressing issues that have been mostly neglected in contemporary scholarship. It aims to offer insights in a historical context about the ways in which African and Asian regions and studies engage with each other and explore them from a variety of standpoints and frameworks. (Kitagawa, 2016)

Japan has recently been heavily involved in building a global system of political economy. Japan's official development assistance charter, agreed in 1992 and revised in 2003, has been the basis of Japan's official development assistance policy. In February 2015 Prime Minister Shinzo Abe's cabinet also agreed the "Development Cooperation Charter : For peace, prosperity and a better future for everyone".

It states :

"With respect to Africa, Japan will provide assistance through joint efforts of the public and the private sector through the operation of the Tokyo International Conference on African Development (TICAD) so that Africa's remarkable growth in recent years based on expanding trade, investment and consumption will lead to further development for both Japan and Africa. Japan will take particular note of Africa's initiatives toward regional development and integration at the sub-regional level. Meanwhile, Africa still has countries that are prone to conflict or are burdened with an accumulation of serious development challenges. Bearing this in mind, Japan will continue to actively engage in assistance for peacebuilding and assistance to fragile states from the perspective of human security, providing necessary assistance with a view towards establishing and consolidating peace and stability, and solving serious development challenges in the region." (Cabinet Office, "Cabinet decision on the Development Cooperation Charter ", February 10, 2015)

In order to appropriately bring several areas concerned, including Africa, into Japan's global perspective, it is necessary to indicate the reality of its relations with these areas and the factors that defined its relations in the past. (Kitagawa, 2012)

This book is on Japan's Economic Relations with Africa in a Historical Perspective, based on pre-war Japanese consular reports. (Kitagawa, 1990, 1997, 2003, 2006, 2015) — It focuses on the emergence of the economic relations between Japan and Africa. It investigates how and why these relations developed, and when and where they did. An attempt is made to identify the forms and structures upon which these historical relations were built and the question of whether these relations were characterized by equality/reciprocity or by imperialism/dependency is considered. Until recently, little attention has been paid to the subject of Japanese African relations and, therefore, there are no set ideas or methodological approaches which have been established by academic circles with regard to this topic. (Agbi, 1982 ; Kitagawa, 1988, 1989a, 1989b; Morikawa, 1985) This book consists of a provisional synthesis of research on Japan's relations with Africa based on an extensive examination of pre-war Japanese consular and other investigative reports regarding economic conditions in Africa.

The historical development of relations between Japan and Africa are examined within two frameworks. The first is the growth of the global system of production and exchange, and the second is the internal dynamics of Japanese political economy. The order of discussion in this introduction is as follows: (1) a brief historical survey of Japan and Africa in the international economy between the Wars, (2) a brief explanation of the contents of this book.

1 Japan, Africa and the International Economy between the Wars
The expansion of the Japanese economy into Africa during the inter-war period was fundamentally influenced by the economic situation prevailing within the European spheres of influence on the African continent, by changes in the nature of the international economy, and by changes in the internal political economy of

2

Japan at this time.

In the mid-1880s, the "Partition of Africa" began. This was a product of and the last stage in the "Age of Empire" which resulted from long time rivalries between European Powers (Hobsbawm. 1987; Robinson. 1972) The integration of Sub-Saharan Africa into the global system of production and exchange under the colonial rule of European Powers was the last stage in this world-wide transformation process.

The international economy in the period between 1896 and 1914 was no fixed and static entity. This was a period of expansion but also of instability. On the one hand, there was a substantial increase in world trade and more investment in Africa, and also this period witnessed the construction of colonial economies reaching new heights. (Munro, 1976) On the other hand, the diffusion of industrialization and competition among European industrial powers destabilized the hitherto existing framework of the international economy and it became a multi-centered, instead of a British-centered, system. European scrambles for new colonies contributed significantly to the outbreak of the First World War. After the War, it became evident that the predominant position in the international economy had shifted from Great Britain to the United States, and the distinctively self-sufficient Soviet system emerged along side the capitalist world economy. In the period between the Versailles Conference and the outbreak of World War II, it should be noticed that confidence in capitalism waned and colonialism faced a crisis as Africans created disturbances by resisting colonial rule. (Munro, 1976; Aldcroft, 1987; Adu Boahen, 1987) European imperial powers responded by attempting to protect their colonial markets for themselves and by increasing the exploitation of their colonies by the implementation of a variety of land and labor policies. Many African societies were thus brought to the brink of destruction as they were further incorporated into the exploitative and dualistic structure constructed by European settlers.[3]

The characteristics of the modern African economy became apparent during the colonial period. European powers' rule, the experience of colonization and African people's reactions were in no way universal across the whole of Africa. All the same, the impact of the colonial rule was revolutionary politically, economically and socially. It is very significant that Africa's diverse societies and cultures were organized into the colonizing countries and the scale and organizing principles of the continent's political and economic systems changed rapidly during the colonial era that lasted for only eight decades.

It is in this context that the expansion of the Japanese economy overseas must be seen. This expansion was closely related to the development of Japanese capitalism. From the mid-1850s Japan was forced to link her political economy to the international economy on the basis of unequal treaties forced upon her by European Powers. The predominant ideology of free trade and the principle of comparative advantage in the middle of the nineteenth century seriously affected Japan. When it finally joined the ranks of imperial powers, Japan was a latecomer imperialist. It was not until after the Sino-Japanese and Russo-Japanese Wars that Japan's modernization was sufficient to allow large scale overseas imperial expansion. Japan's failure to grasp the nature of the structural changes underlying both European and non-European imperialism led her to the belated attempt at a Greater East Asia Co-Prosperity Sphere. The enthusiasm with which Japan undertook this eventually led to the destruction of the Japanese Empire in the late 1930s. (Beasley, 1987; Irie, 1966)

From the beginning of the Meiji Era, Japan's domestic policy had been guided by the concept of "Fukoku Kyohei," the need to enhance the wealth of the country and to strengthen the nation's military capacity. This meant that serious attention had to be given to national defense against the neighboring countries, particularly Russia. There was an urgent need to overcome a position of weakness in the international economy by modernizing the national economy. While Japan might logically have been regarded as a latecomer imperial nation along with Russia, her strategic considerations forced her to promote an argument for working with the advanced European imperial powers. Two complementary aspects of the Japanese overseas policy can be identified. One was the formal and strategically inspired policy that was backed by militarists, colonial bureaucrats and chartered companies such as the Manchurian Railway Company which had special interests in Manchuria and thus wanted to limit Russia's southward advance into that region. The other was an informal economic imperial policy promoted by the Ministry of Foreign Affairs, private industrialists and trading companies that aimed to establish favorable trading conditions in China and other overseas areas through an economic alliance with Great Britain, the United States and other countries.[4] (Beasley, 1987; Martin, 1986; Nish, 1986; Nagaoka, 1976; Murakami. 1984; Ono. 1985; 1920 Nendai Kenkyu Kai, 1983; Shakai Keizaishi Gakkai, 1982)

2 Contents of this Book

The order of discussion in this book is as follows. Chapter 2 explains the emergence of the collection and dissemination of overseas commercial information and draws an overview of Japan's pre-war economic reports concerning Africa. Chapter 3 discusses an overview of the development of trade between Japan and Africa in the inter-war period and refers to the opening of shipping lines as a facilitator of advance of Japanese trading into Africa. Chapter 4 and 5 investigates into Japan's trade with South Africa and examines some aspects of relations between Japan and South Africa in the pre-war period. Chapter 6 deals with some issues of Japan's trade with East Africa, Chapter 7 discusses Japan's trade with West Africa, and chapter 8 considers Japan's trade with Central Africa. After discussing pre-war

Japan's economic relations with Africa, Chapter 9 takes look at post-war Japan's interest in newly independent Africa in the late 1950s and early 1960s. Finally in concluding Chapter 10, this book very briefly makes retrospective and prospective for Japan's policy on Africa until the beginning of the twenty-first century.

Notes

1   In June 2014, at their meeting held in Malabo, Equatorial Guinea, the Executive Council, through its Decision EX. CL/821 (XXV) took note of the Report of the Commission on the development of the African Union Agenda 2063, as well as the two Draft documents, one being the comprehensive Technical Document and the other the Popular Version of Agenda 2063, both entitled "African Union Agenda 2063 – The Africa We Want". (*Report of The Commission on the African Union Agenda 2063, Assembly of the Union*, Twenty-Fourth Ordinary Session 30 - 31 January 2015 Addis Ababa, Ethiopia)

2   TICAD stands for "Tokyo International Conference on African Development". It was launched in 1993 to promote high-level policy dialogue between African leaders and development partners. TICAD is led by Japan and co-organized by the UN, UNDP, the World Bank and the African Union. With the inception of TICAD, Japan became the first country to pioneer a pan-African development partner forum. TICAD initiatives include advocating African "ownership" and the international communities "partnership". The first five TICAD meetings were held at five yearly intervals in Japan and from 2016 they will be held every three years, hosted alternately in Africa and Japan. (Kitagawa, 2012 ; Amakasu Raposo, 2014a, 2014b)

3   Colonial governments employed a variety of active economic and political measures to extend their influence over indigenous peoples in Africa. These included taxation, the reapportionment of land, the promotion of mono-culture crop for exports, the importation of manufactured goods, the inducement of investment in mining and plantations by metropolitan capitalists, and the provision of infrastructure. Their economic goal was to build a financial base for the privileged relations of their metropolitan countries with their colonies, and to extend colonial rule beyond the existing boundaries of their political and economic influence. Because of these policies, the autonomy of African societies was seriously undermined and local African economies became highly dependent upon overseas metropolitan economies. Few links were developed between African economies so that little economic integration of dependent colonies was generated. As a result, a great deal of uneven development took place in these indigenous societies. (Munro, 1976)

4   It should be added that both policies were closely connected to each other. Further consideration is necessary on this point.

References

Adu Boahen. A., (1987), *African Perspective on Colonialism,* Johns Hopkins University Press, Baltimore.

Agbi, S.O., (1982), "The Japanese contact with, and knowledge of Africa, 1868-1912", *Journal of Historical Society of Nigeria,* 11 (1), pp. 153-165.

Aldcroft, D.H., (1987), *From Versailles to Wall Street,* 1919-1929, Penguin Books, Harmondsworth.

African Union, (2015), *Agenda 2063 ; The Africa We Want,* Final Edition, African Union Commission.

Barker. T.C., (1981), "Consular reports: A rich but neglected historical source", *Business History,* 23 (4), pp. 265-266.

Beasley, W.G., (1987), *Japanese Imperialism:* 1894-1945, Clarendon Press, Oxford.

Hobsbawm. E.J., (1987), *The Age of Empire, 1875-1914,* Pantheon Books, New York.

Irie, A., (1966), *Nihon no Gaiko: Meiji Ishin kara Gendai made [Japanese Diplomacy : From Meiji*

Restoration to the Present Time] (in Japanese), Chuo Koron, Tokyo.

Kitagawa, K., (1988), "A study of Japan's pre-War economic research on Africa: A preliminary Investigation" (in Japanese). Kansai University of Foreign Studies, *Kenkyu Ronshu,* 48, pp. 171-191.

Kitagawa, K., (1989), "A study of economic conditions in Africa in the pre-War period seen through Japanese consular reports - An analysis of *'The journal of commercial reports'*" (in Japanese), Kansai University of Foreign Studies, *Kenkyu Ronshu,* 50, pp. 303-320.

Kitagawa, K., (1989), "A study of economic conditions in Africa in the pre-War period seen through consular reports - An analysis of *'official commercial reports'*" (in Japanese), Japan Association for African Studies, *Ahurika Kenkyu (Journal of African Studies),* 35, pp. 47-63.

Kitagawa, K. ed., (2016), *Africa and Asia Entanglements in Past and Present : Bridging History and Development Studies,* Asian and African Studies Group, Faculty of Economics, Kansai University.

Kitagawa, K., (1990), "Japan's Economic Relations with Africa between the Wars ; A Study of Japanese Consular Reports", Kyoto University, *African Study Monograph,* Vol. 11, No. 3, pp. 124-141.

Kitagawa, K., (1997), *A Study in the History of Japanese Commercial Relations with South Africa [Nihon-Minami Africa Tsusho Kankeishi],* International Research Centre for Japanese Studies, Monograph Series, No. 13.

Kitagawa, K., (2003), "Japan's Trade with South Africa in the Inter-War Period", in Chris Aden and Katsumi Hirano ed., *Japan and South Africa in a Globalizing World : A Distant Mirror,* Hampshire, Ashgate, pp. 25-44.

Kitagawa, K., (2006), "Japanese Competition in the Congo Basin in the 1930s", in A.J.H. Latham and Heita Kawakatsu eds., *Intra-Asian Trade and the World Market,* London, Routledge, pp. 135-167.

Kitagawa, K., (2013), "Retrospective and Prospective for Japanese Policy on Africa : Focusing on the Tokyo International Conference on African Development (TICAD) Process", *Kansai University Review of Economics,* No. 15, pp. 1-28.

Kitagawa, K., (2015), "Japan's Trade with West Africa in the Inter-War Period : A Study of Japanese Consular Reports", *Kansai University Review of Economics,* No. 17, pp. 1-28.

Martin, B., (1986), "The politics of expansion of the Japanese: Imperialism or Pan-Asiatic mission", in W.J. Mommsen & J. Osterhammel. eds., *Imperialism and After: Continuities and Discontinuities,* George Allen & Unwin, London, pp. 63-82.

Mazrui, Ali and Adem, Sefudein, (2013), *Afrasia :A Tale of Two Continents,* University Press of America.

Morikawa, J., (1985), "The myth and reality of Japan's relations with colonial Africa, 1885-1960", *Journal of African Studies,* 12 (1), pp. 39-46.

Moss. J. & J. Ravenhill, (1985), *Emerging Japanese Economic Influence in Africa: Implications for the United States,* University of California, Berkeley.

Munro, J.F., (1976), *Africa and the International Economy, 1800-1960: An Introduction to the Modern Economic History of Africa South of Sahara,* Dent. London.

Murakami, K., (1984), "Japanese capitalism and the colonies" (in Japanese), in Shakai Keizaishi Gakkai, ed., *Shakai Keizaishigaku no Kadai to Tenbo [Prospects for the Study of Economic and Social History],* Shakai Keizaishi Gakkai, Tokyo, pp. 193-200.

Nagaoka, K., (1976), "Studies of imperialism in Japan" (in Japanese), in Shakai Keizaishi Gakkai ed., *Shakai Keizaishigaku no Kadai to Tenbo [Prospects for the Study of Economic and Social History]* Shakai Keizaishi Gakkai, Tokyo, pp. 145-153.

Nish, I.H., (1986), "Some thoughts of Japanese expansion", In W.J. Mommsen & J. Osterhammel Eds., *Imperialism and After: Continuities and Discontinuities,* George Allen & Unwin, London, pp. 82-89.

Ono, K. ed., (1985), *Senkankino Nihon Teikokushugi [Japanese Imperialism Between the Wars]* (in

Japanese), Sekai Shisosha, Tokyo.

Robinson, R.E., (1972), "Non-European foundations of European imperialism", in R. Owen & B. Sutcliffe eds., *Studies in the Theory of Imperialism*, Longman, London, pp. 117-142

Shakai Keizaishi Gakkai, (1982), *1930 Nendai no Nihon Keizai: Sono Shiteki Bunseki [A Historical Analysis of Japanese Economy in the 1930s]* (in Japanese), Shakai Keizaishi Gakkai, Tokyo.

1920 Nendai Kenkyukai, (1983), *1920 Nendai no Nihon Shihonshugi [Japanese Capitalism in the 1920s]* (in Japanese), 1920 Nendai Kenkyukai, Tokyo.

Ch 2
Japanese Consular Reports and Commercial Information of Africa

It was generally believed in Japan that, in order to compete with European nations, the development of trade was not really an option, but rather, a dire necessity. Being an island nation devoid of adequate natural resources for capitalist development, Japan had to depend heavily on foreign trade to acquire raw materials, fuels and agricultural products which it lacked (Moss & Ravenhill, 1985). Japan's survival as a latecomer imperialist depended upon the development of an institutionalized system for the collection and dissemination of commercial information throughout the country. In order to collect overseas commercial information, the Ministry of Foreign Affairs founded the Consulate System and Consular Reporting System, and also the Ministry of Agriculture and Commerce opened the Overseas Commercial Museums and dispatched Overseas Business Trainees as well.[1]

1 Japanese Consulate and Consular Reporting System

Japanese scholars have come to appreciate the value of consular reports as invaluable historical sources (Tsunoyama, 1979. 1981, 1986; Barker, 1981;Takashima, 1979, 1986). They have been used effectively, for instance, to clarify the information strategy of the so-called "Commercial State of Japan (Tsusho Kokka Nihon)" (Tsunoyama, 1988) Unlike various other kinds of diplomatic documents sent from government establishments abroad, consular reports provided detailed information on a wide variety of commercial topics by agents stationed all over the world who carried out regular investigations. These reports contained the names of local traders and commercial houses, indications of changing prices or demand for various goods, information about changes in consumer tastes, expected crop yields for agricultural products, import and export duties, foreign exchange rates and the like.

Japanese consular reports were printed and made available to merchants and businessmen from 1881 to 1943. The titles of these journals which contained reports changed frequently and difficulties arise when one attempts to assembly a complete series for study. (Table 2-1)

Although only a small number of early reports regarding Africa appeared initially in the *Tsusho Isan [Journal of Commercial Reports]*, it was not until after the First World War that a variety of reports on economic conditions in Africa began to appear. However, these reports were neither sent directly from Africa nor based on field surveys. They came, instead, from various locations in Asia, Europe and North America where the information was gleaned from local newspapers, reports issued by colonial governments, conversations at international conferences of imperial powers and the like.

During World War I, commercial information on the African continent began to be collected by Japan's Honorary Consul at Cape Town in South Africa. The first Japanese consulate had been opened in Cape Town in August, 1918. Another Consulate was then opened at Port Said in December 1919. The Japanese government clearly regarded Egypt and South Africa as Japan's most important trading partners on the African continent. In March 1926 a Consulate General was opened in Alexandria, after which the following were established in this order: a

Table 2-1 Trade Journals included Consular Reports

Title	Period	Publishing House	Frequency
Report of Commerce	1881-1886	Ministry of Foreign Affairs	semiannually
Commercial Reports	1886/12-1889/12	Ministry of Foreign Affairs	every three month
Official Gazette	1890/1-1905/12	Ministry of Foreign Affairs	daily
Journal of Commercial Reports	1894/1-1913/3	Ministry of Foreign Affairs	monthly
Official Commercial Reports	1913/4-1924/12	Keiseisha Publishing Co. (first half) The Imperial Local Administration Society (second half)	twice a week
Daily Overseas Commercial Reports	1925/1-1928/3	The Imperial Local Government Administration	daily
Weekly Overseas Economic Conditions	1928/4-1934/12	Ministry of Foreign Affairs	every Monday
Overseas Economic Conditions	1935/1-1943/10	Ministry of Foreign Affairs	twice a week

Source : Tsunoyama, S. ed., (1986), *A Study of Japanese Consular Reports*, Tokyo, Dobunkan.

Table 2-2 Japanese Diplomatic and Consular Offices in Africa, 1918-1942

Year	Diplomatic and Consular Offices	Trade Organization
August 1918	Consulate in Cape Town	
December 1919	Consulate in Port Said	
March 1926	Consulate General in Alexandria	
October 1927		Trade Correspondent in Mombasa
November 1927	Japanese Commercial Museum in Cairo	
February 1932	Consulate in Mombasa	
December 1933		Trade Correspondent in Nairobi
May 1934		Trade Correspondent in Casablanca
January 1936	Legation in Cairo Legation in Adis Ababa	
December 1936	Legation in Adis Ababa (closed) Legation in Casablanca	
October 1937	Legation in Cape Town	Trade Mediation Center in Alexandria
November 1938		Trade Mediation Center in Casablanca
December 1938		Trade Mediation Center in Nairobi
February 1939		Trade Mediation Center in Lagos
August 1942	Legation in Cairo and Cape Town (closed)	

Source : Nishino, T., 1963, "On Economic Research in Africa Between the Wars (part 1) : an aspect of African Studies in Japan", *African Studies [Ahurika Kenkyu]*, 1-1,

Consulate in Mombasa (1932), a Legation in Cairo (1936), a Consulate in Addis Ababa (1936), a Consulate in Casablanca (1936), and a Legation in Cape Town (1937). This new information-oriented commercial strategy that was based upon local data provided by a network of consular agents was successful in increasing the extent and quality of commercial information sent directly from Africa.[2] (Table 2-2)

The commercial information regarding Africa was sent by overseas business trainees, secretaries of Japanese Embassy, commercial and technical experts dispatched overseas, and by trade correspondents. Trade mediation centers were founded in Mombasa (1927), Nairobi (1933), and Casablanca (1934) to collect

Figure 2-1 Collection and Dissemination of Commercial Information

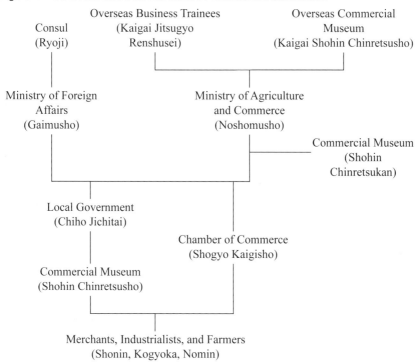

Source : Tsunoyama, (1981).

commercial information and to support the business activities of Japanese traders and industrialists. In addition, various kind of market research provided by the trade missions sent by local governments, private companies and trade associations were useful sources of economic information regarding Africa.

The commercial information which was sent in from around the world, including Africa, was initially collected by the Ministry of Foreign Affairs and the Ministry of Agriculture and Commerce. This information was then disseminated to local governments, chambers of industry and commerce, and local commercial museums by various offices including the Ministry of Foreign Affairs' Bureau of Trade and Commerce (Gaimusho Tsushokyoku) and the Ministry of Commerce's Bureau of Trade (Shomusho Boekikyoku).[3] Relevant information was finally passed on to small and middle-sized industrialists, traders and farmers. To a surprising degree, these offices in charge of handling the information attempted to reply as often as possible to inquiries by people at the lowest level. (Fig. 2-1)

2 Japanese Consular Reports of Africa

As time passed, the number of commercial reports coming in from Japanese consuls residing in various parts of Africa increased steadily and the range of topics grew in number as well. The following brief survey of subjects covered in the series of consular reports mentioned earlier will suffice to show what these reports focused on. (Table 2-1)

In the period of the *Official Commercial Reports* (1913-1924), for example, information regarding form South Africa was sent form the honorary consul, Julius Jeppe, and then Japanese consuls in the Cape Town Consulate, Yaoichi Shimizu and Ban Uehara. The information was on the general trend of foreign trade in South Africa, commercial agents in South Africa, sales conditions of cotton piece goods and general merchandize, port and railway building in South Africa.

In the *Daily Overseas Commercial Reports* (1925-1928), the topics which appeared were the trends in Japanese trade with South Africa, competition of commodity sales among Britain, Germany, and the United States in the South African market and their commercial policy, an investigative reports on the commercial activities of Indian merchants and on the life of European people in South Africa, and reports on cotton cloth imports of South Africa. The Japanese consuls who sent this information were Tadanao Imai and Yoshitaro Kato.

Thereafter in the age of the *Overseas Economic Conditions* (Weekly in1928-1934, twice a month in 1935-1943), reports of South Africa increased substantially on such matters of grave concern as the South African industrial policy, anti-Japanese movement, the British commercial policy to the cotton cloth market, and the sale campaign on Japanese cotton cloth. This information was sent from successive Japanese consuls, deputy consuls or ministers in Cape Town whose names are Tadanao Imai, Chiaki Seki. Takeshige Yamazaki, Tatsuo Hongo, Naojiro Nishikida, Chosaku Mogaki, Nobuo Fujimura, Tomotsune Ota, Kenichiro Zusi, Takeo Kinoshita, Kenkichi Yoshida, and Kenichi Okada.[4] (Kitagawa 1997 : 23-29)

The reports on North Africa initially focused entirely on Egypt, but afterwards, occasional reports on Tunis, Algeria, French and Spanish Morocco were added. Special attention was frequently paid to the number and tonnage of ships passing through the Suez Canal, but there were also reports on prospective cotton crops, on Japanese merchandise such as cotton textiles and knitwear, matches and brushes.

Reports on South Africa focused on the Union of South Africa, Southern and Northern Rhodesia, and South West Africa. The high priority of this area for the Japanese government and businessmen was due to the large scale demand there for Japanese goods. The particularly wide range of reports on the Union of South Africa included reports on foreign trade, on mining, on the market for wool and wool products, on port and harbor facilities, on expected yields of cotton crops, and on the sale of Japanese general merchandise such as cotton goods, medicines, glass bottles, matches, textiles, cement, fishing instruments, etc.

In East Africa the main areas where Japanese goods were sold included Sudan, Ethiopia, Kenya, Uganda, Portuguese East Africa, Zanzibar, Nyasaland and Madagascar. In these areas as well, special attention was paid to cotton crop prospects and the potential East African markets had to absorb Japanese goods.

In contrast, Japanese interest in West African markets was delayed. Nevertheless, there were Japanese who were attracted to the possibility of markets in the Gold Coast, Belgian Congo, Nigeria, and French West Africa. In these markets, Japan's most promising exports were cotton goods.

3 Pre-War Japan's Governmental Investigative Reports Regarding Africa

In the pre-war period government investigation of economic conditions in Africa were focused almost exclusively on Southern and Eastern Africa and in particular on the Union of South Africa and British East Africa (Kenya, Uganda. And Tanganyika).

The earliest economic research report on South Africa was published in 1903 by the Consul in Singapore and a person employed temporarily by the Ministry of Agriculture and Commerce. (Hisamizu & Katsube, 1903) They spent two months in South Africa immediately after the end of the Anglo-Boer War, almost a decade before the establishment of the Union of South Africa. In 1917, report on the foreign trade in South Africa was published by the Department of Agriculture and Commerce (No Shomusho) as one of its industrial and commercial reports (Shoko Isan). (Nunokawa, 1917) This was written by Magoichi Nunokawa who was sent to South Africa in order to investigate the possibility of sending Japanese immigrants to Southern Africa, as well as more Japanese merchandise. His report frankly admitted that the 1913 Immigration Act directed against Asians would undoubtedly hinder the development of increased trade with Japan. In 1927, research report on the Union of South Africa was sent to and published by the Ministry of Foreign Affairs' Bureau of Trade and Commerce (Gaimusho Tsushokyoku). (Imai, 1927) This was intended to provide commercial information regarding South Africa to traders and industrialists who wished to develop ties with counterparts in South Africa.

The earliest report on the economic conditions in Eastern Africa was written and published by the Consul at Cape Town in 1924. (Imai, 1924) It surveyed major industries and the nature of trade in British East Africa, and reported that there was plenty of potential for increasing exports of Japanese cloth to East Africa but that there were also some difficulties due to the financial and credit systems of Indian merchants. (Imai, 1924) In 1927, the Japanese government wanted to encourage the development of trade with East Africa and sent an investigative commission headed by Ujiro Oyama. The Oyama team conducted research in Kenya, Uganda,

Tanganyika, Zanzibar, Madagascar, Abysinnia and Portuguese East Africa from September 1927 to February 1928. Their three volume reports were published by the Ministry of Foreign Affairs' Bureau of Trade and Commerce. (Oyama, 1928a, 1928b; Irie, 1928) K. Irie, an investigator of the Oyama team, argued that in order to encourage the development of Japan's trade with East Africa it was necessary to shorten the time of the voyage between Japan and East Africa, to establish a Japanese Consulate, and to open local branch offices of business banks. (Irie, 1928) In addition to these, the investigative report on Portuguese East Africa, the research report on the economic conditions of the Middle East and Africa, and the report on the maritime products industries in Africa were published one after another by the government offices concerned.[5] (MFA, 1936; MLBWA, 1927; MFA, 1930)

4 Reports from Overseas Business Trainees and Trade Correspondents

Commercial Information regarding Africa which was collected by the Ministry of Agriculture and Commerce (later the Ministry of Industry and Commerce) appeared in such journals as *Trade News* and *the Home and External Current News of Industry and trade*. These included reports of general conditions on annual trade, tariffs and regulation of exports and imports, and research on the demand of Japanese goods in the African market. These were sent by the overseas business trainees, trade correspondents, and trade mission.[6]

5 Reports from Trade Missions dispatched by Local Government

In some trade journals published in such principal cities as Osaka, Yokohama and Kobe, there appeared commercially important information regarding economic conditions in Africa. For Example, in the *Commercial Reports* (1915-1944), issued by the Osaka Commercial Museum, consular reports were sometimes reproduced, and exhibits and explanations on sample commodities sent from overseas countries were included in order to disseminate the knowledge to local merchants and industrialists. Since the middle of 1920s, the amount of economic information regarding Africa increased substantially, and market research reports by the staff of commercial houses in Osaka about such commodities as towel, toothbrush, toys, cosmetics, cotton blanket, and the like began to appear in this journal. In addition, in Osaka, the Trade Association for Exports to Africa was founded in 1929 and it dispatched researchers to obtain detailed information on market performance and structure in Africa.[7]

In the *Studies of East Asian Trade* (1916-1944) issued by the Industrial Research Division of Osaka City, much attention was paid on market research on cotton goods and general merchandize in Africa. Particularly, more attention was paid on sales conditions of such manufactures as towel, brush, glass bottle, toys, cotton blanket, and cotton piece goods which were produced in Osaka district. In addition, the *Bulletin* issued by the Chamber of Commerce and Industry, in principal cities, played an important role in disseminating economic information. For example, the *Monthly Report* (1909-1943) issued by the Osaka Chamber of Commerce, whose title changed several times, provided the business world in Osaka with useful overseas economic information including Africa. In particular, after the World War I, discussions of the commercial strategies to facilitate Japanese commodities break into African market appeared occasionally. Moreover, the Osaka Chamber of Commerce and Industry held a series of lectures on general economic conditions in Africa and granted subsidies to concerned business firms to encourage the development of trade with Africa.[8]

Notes

1   Therefore, in order to clarify the whole system of collecting overseas commercial information, it is essential to investigate not only reports sent from overseas business trainees and Overseas Commercial Museums but also kinds of publications from the Ministry of Agriculture and Commerce.

2   In addition to these consulate, trade office correspondents and trade mediation centers were also established at Mombasa (1933), and Casablanca (1934) to provide various kinds of services and information to Japanese traders and industrialists visiting these locations.

3   Others include the Bureau of Colonization (Takushoku Jimukyoku), the Ministry of Agriculture and Commerce's Bureau of Commerce and Industry (Noshomusho Shokokyoku), and the Ministry of Communication's Bureau of Waterways Administration (Teishinsho Kansenkyoku).

4   In the pre-war period government investigation of economic conditions in Africa was focused almost exclusively on Southern and Eastern Africa and specifically on the Union of South Africa and the British East Africa (Kenya, Uganda, Tanganyika). The earliest economic research report on South Africa was published in 1903 by the Consul in Singapore and a person employed temporarily by the Ministry of Agriculture and Commerce. S. Hisamizu and K. Katsube, "Report of an investigation commission to South Africa", in the *Journal of Commercial Reports [Tsusho Isan]*, No. 27, 1903. And the earliest report on the economic conditions in Eastern Africa was written and published by the consul at Cape Town in 1924. It surveyed major industries and the nature of trade in the British East Africa, and reported that there was plenty of potential for increasing exports of Japanese cloth to East Africa but that there were also some difficulties due to the financial and credit systems of Indian merchants. (Tadanao Imai, *Conditions in British East Africa*, the Ministry of Foreign Affairs' Bureau of Trade and Commerce, 1924.)

5   Investigations by the Japanese government into the economic conditions in West Africa were rare, but the Ministry of Foreign Affairs' Bureau of Trade and Commerce did publish a report titled *Economic Conditions in the Belgian Congo [Berugiryo Kongo Keizai Jijo]* in1927.

6   About reports from Overseas Business Trainees dispatched by the Ministry of Agriculture and Commerce, for example, see "Treatment of Japanese in Transvaal" by Masaji Katagiri, "A Detailed Account on the Rejection of Japanese Immigration in Transvaal" by Kanzo Iwasaki in Diplomatic Archives of MOFA, File 3-8-2-219 "Issues on Treatment to Japanese in South Africa and Zanzibar". See also Komahei Furuya, "The Present Condition of South African Trade and Hopeful Japanese Goods", in *Trade News*, Vol. 3, No. 2, 1916. Magoichi Nunekawa, "A View of Japanese Trade with South Africa", in *Trade News*, Vol. 3, No. 8, 1916.

7   Yaoichi Shimiuzu, "Conditions of South African Overseas Trade", Osaka Commercial Museum,

Commercial Reports, No. 40, 1920. Osaka Trade Association of Exports to Africa [Osaka Ahurika Yushutsu Kumiai], "Investigative Reports in Eastern and Southern Africa", *Commercial Reports*, No. 294, 1932. Mr. Ajioka (Correspondent residing at Cape Town), "Overseas Trade of South Africa", *Commercial Reports*, No. 375, 1938.

8 Economic investigative reports published individually by each private firm and trader should not be overlooked. The Federation of Japanese Cotton Yarn and Piece Goods Export Association made research in East Africa as an export market of Japanese cotton textiles and published *Research Report of Overseas Cotton Textile Market* in 1928 which paid much attention to the period and situation of the demand for cotton goods, the purchasing power of African people, and the habits of commercial dealing. Osaka Shosen Kaisha (OSK) sent Masao Tajima as investigator to the East African coast in order to do research on agriculture and industry, on commercial structures and port facilities of East Africa. See *Report of Economic Conditions in East Africa*, OSK, Osaka, 1924. Yokohama Specie Bank sent Hiroshi Unagami and Yaichi Ouchi to investigate into economic conditions in Africa with the result that two excellent reports, *Investigative Reports* (1926) and *Research on Western African Coastal Area* (1932) were published respectively.

References

Hisamizu, S. & K. Katsube, (1903), "Report of an investigation commission to South Africa", in the Ministry of Foreign Affairs' Bureau of Trade and Commerce (in Japanese). *Tsusho Isan [The Journal of Commercial Reports].* 27, pp. 1-45.

Imai. T., (1924), *Eiryo Higashi Ahurika Jijo [Conditions in British East Africa]* (in Japanese), The Ministry of Foreign Affairs' Bureau of Trade and Commerce, Tokyo.

Imai, T., (1927), *Nan A Renpo Gaikan [A General View of the Union of South Africa]* (in Japanese), The Ministry of Foreign Affairs' Bureau of Trade and Commerce, Tokyo.

Irie, A., (1966), *Nihon no Gaiko: Meiji 1shin kara Gendai made [Japanese Diplomacy : From Meiji Restoration to the Present Time]* (in Japanese), Chuo Koron, Tokyo.

Irie, K., (1928), *Higashi Ahurika Keizai Jijo Chosa Hokokusho [Research Report on Economic Conditions in East Africa]* (in Japanese), The Ministry of Foreign Affairs' Bureau of Trade and Commerce, Tokyo.

Kitagawa, K., (1988), "A study of Japan's pre-War economic research on Africa: A preliminary Investigation" (in Japanese), Kansai University of Foreign Studies, *Kenkyu Ronshu*, 48, pp. 171-191.

Kitagawa, K., (1989), "A study of economic conditions in Africa in the pre-War period seen through Japanese consular reports - An analysis of 'The journal of commercial reports'" (in Japanese). Kansai University of Foreign Studies, *Kenkyu Ronshu*, 50, pp. 303-320.

Kitagawa, K., (1989), "A study of economic conditions in Africa in the pre-War period seen through consular reports - An analysis of 'official commercial reports' " (in Japanese), Japan Association for African Studies, *Ahurika Kenkyu (Journal of African Studies)*, 35, pp. 47-63.

MAF (The Ministry of Agriculture and Forestry [No Rin Sho]), (1936), *Ahurika Suisan Chosa Hokoku [Research Report in Maritime Industries in Africa]* (in Japanese), MOAF, Tokyo.

MCBWA (The Ministry of Communication's Bureau of Waterways Administration [Teishinsho Kansenkyoku]), (1927), *Porutogaruryo Higashi Ahurika Jijo [Conditions in Portuguese East Africa]* (in Japanese), MCBWA, Tokyo.

MOFA (The Ministry of Foreign Affairs [Gaimusho]), (1927), *Berugiryo Kongo Keizai Jijo [Economic Conditions in the Belgian Congo]* (in Japanese), MFA, Tokyo.

MOFA, (1930), *Kinto Ahurika Keizai Jijo Chosa Hokoku, Ahurika no Bu [Research Report on Economic Conditions in Middle East and Africa: Section on Africa]* (in Japanese), MOFA, Tokyo.

MOFA, (1932), *Ahurika Keizai Jijo Tenbo [A View of Economic Conditions in Africa]* (in Japanese),

MFA, Tokyo.

Morikawa, J., (1985), "The myth and reality of Japan's relations with colonial Africa, 1885-1960", *Journal of African Studies*, 12 (1), pp. 39-46.

Moss. J. & J. Ravenhill, (1985), *Emerging Japanese Economic Influence in Africa: Implications for the United States*, University of California, Berkeley.

Naikaku Tokeikyoku, (1916, 1920, 1925, 1930, 1939, 1940), *Dai Nippon Teikoku Tokei Nenkan [Annual Foreign Trade Statistics of Imperial Japan]* (in Japanese), Naikaku Tokeikyoku, Tokyo.

NJKK (Nichimen Jitsugyo Kabushiki Kaisha), (1962), *Nichimen 70 Nenshi [A 70 Year History of Nichimen]* (in Japanese). NJKK, Osaka.

NBSK (Nihon Boeki Shinko Kyokai), (1941), *Ahurika-shu Muke Honpo Zakka Yushutsu Boeki no Bunseki [An Analysis of the Exports of General Merchandise to Africa]* (in Japanese) *Chosa Iho*, 6. NBSK, Osaka.

Nunokawa, M., (1917), *Minami Ahurika Boeki Jijo [Conditions of Foreign Trade in South Africa]* (in Japanese), Industrial and Commercial Report of the Ministry of Agriculture and Commerce (No Shomusho Shoko Isan), Tokyo.

OSK (Osaka Shosen Kaisha), (1924), *Higashi Ahurika Keizai Chosa Hokokusho [Report of Economic Conditions in East Africa]* (in Japanese), OSK, Osaka.

OSK, (1934), *Nishi Ahurika Keizai Chosa Hokokusho [Report of Economic Conditions in West Africa]* OSK, Osaka.

OSMSKK (Osaka Shosen Mitsui Senpaku Kabushiki Kaisha), (1966), *Osaka Shosen Kabushiki Kaisha 80 Nenshi [A 80 Year History of OSK]*, OSMSKK, Osaka.

Oyama, U., (1928a), *Eiryo Higashi Ahurika Jijo [Conditions in British East Africa]* (in Japanese), The Ministry of Foreign Affairs' Bureau of Trade and Commerce, Tokyo.

Oyama, U., (1928b), *Abisinia Jijo, Madagasukaru Jijo, Porutogaruryo Higashi Ahurika Jijo [Conditions in Abyssinia, Madagascar and Portuguese East Africa]* (in Japanese), The Ministry of Foreign Affairs' Bureau of Trade and Commerce, Tokyo.

Shakai Keizaishi Gakkai, (1982), *1930 Nendai no Nihon Keizai: Sono Shiteki Bunseki [A Historical Analysis of Japanese Economy in the 1930s]* (in Japanese), Shakai Keizaishi Gakkai, Tokyo.

1920 Nendai Kenkyukai, (1983), *1920 Nendai no Nihon Shihonshugi [Japanese Capitalism in the 1920s]* (in Japanese), 1920 Nendai Kenkyukai, Tokyo.

Takashima, M., (1979), "Consular reporting system and the reports of consulate" (in Japanese). *Keizai Riron*, 168, pp. 62-85.

------ (1986), "Development of consular reporting system and the publishing of consular reports" (in Japanese), in S. Tsunoyama, ed., *Nihon Ryoji Hokoku no Kenkyu [A Study in Japanese Consular Reports]*, Dobunkan, Tokyo, pp. 71-117.

Tsunoyama, S., (1981), "Japanese consular reports.", *Business History*, 23 (4), pp. 284-287.

Tsunoyama, S., (1979), "On the consular reports" (in Japanese). *Keizai Riron*, 167, pp. 1-19.

Tsunoyama, S., (ed.), (1986), *Nihon Ryoji Hokoku no Kenkyu [A Study in Japanese Consular Reports]* (in Japanese), Dobunkan, Tokyo.

Tsunoyama, S., (1988), *"Tsusho Kokka" Nihon no Joho Senryaku [Information Strategy by "Commercial State" Japan]* (in Japanese), Nihon Hoso Kyokai, Tokyo.

Ch 3
Japan's Economic Relations With Africa Between the Wars: An Overview

1 General Trends

It was not until the outbreak of the Sino-Japanese War that Japan's overseas trade underwent a fundamental change, as ventures in direct trade were launched. At the same time, Japanese traders themselves gained more control over external commerce. Until then, most of Japan's trade was handled by European and Chinese merchants residing in specified treaty ports. By the end of the Russo-Japanese War, there had evolved two distinctive areas and styles of overseas trade: (1) trade with Europe, North America, Australia, and British India which was generally handled by large trading companies engaging almost exclusively in this kind of commerce, and (2) trade with Korea, China, and other areas, including Africa and the Middle East, which tended to be handled more by small and middle-size merchant houses. It was only after the outbreak of the First World War that spectacular but short-lived advance of Japanese merchandise into Africa was seen.

In the aftermath of the war, however, Japanese trade suffered a severe setback as European powers regained their markets and adopted measures in keeping with increasingly popular ideas of imperial self-sufficiency. The newly-founded Republic of China also adopted high tariff policies to hurt its rivals, as did British India. The British Empire as a whole moved towards greater protection of its commonwealth markets. At the same time, Japanese industrialists and merchants who made or dealt in cotton textiles and other miscellaneous merchandise and who had increased number during the war, now found the domestic market in Japan insufficient to absorb their surplus goods. Given this situation, it was inevitable that greater attention came to be paid to new markets which had not received much attention in the past. These included the Balkan States, the Middle East, South America and Africa. With the abolition of the gold standard in 1931, the value of the Japanese yen fell and set the stage for the promotion of Japanese exports (NBSK, 1941)

This situation strengthened Japan's potential relations with various areas in Africa. Despite the temporary increase in exports to Africa which resulted from the dislocation of trade between Europe and Africa during the First World War,

Table 3-1 Japan's Trade with Africa, 1912-1939 (100,000Yen)

Year	Egypt		Cape/Natal, Union of South Africa		East Africa/Others			
	Ex	Im	Ex	Im	Ex	Im	Ex	Im
1912	8	63	4.5	0			-	-
1913	13	71	4.7	0.4			-	-
1914	18	63	4.9	0			-	-
1915	9	61	10.0	0.1			-	-
1916	53	58	42	0.07			4	2
1917	135	109	67	188			5	100
1918	284	91	183	294			13	6
1919	159	161	81	371			6	14
1920	305	132	82	738			8	12
1921	49	122	38	28			2	19
1922	64	105	48	37			4	26
1923	180	206	47	6			24	14
1924	270	170	57	9			83	40
1925	252	326	95	13	-	-	81	75
1926	230	319	107	9	-	-	93	84
1927	290	246	116	10	-	-	105	106
1928	237	203	116	13	64	62	20	42
1929	313	258	131	14	131	114	28	38
1930	289	162	141	16	106	44	31	16
1931	228	135	192	13	108	22	58	10
1932	418	197	164	26	157	34	116	16
1933	556	264	267	43	231	143	317	32
1934	729	462	295	82	374	213	424	37
1935	538	513	327	47	223	26	746	105
1936	409	507	415	225	270	291	882	106
1937	327	741	537	888	401	241	1160	191
1938	139	363	352	95	225	60	655	87
1939	156	503	468	92	228	196	675	135

Source : Naikaku Tokeikyoku, 1996, 1920, 1925, 1930, 1939, 1940
Note : After 1925, others is divided into East Africa and others. East Africa includes Kenya, Uganda and Tanganyika. After 1930, Union of South Africa is used instead of Cape/Natal.

19

Table 3-2 Japan's Trade with Africa by Areas, 1939 (%)

Export		Import	
South Africa	30.6	Egypt	54.2
Kenya	14.9	Kenya	21.2
Egypt	23.7	South Africa	9.9
Mozambique	7.0	Eritrea	4.3
Anglo-Egyptian Sudan	5.8	Anglo-Egyptian Sudan	3.0
Belgian Congo	5.6	Others	7.8
Nigeria	1.9		
Cameroon	1.9		
Others	8.6		

Source : NBSK (Nihon Boeki Shinko Kyokai), (1941), *Ahurika-shu Muke Honpo Zakka Yushutsu Boeki no Bunseki [An Analysis of the Exports of Japanese General Merchandise to Africa]* (in Japanese) *Chosa Iho*, 6, NBSK, Osaka.

Table 3-3 Japan's Trade with Africa by Kinds, 1939 (%)

Export		Import	
Cotton (bleached)	9.3	Cotton, Ginned Cotton	64.1
Cotton (Unbleached)	9.7	Phosphate	6.4
Cotton (Others)	20.5	Wool	1.7
Artificial Textile	3.7	Others	27.8
Silk Textile	1.1		
Hosiery	3.5		
Woolen Textile	1.4		
Others	47.4		

Source : NBSK (Nihon Boeki Shinko Kyokai), (1941), *Ahurika-shu Muke Honpo Zakka Yushutsu Boeki no Bunseki [An Analysis of the Exports of Japanese General Merchandise to Africa]* (in Japanese) *Chosa Iho*, 6, NBSK, Osaka.
Note : Others includes such general merchandize as pottery, canned foods, glass ware, cotton towel, toys, canvas shoes, tea, shirts and the like.

at which time the quantity of Japan's exports to Africa exceeded her imports for the first time, it was not until after 1923 that Japan's exports to Africa consistently exceeded her imports. This regular state of unbalanced trade, always in Japan's favor after 1923, reflected the extraordinary efforts of the Japanese government and traders to penetrate African markets. The percentage of Japan's total exports to Africa also rose temporarily during the First World War, but declined quickly thereafter. It was only in the 1920s and 1930s that there was a substantial increase in Africa's proportion of Japan's exports.

Both before and after the First World War, until 1936, Egypt was always at the top of the list among African countries importing Japanese commodities (Table 3-1, 3-2). In that year, South Africa rose to first place as an export market for Japanese goods in Africa. Egypt was also at the top of the list of countries from which Japan imported goods until the latter half of the 1930s. Imports from South Africa also rose considerably in the 1930s, but the increase in imports of cotton from East Africa during this decade is the most noteworthy development in Japanese African trade. On the whole, Japan's exports to Africa consisted mostly of cotton textiles and miscellaneous merchandise such as woolen goods, shirts, knitwear, bedding and the like. Imports from Africa were chiefly composed of ginned cotton and other raw materials. (Table 3-3)

2 Opening Shipping Line to Africa
East and South African Route

The opening and development of shipping lines from Japan to Africa played a significant role in advancing Japan's trade with Africa. The Osaka Shosen Kaisha (OSK) opened the first shipping line to South Africa in December 1916. The ships on this line called at Durban, Cape Town, East London and Port Elizabeth, and this contributed considerably to the development of trade with South Africa. Japanese traders also felt the need for a direct route to East Africa. Exports from Japan were being re-exported via Bombay or Aden and the traders were eager to have a direct Japan-East Africa shipping route established. Their requests helped convince the OSK to send teams of investigators to the East African coast, as did the growing general interest in East Africa as a new market. Particular attention was paid in OSK's investigative reports to agriculture and industry, to commercial structures and port facilities of East Africa. Finally, in March 1926, the OSK decided to open the East African line and the Kanada-Maru was sent on a trial run. (OSK, 1924, 1934)

The Japanese government authorized the East African line that same year which made it possible for ships such as the Kanada-Maru, the Panama-Maru, the Shikago-Maru and the Mekishiko-Maru to begin regular services once a month to East Africa. These ships departed from Kobe and turned around in Cape Town, making calls along the way in Moji, Hong Kong, Singapore, Colombo, Mombasa, Zanzibar, Dar es Salaam, Beira, Delagoa Bay and Durban. When the Japan Steamship Company (Nihon Yusen Kaisha, NYK) withdrew its ships from a line to the eastern coast of South America in April 1931, the OSK decided to allocate seven larger ship, such as the Hawai-Maru, or the Arizona-Maru to make brief stops at various ports on the east coast of South Africa once a month on the way to South America. This regular service started in Yokohama and turned around in

Buenos Aires.[1] Although the volume of goods to be transported to and from the East Coast of Africa appeared at first insufficient to justify the launching of this new route, the OSK's determination to survive and prosper led it to undertake this risk. In doing so, it helped to make a significant contribution to the development of Japan's trade with Africa. By 1923 Japanese cotton goods and general merchandise had advanced not only to South Africa but also to the coastal zone of East Africa.

The development of Japan's trade with East Africa from 1931 to 1937 owed much to the principle of free trade established for East Africa initially at the Berlin Conference of 1885.[2] (Morikawa 1985) In contrast, South Africa discriminated against Japanese goods by imposing high tariffs and practicing the kind of protectionism associated with the British imperial preference system. (OSMSKK, 1966) OSK's shipping line between Japanese and various East African ports had to compete with the Japan Steamship Company (NYK), the Bank Line, Andrew Weir & Co., the British India Steamship Navigation Co., Koninklijke Paketvaat Maatshappij, Messagerie Maritime and Norddeutsch Lloyd. But OSK had the good fortune to monopolize the Japan-Southern African route and to compete effectively on the Japan-East African route, because the growth of the commercial traffic and increase in the tonnage and number of ships was marked during this period. After 1932 there were, in addition to the regular routes, special ships sent to East Africa. Between 1934 and 1937, ships owned by Kawasaki, Kokusai and Yamashita Steamship Company were allocated to this route under the control of OSK.

West African Route

The OSK, which had opened new markets for Japanese commodities by establishing a shipping line to East Africa in 1926, continued its surveys of the West African coast. In November 1933, a new, trial line was established with the Arasaka-Maru calling at Lagos, Accra, and Dakar via South Africa. The OSK's *History of African Shipping Lines [Africa Koro Shi]* notes the following: "While Our Empire's commercial supremacy already extends to the northern, eastern, and southern areas of the African continent, in spite of the considerable interest of our Imperial nation in West Africa as the one remaining new market, there is currently a great paucity of materials that could be used to learn about the situation on the ground. Therefore, with the aim of contributing to the state of knowledge on West Africa, our employee Mr. Masao Tajima (currently Executive Director, Sales Manager) was dispatched from Cape Town on this vessel [the Arasuka-Maru—author] to West Africa to investigate conditions there, where he expended great effort in examining conditions in West Africa." (OSK, 1956 : 179)

Until that period, Japanese exports had been either transshipped through various European ports (Liverpool, Hamburg, Marseilles) or shipped on from New York. Goods were shipped to Europe from Japan on services like the NYK Line,

Norddeutscher Lloyd, or Messageries Maritimes, and depended upon lines like the Elder Dempster Line, the Woermann Line, the Deutsche Ost-Afrika Line, and the Hamburg-Bremen Afrika Line for the Europe to West African leg. Goods shipped by mail boats to New York from Japan were sent on to West Africa on regular services run by the American West African Line and the Elder Dempster Line. The establishment of a direct West African service by the OSK would inevitably compete with those services.

However, the import and export trade in West Africa was largely in the hands of European firms, in particular United Africa Company (UAC) and Compagnie Français de L'Afrique Occidentale (CFAO). Furthermore, as these firms used their own vessels for trading, and even if the OSK established a direct line to West Africa, booking sufficient cargo would be problematic without the cooperation of these trading firms. (Muroi, 1992) The following can be found in the *A History of African Shipping Lines:*"In truth, West African trade is largely in the hand of these two firms, and the cargos of our nation's imports are entirely dependent on their mandates. As it is clear that without cooperation between Our Company and these two firms carrying cargo is impractical, our company concluded an FAO in 1936, and sought to organize cargo using this FAO from the dispatch of the Kofuku-Maru in September of the same year. …Cargo taken by CFAO through the FOB costs ten shillings a ton for the first thousand tons and five shillings a ton thereafter. This deal applied for a year beginning from October 1936, under the title of the Special Address 7 & Inward Freight Commission." (OSK, 1956 : 195)

However, the situation became more favorable from 1935 onward:"As the direct charters undertaken by the vessels of the two West African firms, UAC and CFAO, are patterned on boosting their results when collecting Our Nation's goods (at intermediate ports, taking on rice at Rangoon and sacking at Calcutta), this is an opportunity that Our Company cannot let slip. Therefore, tremendous effort was expended on dispatching vessels seven times at two- to three-month intervals, with the Atorasu-Maru No. 2 in November of 1935, the Arasuka-Maru No. 3 in December of that same year, the Yamashita class Eifuku-Maru No. 4 (actually a charter) in April of 1936, the Arasuka-Maru No. 5 in July, the International class Kofuku-Maru No. 6 in September, and the Kawasaki-class Denmak-Maru No. 7 in January 1937, establishing this route on secure foundations." (OSK 1956 : 181)

In this way, assigning the second and third vessels by December 1935, OSK had secured this route. However, maritime transport of the period had the following issue: "Looking at trade occurring between the various nations of the world currently, everywhere there is an adherence to economic nationalism—with the establishment of tariff barriers and quotas, no extreme trade control, the implementation of strict import restrictions, and each nation's focus on their own vessels and cargos with regard to marine transport. Consequently, there can be

Figure 3-1 Navigation Route of Osaka Shosen Kaisha (OSK)

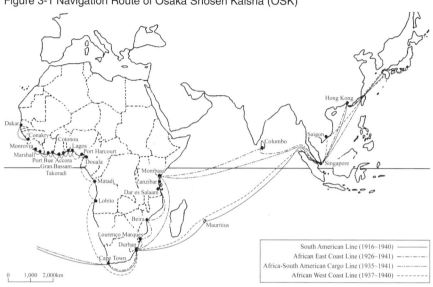

Source : OSK (Osaka Shosen Kaisha), 1956, *History of African Shipping Lines [Ahurika Koro Shi]*.

no positive outlook for the spread overseas of Our Empire's commodities, and specifically Our Nation's products to West Africa, while direct connections remain limited, given the unavoidable burden of the great expense and vast amount of time that results from the detour of the transshipment to Europe. … " (OSK, 1956 : 184)

Nonetheless, the OSK's situation improved favorably enough so that "from the beginning of 1935, direct and indirect requests for aid were accepted by the Ministry of Communications and Transportation, and, beginning April 1937, the routes were licensed by a decree of this agency, marking the moment when, after many twists and turns, this route became supported as a regular maritime line" (p. 184). In this way, the West African line was established as a regular route. It ran six times a year and was serviced by the Atorasu-Maru, Shunko-Maru, and Arasuka-Maru under the authority of the Ministry of Communications and Transportation. (OSMSKK, 1966 : 373-374)

Prior to the OSK operating a direct route to West Africa, the development of Japanese trade with the region, excluding Belgian Congo and Portuguese West Africa, was hindered by tariff barriers and quotas. However, Africans, with low standards of living and minimal buying power, welcomed high-quality, cheap Japanese commodities, and export trade to West Africa expanded. Nevertheless, from the middle of 1937 onward, the situation changed because of the outbreak of the Sino-Japanese war. As the war progressed, business discussions were gradually troubled by the introduction of import exchange controls and the rising cost of commodities due to problems with sourcing raw materials, while the buying power of peasants in Nigeria and the Gold Coast declined simultaneously, and the closure and bankruptcy of small and medium firms continued apace. Belgian Congo and French West Africa fell into similar straits, and the export trade with West Africa ebbed away.

A survey of Japan's exports to West Africa shows that the goods carried on outward voyages primarily consisted of textiles and cotton goods, rayon (artificial silk), blankets, enamel goods, rubber boots, ceramics, zinc etchings, hats, and canned goods. The main goal of this route was transporting goods to West Africa, but West African cargo might not have been enough to fill the ship's hulls. Therefore, both freighters and regular liners were packed out with cargo for South Africa or, when putting into port at Saigon, were packed out with rice for West Africa there. Subsequently, West African market conditions showed some signs of improvement, but no one expected a fundamental economic recovery. At the end of 1938, a partial recovery was brought about by measures encouraging exports to West Africa, such as establishing a West African trade office and transferring goods formerly transshipped via Europe onto OSK's West African line because of the unstable political situation in Europe. Although 1939 saw steady speculative buying of small and medium firms by those anticipating economic recovery, increasing import restrictions in various West African countries, continuing low prices for agricultural commodities, and the reduced purchasing power of the African population meant that demand remained slow. However, in September 1939, with the British and French declaring war on Germany, regular shipping from those countries was terminated, and there were shortages of European goods in West Africa, instantly depleting the stock that had built up since 1937 and raising market prices. Moreover, a shortage of freighter capacity became apparent in rice transports from Saigon to West Africa. Subsequently, however, in July 1940 the voyage of the Nan'a-Maru terminated Japanese shipping to West Africa due to Japan's accession to the Tripartite Pact. (OSK, 1956 : 196-198, 203)

Notes

1   Ports of Call along the way were Nagoya, Osaka, Kobe, Moji, Hong Kong, Singapore, Colombo, Mombasa, Zanzibar, Dar es Salaam, Laurenço Marques, Durban, Port Elizabeth, Cape Town, Rio de Janeiro, and Santos.

2   Japan's earliest economic interest in Black Africa was in the so called Congo Basin Area which was accorded the status of a free trade area by Article III of the Berlin Act of 1885. (Morikawa, 1985)

References

Adu Boahen. A., (1987), *African Perspective on Colonialism.* Johns Hopkins University Press, Baltimore.

Agbi, S.O., (1982), "The Japanese contact with, and knowledge of Africa, 1868-1912", *Journal of Historical Society of Nigeria,* 11 (1), pp. 153-165.

Aldcrofr, D.H., (1987), *From Versailles to Wall Street,* 1919-1929, Penguin Books, Harmondsworth.

Barker. T.C., (1981), "Consular reports: A rich but neglected historical source", *Business History,* 23 (4), pp. 265-266.

Beasley, W.G., (1987), *Japanese Imperialism:* 1894-1945, Clarendon Press, Oxford.

Hisamizu, S. & K. Katsube, (1903), "Report of an investigation commission to South Africa", in the Ministry of Foreign Affairs' Bureau of Trade and Commerce (in Japanese). *Tsusho Isan [The Journal of Commercial Reports],* 27, pp. 1-45.

Hobsbawm. E.J., (1987), *The Age of Empire, 1875-1914,* Pantheon Books, New York.

Imai. T., (1924), *Eiryo Higashi Ahurika Jijo [Conditions in British East Africa]* (in Japanese), The Ministry of Foreign Affairs' Bureau of Trade and Commerce, Tokyo.

--- (1927), *Nan A Renpo Gaikan [A General View of the Union of South Africa]* (in Japanese). The Ministry of Foreign Affairs' Bureau of Trade and Commerce, Tokyo.

Irie, A., (1966), *Nihon no Gaiko: Meiji 1shin kara Gendai made [Japanese Diplomacy : From Meiji Restoration to the Present Time]* (in Japanese), Chuo Koron, Tokyo.

Irie, K., (1928), *Higashi Ahurika Keizai Jijo Chosa Hokokusho [Research Report on Economic Conditions in East Africa]* (in Japanese), The Ministry of Foreign Affairs' Bureau of Trade and Commerce, Tokyo.

Kitagawa, K., (1988), "A study of Japan's pre-War economic research on Africa: A preliminary Investigation" (in Japanese), Kansai University of Foreign Studies, *Kenkyu Ronshu,* 48, pp. 171-191.

Kitagawa, K., (1989), "A study of economic conditions in Africa in the pre-War period seen through Japanese consular reports - An analysis of 'The journal of commercial reports'" (in Japanese). Kansai University of Foreign Studies, *Kenkyu Ronshu,* 50, pp. 303-320.

Kitagawa, K., (1989), "A study of economic conditions in Africa in the pre-War period seen through consular reports - An analysis of ' official commercial reports'" (in Japanese), Japan association for African Studies, *Ahurika Kenkyu (Journal of African Studies),* 35, pp. 47--63.

Martin, B., (1986), "The politics of expansion of the Japanese: Imperialism or Pan-Asiatic mission", in W.J. Mommsen & J. Osterhammel, eds, *Imperialism and After: Continuities and Discontinuities,* George Allen & Unwin, London, pp. 63-82.

MOAF (The Ministry of Agriculture and Forestry [No Rin Sho]), (1936), *Ahurika Suisan Chosa Hokoku [Research Report in Maritime Products Industries in Africa]* (in Japanese), MOAF, Tokyo.

MCBWA (The Ministry of Communication's Bureau of Waterways Administration [Teishinsho Kansenkyoku]), (1927), *Porutogaruryo Higashi Ahurika Jijo [Conditions in Portuguese East Africa]* (in Japanese), MCBWA, Tokyo.

MOFA (The Ministry of Foreign Affairs [Gaimusho]), (1927), *Berugiryo Kongo Keizai Jijo [Economic Conditions in the Belgian Congo]* (in Japanese), MFA, Tokyo.

MOFA, (1930), *Kinto Ahurika Keizai Jijo Chosa Hokoku, Ahurika no Bu [Research Report on Economic Conditions in Middle East and Africa: Section on Africa]* (in Japanese), MOFA, Tokyo.

MOFA, (1932), *Ahurika Keizai Jijo Tenbo [A View of Economic Conditions in Africa]* (in Japanese), MOFA, Tokyo.

Morikawa, I., (1985), "The myth and reality of Japan's relations with colonial Africa, 1885-1960", *Journal of African Studies,* 12 (1), pp. 39-46.

Moss. J. & J. Ravenhill, (1985), *Emerging Japanese Economic Influence in Africa: Implications for the United States,* University of California, Berkeley.

Munro, J.F., (1976), *Africa and the International Economy, 1800-1960: An Introduction to the Modern Economic History of Africa South of Sahara,* Dent, London.

Munro, J.F., (1990), "Africa and the Sea-Reflections on the Maritime History of Africa" *(unpublished paper)* Paper presented at the Meeting of Area Studies Centre of Keio University, July 10, 1990, Tokyo, Japan.

Murakami, K., (1984), "Japanese capitalism and the colonies" (in Japanese), in Shakai Keizaishi Gakkai, ed., *Shakai Keizaishigaku no Kadai to Tenbo [Prospects for the Study of Economic and Social History]*, Shakai Keizaishi Gakkai, Tokyo, pp. 193-200.

Muroi, Yoshio, (1992), *Rengo Ahurika Kaisha no Rekishi, 1879-1979: Naijeria Shakai Keizaishi Josetsu [History of the United Africa Company 1879-1979 : an introduction to Social and Economic History in Naigeria]*, Dobunkan, Tokyo.

Nagaoka, K., (1976), "Studies of imperialism in Japan" (in Japanese), in Shakai Keizaishi Gakkai ed., *Shakai Keizaishigaku no Kadai to Tenbo [Prospects for the Study of Economic and Social History]* Shakai Keizaishi Gakkai, Tokyo, pp. 145-153.

Naikaku Tokeikyoku, (1916, 1920, 1925, 1930, 1939, 1940), *Dai Nippon Teikoku Tokei Nenkan [Annual Foreign Trade Statistics]* (in Japanese), Naikaku Tokeikyoku, Tokyo.

NJKK (Nichimen Jitsugyo Kabushiki Kaisha), (1962), *Nichimen 70 Nenshi [A 70 Year History of Nichimen]* (in Japanese). NJKK, Osaka.

NBSK (Nihon Boeki Shinko Kyokai) (1941), *Ahurika-shu Muke Honpo Zakka Yushutsu Boeki no Bunseki [An Analysis of the Exports of General Merchandise to Africa]* (in Japanese) *Chosa Iho*, 6, NBSK, Osaka.

Nish, I.H., (1986), "Some thoughts of Japanese expansion", in W.J. Mommsen & J. Osterhammel eds., *Imperialism and After: Continuities and Discontinuities*, George Allen & Unwin, London, pp. 82-89.

Nunokawa, M., (1917), *Minami Ahurika Boeki Jijo [Conditions of Foreign Trade in South Africa]* (in Japanese), Industrial and Commercial Report of the Ministry of Agriculture and Commerce (No Shomusho Shoko Isan), Tokyo.

Ono, K. ed., (1985) *Senkanki no Nihon Teikokushugi [Japanese Imperialism Between the Wars]* (in Japanese), Sekai Shisosha, Tokyo.

OSK (Osaka Shosen Kaisha), (1924), *Higashi Ahurika Keizai Chosa Hokokusho [Report of Economic Conditions in East Africa]* (in Japanese), OSK, Osaka.

OSK, (1934), *Nishi Ahurika Keizai Chosa Hokokusho [Report of Economic Conditions in West Africa]* OSK, Osaka.

OSK, (1956), *Ahurika Koro-shi [History of African Shipping Lines]*, Osaka.

OSMSKK (Osaka Shosen Mitsui Senpaku Kabushiki Kaisha), (1966), *Osaka Shosen Kabushiki Kaisha 80 Nenshi [A 80 Year History of OSK]* OSMSKK, Osaka.

Oyama, U., (1928a), *Eiryo Higashi Ahurika Jijo [Conditions in British East Africa]* (in Japanese). The Ministry of Foreign Affairs' Bureau of Trade and Commerce, Tokyo.

Oyama, U., (1928b), *Abisinia Jijo, Madagasukaru Jijo, Porutogaruryo Higashi Ahurika Jijo [Conditions in Abyssinia, Madagascar and Portuguese East Africa]* (in Japanese), The Ministry of Foreign Affairs' Bureau of Trade and Commerce, Tokyo.

Robinson, R.E., (1972), "Non-European foundations of European imperialism", in R. Owen & B. Sutcliffe eds., *Studies in the Theory of Imperialism*, Longman, London, pp. 117-142.

Shakai Keizaishi Gakkai, (1982), *1930 Nendai no Nihon Keizai: Sono Shiteki Bunseki [A Historical Analysis of Japanese Economy in the 1930s]* (in Japanese), Shakai Keizaishi Gakkai, Tokyo.

1920 Nendai Kenkyukai, (1983), *1920 Nendai no Nihon Shihonshugi [Japanese Capitalism in the 1920s]* (in Japanese), 1920 Nendai Kenkyukai. Tokyo.

Takashima, M., (1979), "Consular reporting system and the reports of consulate" (in Japanese), *Keizai Riron*. 168, pp. 62-85.

Takashima, M., (1986), "Development of consular reporting system and the publishing of consular

27

reports" (in Japanese), in S. Tsunoyama, ed., *Nihon Ryoji Hokoku no Kenkyu [A Study in Japanese Consular Reports]*, Dobunkan, Tokyo, pp. 71-117.

Tsunoyama, S., (1981), "Japanese consular reports." *Business History*, 23 (4), pp. 284-287.

Tsunoyama, S., (1979), "On the consular reports" (in Japanese). *Keizai Riron*, 167, pp. 1-19.

Tsunoyama, S., (ed.), (1986), *Nihon Ryoji Hokoku no Kenkyu [A Study in Japanese Consular Reports]* (in Japanese), Dobunkan, Tokyo.

Tsunoyama, S., (1988), *"Tsusho Kokka" Nihon no Joho Senryaku [Information Strategy by "Commercial State" Japan]* (in Japanese), Nihon Hoso Kyokai, Tokyo.

Yoshida, M., (1974), "Japanese merchant house and cotton ginnery in East Africa before World War II" (in Japanese), *Gekkan Ahurika [Monthly Africa]*, 14 (9), pp. 22-25.

Ch 4
Japan's Trade with South Africa

1 Japan's Early Economic Interests in South Africa

A detailed and positive description of the African continent as a Japanese commodity market was given in *A View of Economic Conditions in Africa [Ahurika Keizai Jijo Tenbo]* published in 1932. (MOFA, 1932) In this report, African markets were divided into four groups. From the Japanese perspective, Group A which included Egypt, Sudan, French and Spanish Morocco and Group C which comprised the Union of South Africa, Southern and Northern Rhodesia were regarded as the most important trading areas. In the 1930s more attention came to be focused on Group B, or what was essentially the British East Africa. (MOFA, 1932)

In the aftermath of the First World War, Japanese trade suffered severe setback as European powers regained their markets and adopted measures in keeping with increasingly popular ideas of imperial self-sufficiency. The newly founded Republic of China also adopted a high tariff policy against its rivals, as did the British India. The British Empire as a whole moved towards greater protection of its Commonwealth markets. At the same time, Japanese industrialists and merchants who made or dealt in cotton textiles and other miscellaneous merchandise and who had increased in number during the war, now found the domestic market in Japan insufficient to absorb their surplus goods. Given this situation, it was inevitable that greater attention came to be paid to new markets which had received little attention previously. These included the Balkan States, the Middle East, South America and Africa. With the adoption of the gold standard in 1931, the value of Japanese yen fell and set the stage for the promotion of Japanese exports. (Kitagawa, 1988; JTPA, 1941)

There is historical evidence which shows early Japanese economic interests in South Africa, and a small amount of Japanese goods had already been traded in South Africa before 1910, when the Union of South Africa was formed.

Hisamizu Mission : "Report of the Mission to South Africa [Nan-A Shisatsu Fukumeisho]", 1902.[1] (Diplomatic Archives of MOFA, File 6-1-6-2-5-2)

Saburo Hisamizu, Japanese consul in Singapore, and Kuniomi Katsube, part-time investigator for the Ministry of Agriculture and Commerce, undertook investigation on economic conditions in Cape, Natal, Transvaal and the Orange Free State for two months from 3 August to 5 October in 1902. This investigation was undertaken immediately after the Anglo-Boer War (1899-1902), and as peace in South Africa recovered, it was inevitable that foreign trade was on the inflow of goods for everyday life.

After Hisamizu and Katsube observed South African mining industries, particularly De Beers mines, and agriculture as well as analysed its foreign trade, they stated : "it can be safely said that trade between Japan and South Africa has not shown the slight movement. Nevertheless, Japanese general merchandize are unfailingly found in several shops of almost every town. It can be assumed that those merchandize are mostly either re-exported from Britain or brought there by Indian merchants". (MOFA, 1903)

In their report, they showed Japanese goods had already been brought into the South African market through the Indian Commercial networks and their recognition of the beginning of the 20th century as "the Age of Peaceful War", when Japan should attempt to be an unshakeable "commercial state", and Japanese trade policy should aim at such countries that had much purchasing power without development of industrial productivity.

Nunokawa Mission: "Condition of Foreign Trade in South Africa *[Minami Ahurika Boeki Jijo]*", 1917, (Nunokawa, 1917)

Japanese government and traders made concerted efforts to advance into the South African market during the war period. Magoichi Nunokawa, part-time investigator for the Ministry of Agriculture and Commerce, left Japan in September 1916 and on 23 October arrived in Cape Town. After researching several districts in the Union of South Africa, he came back to Japan in January 1917.

The purpose of this mission was to conduct an investigation into the reality that in spite of rapid increase of Japanese trade with South Africa during the First World War, Japanese middlemen could not do their business activities freely under the 1913 Immigration Act which prohibited Asian immigrants. This investigation was undertaken in order to take some kind of measures by which Japanese merchants would be guaranteed to immigrate and reside in South Africa and develop Japanese trade with South Africa.

Nunokawa reported that during the First World War South African imports from Japan substantially increased because of dislocated inflow of consumer goods from European countries, which sent their prices up and consequently created demand for Japanese manufactured goods. At that time the Mikado & Co. which was opened by Komahei Furuya in Cape Town at the end of nineteenth century was the oldest Japanese store which dealt in Japanese goods. (Aoki, 1993; Diplomatic Archives of

MOFA, File 6-1-6-2-5-2) Some of South African middlemen and merchant houses tried to deal with Japanese traders directly and to acquire Japanese goods through the hands of European merchants residing in Japan. Japanese exports were cotton piece goods, knitwear and other general merchandize and her imports were wattle bark, oxhide, goatskin, wool and aloes.

There were two serious problems to the development of Japanese trade with South Africa. The first problem involved the manner in which business settled accounts. The British merchants in South Africa had a firm financial base to do business at their direction. When they imported Japanese goods, they usually ordered from Japanese traders through their interested concerns in Britain and gave them an order to send commodities directly to South Africa. When Japanese merchants received orders from South African traders, they instructed Japanese traders to offer the long term credit. But the unavailability of long term credit to which South African traders had been given access by European traders was one of unfavourable conditions. The second problem was that Japanese traders had to find reliable counterpart agents in South Africa because Japanese businessmen were prohibited from residing and doing business under the 1913 Act in South Africa. (Nunokawa 1917 : 88-89, 98-99) Nunokawa negotiated with the South African government to reach an agreement to exchange 'Note of Understanding', but these discussion were suspended as a result of the British government's official notice to South African government.[2] (Diplomatic Archives of MOFA, File 3-8-2-219)

2 Japanese Goods in South African Market

South African share of total Japanese exports to Africa was 34% in the 1910s, 25.3% in the 1920s, and 22.5% in the 1930s. Its contribution to the total Japanese imports from Africa was 23.9%, 17.2% and 12.7% in the three consecutive decades respectively. South African export to Japan consisted of wattle bark, oxhide, goatskin, wool, aloes, maize, and asbestos. (Table 4-1, 4-2)

South African imports from Japan consisted of rayon piece goods, cotton piece goods, silk piece goods, china and pottery ware, furnishing drapery, artificial silk, toys, bicycles, women's outer garments, oak timber and enameled ware.

It is difficult to show to what extent Japanese cotton goods made up all the cotton piece goods imported to South Africa from abroad. We know that at least prior to 1914 the United Kingdom consistently supplied over 80% of this trade, and this proportion was well maintained until 1923, when nearly 85% of South Africa's cotton piece goods imports were of United Kingdom manufacture. Since then, however, there has been a steady and serious loss of her trade, the percentage falling year by year. Japan gained a large share of the trade since 1923, its increase recorded each year.[3]

What kind of cotton piece goods were imported into the South African market?

Table 4-1 Japanese Trade with South Africa, 1910-1939 (1,000 Pound)

Year	Import from Japan	Export to Japan
1910	78	-
1911	94	-
1012	104	-
1913	109	-
1914	110	0.1
1915	221	0.7
1916	540	14
1917	730	2842
1918	2633	2816
1919	1754	3752
1920	1436	5981
1921	747	467
1922	628	155
1923	525	66
1924	699	87
1925	846	93
1926	1116	89
1927	1046	116
1928	1233	106
1929	1399	87
1930	1557	101
1931	2446	100
1932	1209	158
1933	2064	428
1934	2241	341
1935	2656	428
1936	3065	2335
1937	3869	3308
1938	2785	406
1939	2893	771

Source : "Annual Reports of South Africa" in *Official Commercial Reports, Daily Overseas Commercial Reports, and Overseas Economic Conditions.*

Table 4-2 Japanese Trade with South Africa by Kinds, 1930-36 (Pound)

year	Export from South Africa			Import to South Africa		
	wattle	wool	asbestos	cotton textile	artificial textile	silk textile
1930	68574	991	-	342828	13417	580526
1931	75873	15953	7017	636160	237625	681967
1932	61806	62078	4367	341195	195203	250402
1933	48156	157606	16131	391943	322729	369752
1934	39294	237077	23195	297744	450740	296955
1935	39788	217208	30497	469000	471000	294000
1936	40430	2087552	28357	488000	432000	239000

Source : "Annual Report of Overseas Trade of South Africa (1936)" in *Overseas Economic Conditions*, No.6, 1938.

Japanese cotton piece goods imported into South Africa mostly consisted of unbleached grey cloth in terms of both volume and value. Unbleached drills manufactured by Toyo Boseki Company were used as lining of women's clothes for African people living in rural and urban areas. Jeans with the Yorakucho or Building trademark imported from Japan were used for lining and pocket cloth. Sheeting was mostly imported from Japan and the United Kingdom. Japanese goods were 36-inch coarse cotton with Kyuryu trademark manufactured by Kanebo Company. These were used for making overall, dust coats, and clothes for African shop assistants. Sheeting with the Rugby trademark and ducks were used for shoe lining, sails and tents.

In the case of bleached cloth, this line formed 10% of Japanese cotton piece goods imported in South Africa. 70% of this class was sheeting. High quality goods of drills were imported from the United Kingdom and low quality goods were imported from Italy, which were demanded for clothes material. Japanese khaki drill with Cat and Goldfish trademark and jeans with trademarks of Wild Boar, Public Hall and Kindergarten also advanced in the South African market. The majority of sheeting was made up of the United Kingdom manufactures with trademarks of Horrocks, Fish and Tiger, which were used as clothes material and cloth for bags. Kaffir sheeting was usually used for making African women's clothes.

In the case of processed cotton cloth imported from Japan, printed cloth accounted for 10%, and jeans and poplin accounted for 30% of total import value of these classes. They were used for shirts and lining materials of suits and dresses. Striped drills (yarn dyed) was usually used for cotton cloth and

Japanese goods were used as shuka for African people. Dyed drills were mostly used for manufacturing clothes and shirts, most of which were United Kingdom manufactures with the Spinners trademark. Japanese gabardines (printed) with trademark of Cat and Goldfish and Kanebo-3460 advanced in the South African market as well.[4] (Kitagawa, 1997 : 63-64)

3 Japanese Trading Firms in South Africa

The World War I provided a good opportunity for the Japanese textile industry to make great strides and become competitive in the world market. The textile industry's sudden rise was made possible by the existence of cheap land and good quality labour, the neighboring Asian market, the development of maritime transport and the growth of trading companies. There were also many innovations in the domestic machinery industry, in the rationalization of management practice, in the effective combination of technology, capital and labour, and in founding associations of textile industrialists and traders. It was critically important for these industries to be able to secure cheap labour, to import sufficient quantities of high quality materials and to find favourable outlets for its manufactured goods.

To get a total and precise picture of the hectic activities of the Japanese commercial houses that were involved in trading in the South African market, a lot of work needs to be done to collect historical sources not only from the fragmented information found in the Japanese consular reports on companies but also from the various kinds of other documents. At any rate, Japanese consular reports showed that South African imports of Japanese manufactured goods suddenly increased because of the dislocating inflow of consumer goods from European countries. And also in 1916 when Australian wool was bought exclusively by Britain, Japanese commercial houses that were rejected access to Australian wool became much more interested in South African wool. Thus in 1917, such influential trading companies as Kanematsu, Mitsui, and Takashimaya played an active role in purchasing in South Africa. In addition, Okakura-Gumi, Hara Exporting Company, Japan Wool Spinning, Nihon Menka, Tokyo Wool, Nozawa-Gumi, and Mikado sent experts to investigate conditions in the South African wool market. (Nunokawa, 1917: 104-105)

In the latter half of 1920s, Mikado & Company, which was the first in starting trade with South Africa, cooperated with Morimura Trading Company to set up a branch office in Kobe. Yokohama Silk House, a Branch of Japan-Africa Trading House in Yokohama, was established in Cape Town. In the middle of the 1930s, influential trading houses engaged in South African trade, being notably Mitsui, Mitsubishi, Kanematsu, Sekiya Trading House, Iwai Shoten and Hattori Shoten. (Kanematsu, 1934 : pp. 88, 110; Takashimaya 1965; Iwai Shoten, 1963; Mitsui, 1951, 1986)

In addition to these large trading companies, the activities of small and middle-sized Japanese commercial houses should not overlooked. Office agents of small trading companies in Osaka and Kobe were stationed in South Africa and engaged in selling Japanese general merchandise. Those goods were also brought into the South African market by the Indian merchant houses there, and by Indian and British traders residing in Japan. (Kitagawa, 1997 : 40-41; Padayachee and Morrel, 1991)

4 Trade Issues in South Africa and Japan's Wool buying Strategy
There were various difficulties caused by Japan's advance into South African markets. The most grave was the Anti-Asian sentiment and movement. Japanese being Asians were among its victims.

Since the Union in 1910, South Africa had made much progress in development, but because of market conditions, transport difficulties and other problems, none of the advances were on a very large scale, except for gold mining. The Union's progress in agriculture and mining was important to Japanese manufacturers because they enhanced the country's purchasing capacity. The expansion of overseas trade in the twenty five years since Unification had not been great. The failure of overseas trade to grow was evidence that the Union was becoming self-supporting : more domestic products were being used and fewer manufactured goods were being imported. So South Africa was faced with the serious problem of dealing with a large export surplus and a particular concern was the overproduction of many agricultural products.

Consequently the expansion of the internal market for such products was drawing the attention of the government. At first to find a new outlet for employment the government hoped to develop base metal resources. The next area of growth was secondary industry, which the Government hoped would use local agricultural and forest products. Finally the issue which influenced all of these matters was the question of tariff protection. The first Customs Tariff Act in 1925 was primarily designed to encourage industrial development following a report by the Board of Trade and Industry (BTI). The 1925 Tariff offered assistance to the manufacturing industries with increased import duties: a rebate of import duties on many raw materials and the power to impose dumping duties.[5] (Imai 1927: 77)

The policy of protecting secondary industries with the custom tariff was maintained and many import duties were increased after 1925. There is little doubt that, from 1925 the manufacturing industries became more important as consumers of domestic products of the Union. Although Union found more market for its products, more overseas countries competed for the import trade in South African market. The outstanding change in the import trade was the arrival of competition from Japan.

Japan supplied 4. 9 per cent of imported merchandise in 1931. Its importance as a competitor was declining but it offered a far wider range of goods than ever before, and the decline was almost entirely due to a fall in piece goods. In 1932 Japan supplied 186 items out of a total of 1002 items and in 1934 it supplied 336 items. These items accounted for less than £ 100, in values but indicated the way in which Japanese exporters were continually trying to advance new items to the market.

Piece goods were still the most important line of merchandise although their relative importance was not as great as it had been. In 1931 the value of imports of piece goods represented nearly two-thirds of total imports from Japan. After 1932 imports of Japanese cottons and rayons were severely restricted by specific duties.

While imports of Japanese silks suffered from a decline in demand, other goods were hit by import duties or by dumping duties imposed on nearly all Japanese goods which competed with local manufactures, included men's outer garments, knitted underclothing, felt hats, handkerchiefs, and canvas and rubber footwear.

By establishing branches of Japanese houses in the Union and offices for buying Union products in Japan, trade connections between the two countries were considerably strengthened. Samples and counter-samples were continually being sent and new lines offered experimentally.[6]

Japan appeared to be increasing in importance as a customer of the Union. Wool formed nearly two thirds of the Union shipment to Japan in 1934, but Japan also imported fairly large quantities of wattle bark and extract, asbestos, and smaller quantities of chrome ore and manganese ore. During the Depression of 1929-34, South African farmers suffered poor returns in virtually all crops because of unfavourable price of agricultural products. Their affections were exacerbated by the Government's unwillingness to leave the Gold Standard. The agricultural sector was vociferous in its criticism of the Government's acts positing the Gold Standard. The South African farmers' struggle to contain the drastic decline of prices in these years was complicated by overproduction of their various primary products. The expectations of high fixed prices had led to such expansion of production that the local market was unable to absorb further amount. Sections of agriculture demanded restrictions and the surplus caused South African farmers to look for export markets. This resulted in the export of surpluses on a subsidized basis, and cutting supplies in the local market to keep domestic prices high. This helped farmers who produced for the local market, but did not help those who had no domestic market. The sectors particularly affected in this regard were wool, mohair, wattle bark and extract, and hide and skins.[7]

Given this background, Japan had to create favourable conditions to introduce Japanese manufactures to the South African market, and suppress an anti-Japanese sentiment. So the Japanese Government decided to make a strategic purchase of South African wool. In December 1933, Chosaku Mogaki, Japanese consul in Cape

Town, sent this telegram to Koki Hirota at the Ministry of Foreign Affairs : "As it is thought that at present anti-Japanese sentiment in South Africa is very high, it is unfavourable for Japan to let the situation take its course. The situation involves racist prejudice. This has caused unrest which is apparent in the Japanese-South African Notes of Understanding which is the basis of relations between the two countries. Therefore the Japanese government should buy South African wool even it is adversely Japanese traders and industrialists in order to win the South African wool farmers over to the Japanese side and stabilize the basis of South African political power and further drive a wedge into the economic barriers of the British Empire".[8]

In accord with the recommendation of Nobuo Fujimura, the Japanese consul in Cape Town, on the strategy of buying South African wool, a Conference for the Promotion of Japanese-South African Trade was organized under the leadership of the Japanese government and the business world involved in South African trade. The first conference was held in Osaka on 23 July 1935 and made these resolutions:

1 The extra charge of freight rate to South Africa will be compensated by profit margin of dealing South Africa wool.

2 The upper limit of the profit margin is 30yen per bale.

3 Wool-buying should start from the beginning of the shearing season.

4 The total sum of collecting the extra freight charge will not be announced.

5 If necessary, further committee meeting should be held.

Those represented at the first meeting were : the Ministry of Industry and Commerce, the Ministry of Foreign Affairs, the Consul, the Association for Exporting Wool Cloth and Yarn, the Osaka Export Union of Cotton Cloth and Artificial Silk Goods, the Association of Exporting Traders in Kobe, the Japanese Association for Exporting Hosiery, the Federal Association for Exporting Pottery and China Ware, the Trade Association for Importing Wool, Companies such as Kanematsu, Mitsui, Mitsubishi, Osaka Shosen Kaisha, the Japan Association of Wool Industries, the Association for Exporting Silk and Artificial Silk Goods in Yokohama.[9]

Notes

1 In detail see Diplomatic Archives of the Ministry of Foreign Affairs (MOFA), File 6-1-6-2-5-2 "Report of the Mission to South Africa", in Consul Hisamizu residing Singapore and Report of Mission to South Africa".

2 In detail see "An Outline of Negotiations on the Note of Japanese Immigration in South Africa", and "Issues on Treatment to Japanese in South Africa and Zanzibar", Diplomatic Archives of MOFA, File 3-8-2-219.

3 "Japanese Trade with South Africa Sales Conditions of Japanese Goods in South African Market" (29 April 1916, Yaoichi Shimizu to the Ministry of Foreign Affairs), *Official Commercial Reports*, No. 332, July 1916. "Annual Report on South African Overseas Trade in 1920" (22 September 1921, Tadanao Imai to the Ministry of Foreign Affairs), *Official Commercial Reports*, January

1922. "Annual Report on South African Overseas Trade" (15 July 1924, Tadanao Imai to the Ministry of Foreign Affairs), *Official Commercial Reports*, November 1924.

4 "Annual Report on Overseas Trade of the Union of South Africa (1937)" (25 November 1938, Takeo Kinoshita to the Ministry of Foreign Affairs), *Overseas Economic Conditions*, No. 4, 1939. "Japanese Cotton Cloth in South African Market" 28 November 1939, Kenichi Okada, the Minister extraordinary and plenipotentiary to the Ministry of Foreign Affairs), *Overseas Economic Conditions*, No. 4, 1940, pp. 243-249.

5 "Research on the Trade Relations of Foreign Countries : South Africa" Diplomatic Archives of MOFA, File E329-XI-B6, "Research on the Trade Conditions of Foreign Countries : South Africa" (Vol. 1, Vol. 2), Diplomatic Archives of MOFA, File E329-XI-B6

6 "Annual Report of Foreign Trade in the Union of South Africa" (24 September 1935, Tomotsune Ota to the Ministry of Foreign Affairs), *Overseas Economic Conditions*, No. 6, 1838, pp. 63-69.

7 "Annual Report of Foreign Trade in the Union of South Africa (1929)" (1 July 1930, Takeshige Yamazaki to the Ministry of Foreign Affairs), *Overseas Economic Conditions*, No. 39, 40, 41, 42, 1930. "A General View of Foreign Trade in the Union of South Africa (1932)" (7 July 1933, Chosaku Mogaki to the Ministry of Foreign Affairs), *Overseas Economic Conditions*, No. 37, 1933. "A General View of Foreign Trade in the Union of South of South Africa (1933)" (23 June 1934, Nobuo Fujimura to the Ministry of Foreign Affairs), *Overseas Economic Conditions*, No. 37, 1934. "A General View of Foreign Trade in the Union of South of South Africa" (17 July 1935, Nobuo Fujimura to the Ministry of Foreign Affairs), *Overseas Economic Conditions*, No. 18, 1935.

8 "Fur, Feather and Bone : On Purchase of South African Wool", Diplomatic Archives of MOFA, File E.4.3.2.2-.

9 In detail see "Fur, Feather and Bone : On Purchase of South African Wool", Diplomatic Archives of MOFA, File E.4.3.2.2-2. On the Note exchanged between Japan and South Africa, see Union of South Africa, Notes Exchanged between the Union Government and the Japanese Consul in the Union. Concerning Japanese Immigration into South Africa (Tabled at the House of assembly on the 13 th February 1931) (Document No. A. 1-31 Japanese Consul on Japanese Immigration into South Africa). See also "Issue on the Purchase of South African Wool (1934-1935) and Strategy to South African Government", "Plan for the Purchase of South African Wool" (Nobuo Fujimura to Koki Hirota, 18 December 1934, Fujimura to Hirota, 8 July 1935, Susumu Terao to Saburo Kurusu, 31 July 1935), in "Issue of the Purchase of South African Wool" Diplomatic Archives of MOFA, File E.4.3.2.2-2.

References

Abe, Takeshi, (1989), *Development of Local Cotton Weaving in Japan [Nihon ni okeru Sanchi Menorimonogyo no Tenkai]*, Tokyo University Press.

Aman, W.C., (1927), *Cotton in South and East Africa, South and East Africa Cotton Year-Book, 1926 : An Annual Book of Reference for the Cotton Merchants, Ginners, Planters, and Prospective Settlers*, Longman Green & Co., R.L. Esson & Co.

Ampiah, Kweku, (1990), "British Commercial Policies Against Japanese Expansionism in East and West Africa, 1932-1935", *The International Journal of African Historical Studies*, Vol. 23, No. 4, pp. 619-641.

Annon., "An Outline of Negotiation on the Note of Japanese Immigration in South Africa", Diplomatic Archives of MOFA, File 3-8-2-219.

Annon., "Issues of Treatment to Japanese in South Africa and Zanzibar", Diplomatic Archives of MOFA, File 3-8-2-219.

Annon., "Fur, Feather and Bone On Purchase of South African Wool", Diplomatic Archives of MOFA, File No. 4-3-2-2-2.

Aoki, Sumio, (1993), *Japanese Immigrants and Travellers in Africa [Ahurika ni watatta Nihonnjin]*, Jiji Tsushin.

Bradshaw, R.A., (1992), "Japan and Colonialism in Africa, 1800-1039", Ph.D. Thesis, Ohio University.

Goey, Ferry de (2014), *Consuls and the Institutions of Global Capitalism, 1783-1914*, Pickering and Chatto, London.

Imai, Tadanao, (1927), *The General View of the Union of South Africa [Nan-A Renpo Gaikan]*, The Ministry of Foreign Affairs' Bureau of Trade and Commerce.

Iwai Shoten, (1963), *Iwai Shoten : One Hundred Years. [Iwai Shoten 100 Nenshi]*.

Iwasaki, Kanzo, "A Detailed Account on the Rejection of Japanese Immigration in Transvaal", Diplomatic Archives of MOFA, File No. 3-8-2-219.

Japan Trade Promotion Association (JTPA), [Nihon Boeki Shinko Kai], (1949), *An Analysis of Export Trade of General Merchandize to Africa :1934 [Ahurika muke Zakka Yushutsu Boeki no Bunseki]*, Research Report, No. 6.

Kanematsu, (1934), *Kanematsu : A History of 60 Years [Kanematsu 60 Nenshi]*.

Katagiri, Masaji, "Treatment of Japanese in Transvaal", Diplomatic Archives of MOFA, File No. 3-8-2-219.

Kennedy, C.S., (1990), *The American Consul : A Study of the United States Consular Service, 1775-1914*, New York.

Kitagawa, K., (1988), "A Study of Japan's Pre-War Economic Research on Africa : A Preliminary Investigation [Senzenki Nihon no Ahurika Keizai Jijo Chosa no Kenkyu : Sono Yobiteki Kosatsu]", Kansai University of Foreign Studies, *Kenkyu Ronshu*, No. 48, pp. 171-191.

Kitagawa, K., (1990), "Japan's Economic Relations with Africa between the Wars : A Study of Japanese Consular Reports", Kyoto University, *African Study Monograph*, Vol. 11, No. 3, pp. 125-141.

Kitagawa, K., (1997), *A Study in the History of Japanese Commercial Relations with South Africa [Nihon-Minami Ahurika Tusho Kankeishi Kenkyu]*, International Research Centre for Japanese Studies, Monograph Series, No. 13.

Kitagawa, K., (2003), "Japan's Trade with South Africa in the Inter-War Period", in Chris Aden and Katsumi Hirano eds., *Japan and South Africa in a Globalizing World ; A Distant Mirror*, Hampshire, Ashgate, pp. 25-44.

Kitagawa, K., (2014), "The Relationship between Japan and South Africa before World War II", *Kansai University Review of Economics*, No. 16, pp. 31-57.

Kitagawa, K., (2015), "Japan's Trade with West Africa in the Inter-War Period : A Study of Japanese Consular Reports", *Kansai University Review of Economics*, No. 17, pp. 1-28.

Mitsui Trading Company (1951), *A Short History of Mitsui Trading Company before the World War I [Mitsui Bussan Sho-Shi]*.

Mitsui Trading Company, (1986), *A History of Mitsui Trading Company [Mitsui Bussan no Rekisi]*, Vol. 1.

Nichimen Jitsugyo Kabushiki Kaisha, (1962), *A 70 Year History of Nichimen [Nichimen 70 Nenshi]*, Osaka.

Nunokawa, Magoichi, (1917), "Conditions of Foreign Trade in South Africa [Nan-A Boeki Jijo]", The Ministry of Agriculture and Commerce's Bureau of Trade and Industry, *Journal of Trade and Industry*, No. 45.

Osaka Shosen Kaisha (OSK), (1956), *History of African Shipping Lines [Ahurika Koro Shi]*, OSK, Osaka.

Padayachee, Vishnu and Robert Morell (1991), "Indian Merchants and Dukawalas in Natal Economy, 1889~1914", *Journal of Southern African Studies*, Vol. 19, No. 1, pp.

Platt, D.C. M., (1971), *The Cinderella Service : British Consul since 1825*, London.

Shimizu, Yaoichi, "Japanese Immigrants in South Africa [Nan-A no Nihonjin Imin]", Diplomatic

Archives of MOFA, File 3-8-8-20.

Shirakawa, Ikai, (1928), *Field Report : A Trip to East Africa [Jicchi Tosa Higashi Ahurika no Tabi]*, Hakubunkan.

Sugiyama, Shinya and Linda Grove eds. (1999), *Commercial Networks in Modern Asia [Kindai Ajia no Ryutsu Nettowaku]*, Sobunsha, Tokyo.

Takashimaya 135th Commemorative Publication, (1968), *Takashimaya : A History of 135 Years [Takashimaya 135 Nen-Shi]*.

The Ministry of Foreign Affairs (MOFA), (1932), *A General View of Economic Conditions in Africa [Ahurika Keizai Jijo Tenbo]*, Tokyo.

The Ministry of Foreign Affairs (MOFA), (1903), "Report of the Mission to South Africa [Nan-A Shisatsu Fukumeisho]", *The Journal of Commercial Reports*, No. 22.

"Japanese Trade with South Africa and Sales Conditions of Japanese Goods in South African Market" (Letter on 29 April 1916 from Yaoichi Shimizu to the Ministry of Foreign Affairs), *Official Commercial Reports*, No. 332, July 1916.

"Annual Report on South African Overseas Trade in 1920" (Letter on 22 September 1921 from Tadanao Imai to the Ministry of Foreign Affairs) *Official Commercial Reports*, January 1922.

"Annual Report on South African Overseas Trade in 1923" (Letter on 15 July 1924 from Tadanao Imai to the Ministry of Foreign Affairs), *Official Commercial Reports*, November 1924.

"Annual Report on Overseas Trade of the Union of South Africa (1937)" (Letter on 25 November 1938 from Takeo Kinoshita to the Ministry of Foreign affairs), *Overseas Economic Conditions*, No. 4, 1939.

"Japanese Cotton Cloth in South African Market" (Letter on 28 November 1939 from Kenichi Okada to the Ministry of Foreign Affairs), *Overseas Economic Conditions*, No. 4, 1940.

Ch 5
Pre-War Japan and South Africa

This chapter limits itself to the era before World War II, and considers how movements and experience emerged in South Africa. First, it considers Komahei Furuya, a merchant who advanced into South Africa as early as the end of the nineteenth century. Second, it describes Magoichi Nunokawa, who investigated South Africa's economic situation during World War I. Third, it examines Katsue Mori, a captain of the Osaka Shosen Kaisha (OSK) on the South African route, and Ikai Shirakawa of the *Osaka Asahi Shimbun*, who were involved in exchanges between Japan and South Africa in the 1920s and 1930s, as well as two South Africans from Natal who visited Japan. Fourth, it discusses Robert Wright, an honorary consul in Durban who played an important role in promoting trade between Japan and South Africa during the same era. Finally, it analyzes the views of an intellectual from imperial Japan on building a Boer "emerging nation" under the British imperial regime in South Africa.

1 Komahei Furuya and the "Mikado Shokai"

Let us examine the first person to involve himself in trade between Japan and Africa in the prewar era. According to *An Analysis of export trade of General Merchandize to Africa: 1939 [Ahurika shu muke honpo zakka yushutu boeki no bunseki: showa 14 nen]*, a report compiled by the Japan Trade Promotion Association, the earliest named stores run by Japanese people in prewar Africa were "Mikado Shokai" in Cape Town and "Nanbu Shokai" in Port Said.

The first Japanese field survey report on South Africa was probably "Report of the Mission to South Africa [Nan-a shisatsu fukumeisho]". This "Fukumeisho" was based on a survey that Saburo Hisamizu, a Japanese consul in Singapore, and Kuniomi Katsube, who was commissioned by the Ministry of Agriculture and Commerce, conducted for two months, from August to October, in 1902. The report was published in *Journal of Commercial Reports [Tsusho Isan]* (No. 22, 1903), and it was republished in five parts in Ukichi Taguchi's *Tokyo Economics Magazine [Tokyo Keizai Zasshi]* under the title "British South Africa." It contains a section entitled "A Japanese man in South Africa," and, though his name is not given specifically, it mentions Komahei Furuya of the "Mikado Shokai," as follows:

"The two, who own a Japanese sundry goods shop in an affluent part of town, and who also own a house near the mountains, are a fine example of a Japanese merchant and his wife. There is another who is employed as an assistant. It seems that the shop is greatly prosperous and very profitable; moreover, it seems to be gaining considerable trust among the merchants of Cape Town. Indeed, it even seems that the general secretary of the local chamber of commerce is treating him as a fully-fledged merchant." (*Journal of Commercial Reports [Tsusho Isan]*, No, 22, 1903)

The detailed history of Komahei Furuya, who ran the "Mikado Shokai," is unknown. The Diplomatic Archives of the Ministry of Foreign Affairs of Japan, thereafter Diplomatic Archive of MOFA) has a "List of Japanese nationals in British South Africa" in its collection, including the document "The name list of Japanese Traveler to South Africa [Nan-a tokosha jinmei ikken] (Taisho 5-nen 12-gatsu)" (File No. 3-8-8-20), according to which Furuya was born in the village of Oda, Tsukuba County, in February 1869, moved to South Africa in 1898, and ran a Japanese sundry goods store. It also seems that Furuya had the right to permanent residency because he was living in South Africa before the enactment of its immigration law in 1913. By the end of 1916, the "Mikado Shokai" was employing five Japanese, eight Europeans, and five Africans. Among the Japanese employees, Tokuichi Otsuka (born in 1888) had been working in the store since October 1906 and had permanent residency. The four others had begun working at the "Mikado Shokai" after the establishment of the Union of South Africa: Heishiro Suzuki (born in 1891), who had graduated from Osaka Business School; Sadamu Kurakazu (born in 1890), who had graduated from the Waseda University business school; Takami Iijima (born in 1890), who had graduated from Nagasaki Commercial College; and Arihito Arai (born in 1887), who had graduated from Tokyo High School of Business. Based on their education, it seems likely that they were working at the "Mikado Shokai" as part of the Agriculture and Commerce Ministry's Overseas Business Trainee program. Among other goods, the "Mikado Shokai" originally sold folding screens, silk handkerchiefs, folding and rigid fans, kimonos, Cloisonné vessels, bamboo baskets, umbrellas, and pottery; it later added to its stock knitted cotton underwear, towels, paintbrushes, Japanese socks, and shell buttons. (Aoki, 1993 : 141-190)

At this time, Furuya was commissioned by the Ministry of Japanese Agriculture and Commerce, and he contributed a report entitled "The impact of current affairs on South African trade and goods with hopeful prospects for export" to *Boeki Zasshi [Trade Journal]* (Vol. 3, No. 2, February 1916). In this report, Furuya presented the following problems as needing to be addressed in order for Japan-South Africa trade to develop:

"One can still recognize anti-Japanese tendencies toward our nation's products and merchants in South Africa; three years ago the Union government promulgated and then implemented immigration regulations absolutely banning all Asians. At the time, I met with the South African Union government's Minister of the Interior to appeal for better prospects in the future for Japan-South Africa trade. As a result, I was led to understand that merchants would be allowed to stay for up to five years, but that the government would not grant any new business licenses, meaning that the path for starting new businesses is currently still blocked off. This is a grave problem, tantamount to a ban on trade between Japan and South Africa. Only fifteen Japanese people are staying in Cape Town at present, and the Anglo-Japanese Treaty is yet to be applied here; if things continue as they are, trade ties between Japan and South Africa will surely be severed. It is necessary to formulate some sort of measures while we have the opportunity to do so." (*Boeki Zasshi [Trade Journal]*, Vol. 3, No. 2, 1916)

Incidentally, the year before the formation of the Union of South Africa, Furuya had also petitioned the Japanese government to have the barriers to commercial activities in South Africa removed. The Diplomatic Archives of the Ministry of Foreign Affairs has two letters in their collection that were sent in 1909 from Komahei Furuya to Takaaki Kato, Japan's Plenipotentiary Ambassador to the United Kingdom, in a document entitled "Various matters relating to treatment of this nation's citizens in South Africa and Zanzibar" (1905–1920), (Diplomatic Archives of MOFA, File No. 3-8-2-219) The contents are as follows.

The first letter, dated November 29, 1909, dealt with two matters. First, Furuya was traveling around South Africa with samples, was taking orders, and wanted to expand his sales. There seemed to be no trouble in the colonies of Natal or Cape, but he complained that there was a barrier to entering Orange River Colony unless he had lived there before 1898 or was given permission for a temporary stay. Japanese nationals, as Asians, were prohibited immigrants; obtaining a temporary stay permit required a wait of one month, and, even if he was successful in entering the colony, he was prohibited from dealing in goods. Second, Furuya had planned to open a branch in Johannesburg, but for similar reasons business licenses would not be issued to those with temporary stay permits. However, there were few Japanese people staying there, even compared to other Asians, and it was possible that those applying for exemptions through the local consulate might receive special treatment; so he appealed to the Japanese government to enter into negotiations with the Transvaal government. (Diplomatic Archives of MOFA, File No. 3-8-2-219)

In the second letter, dated December 15, 1909, Furuya recommended the appointment of Julius Jeppe, a Cape Town resident who desired to become an Honorary Consul of Japan. Jeppe had previously applied to Count Jutaro Komura to be appointed to the post, but the latter had refused on the grounds that the time was not yet ripe. Now he was receiving Furuya's recommendation. It was clear that the Union of South Africa would soon be established, and once this happened, the immigration regulations would become the most serious impediment to expanding trade between Japan and South Africa. Furuya was appealing to have an Honorary Consul appointed without delay, so that the Japanese could be left out from the category of prohibited immigrants. (Diplomatic Archives of MOFA, File No. 3-8-2-219)

Later, Julius Jeppe became the Honorary Consul in Cape Town, and he sent information about South Africa's economy to the Trade Bureau of Japan's Foreign Affairs Ministry. The first report, entitled "General outlook on South Africa: 1910" (dated June 1, 1911), was published in *Tsusho Isan [Journal of Commercial Reports]* (No. 62, 1911). However, South Africa would not afford wide latitude to the Japanese to freely conduct business activities until long after World War I, meaning that it was delayed until the start of the worldwide depression of the 1930s. (Aoki, 1993)

2 Magoichi (Seien) Nunokawa and the Survey of South African Economy
When considering the early relationship between Japan and South Africa, one may note the importance of Magoichi (Seien) Nunokawa and his survey research on South Africa during World War I.

Nunokawa was born in 1870 and died in 1944. He was born in Yamagata Prefecture, moved to study in Sendai at the age of 14, and went to Tokyo to study at Keio Gijuku (today's Keio University) at 15. However, he went home after six months, was baptized at 16, and returned to Tokyo aged 17 in the autumn to study at the theology department of the Tokyo English-Japanese School (today's Aoyama Gakuin University). Nunokawa was less interested in theology than in psychology, ethics, or sociology, and eventually dropped out of Aoyama Gakuin after three years.

In the period between the Sino-Japanese War and the Russo-Japanese War, German-style scholarship became predominate, and with this came a flourishing of research into social problems; debates began to develop from the viewpoints of social reformism and socialism. Immediately after the Sino-Japanese War, Nunokawa predicted that economic fluctuations would cause social problems, and he established the Sociological Society, which began publishing *Shakai Zasshi [Sociology Magazine]*. In 1896, Nunokawa consulted with Ukichi Taguchi about the magazine. The publication of *Shakai Zasshi* began in April 1897, and Nunokawa later became involved in editing it. Nunokawa argued about social problems from the viewpoints of social policy and social reformism, and he did not always agree with Taguchi.

According to the article "Professor Taguchi and the Meiji economics academia"

(*Tokyo Keizai Zasshi [Tokyo Economics Magazine]*, No. 1845, January 1916), Nunokawa studied economics at Keio Gijuku as a regular student. He also wrote a short piece himself for *Tokyo Keizai Zasshi* (No. 1591, April 1911), entitled "Matters related to Professor Teiken." According to this piece, in 1895 Nunokawa had served at the Meiji Girls' School, which Ukichi Taguchi's sister, Toko Kimura, had established, and he taught economics to the college students there.

In 1903, Nunokawa joined the Keizai Zasshi Company, and for the seven years until 1909 he was in charge of this magazine's editing. He contributed many essays to it between 1906 and 1911. For instance, in "Popular sentiment after the war" (No. 1334, April 1906) and "The effects of financial fluctuations" (No. 1373, 1907), he warned that problems of prices, unemployment, overpopulation, and hard living conditions needed to be dealt with properly, as it was unknown whether the economic recovery following the end of the Russo-Japanese War would last. In these essays, he argued that economic policy should be formulated from a global standpoint. In order to reign in the spread of plutocracy, which controlled politics at all levels from central to local, he called for the franchise to be expanded; additionally, he stressed the need for a factory law and a workers' insurance law to combat various problems arising from a concentration of capital and an increase in poverty.

The following essays, which are on related matters, are of interest. Nunokawa considered Japan's place in the world and its global policy in the articles "Solving the Tibet Problem" (No. 1335, May 1906), "The fusion of Eastern and Western civilization (parts one and two)" (Nos. 1404 and 1405, September 1907), and "The Japanese have poor knowledge of China" (Nos. 1751 and 1752, May and June 1913). He discussed the ethics of industrialists and politicians and social policy in "Economics and morality" (No. 1375, February 1907), and he also discussed social problems in such works as "An observation on this nation's population problem" (No. 1809, July 1915) and "Observations on the conditions of manual laborers in Tokyo (parts one, two, and three)" (Nos. 1811, 1912, and 1913; July and August 1915). He wrote about economic theory and thought in works such as "The 150th anniversary of Malthus' birth (parts one, two, and three)" (Nos. 1838, 1839, and 1841; February and March 1916) and "Professor Taguchi and the Meiji economics world (parts one, two, and three)" (Nos. 1835, 1836, and 1837; January and February 1916).

Later during the World War I, Nunokawa was commissioned by the Ministry of Agriculture and Commerce, which sent him on an economic survey in the Union of South Africa from September 1916 to January 1917, as well as to Russia for seven months from September 1917, and he wrote many reports. His economic surveys of South Africa were collected in the article "Conditions of Foreign Trade in South Africa [Nan-A Boeki Jijo]" (Ministry of Agriculture and Commerce Bureau of Commerce and Industry, *Shoko Isan*, No. 48, March 1917), and his surveys on Russia, written in the months leading up to and immediately after August 1918, when Japanese troops were first deployed to Siberia, cover the conditions surrounding the Russian Revolution and are of much interest. For example, he published reports including "Current affairs in Russia" (No. 1950, April 1918), "Commercial conditions in Vladivostok" (No. 1937, January 1918), and "Recent conditions of Russo-Japanese trade and its future (parts one and two)" (Nos. 1979 and 1980, November 1918).

It should be noted that "Conditions of Foreign Trade in South Africa" was based on a field survey that Nunokawa, under commission from the Ministry of Agriculture and Commerce, conducted after the establishment of the Union of South Africa. Nunokawa left Japan in September 1916 and arrived in Cape Town in October 23. Having observed areas throughout South Africa, he returned to Japan at the end of January 1917. According to a report by Yaoichi Shimizu, who was at the time stationed in Cape Town and commissioned by the Ministry of Foreign Affairs, Japanese trade with South Africa had rapidly boomed during the World War I, but Asians were prohibited immigrants under the 1913 immigration law, and could not freely engage in commercial activities. It would appear that Nunokawa's survey was conducted in order to explore the background to these problems, given the necessity of formulating all possible measures to enable the continued development of trade between Japan and South Africa and to ensure guarantees for entry and stay into the Union of South Africa for Japanese merchants. According to Nunokawa's report, the Union of South Africa had maintained a trade surplus before the World War I, but this had turned into a deficit during the war. The United Kingdom and other British possessions accounted for an overwhelming proportion of its international trade. Looking at individual goods, the pattern was that South Africa exported minerals, agricultural products, and animal products, while it imported manufactured goods. Looking at trade between Japan and South Africa, exports from the former had increased rapidly during the World War I. This was due to the flow of consumer goods from Europe being cut off during the war and prices rising, meaning that demand for Japanese goods increased. Some South African merchants even tried to trade with Japanese merchants directly or to acquire Japanese goods via foreign merchants staying in Japan. Exports from Japan consisted chiefly of cotton and silk textiles, knitted goods, and sundries, and its imports included wattle bark, cattle and sheep hides, wool, and aloes, whose imports were generally of a low value. (Nunokawa, 1917: 3)

Nunokawa argued that there were two important issues to resolve in order for Japan's trade with South Africa to increase. The first was a problem concerning trade settlement practices. In the Union of South Africa, merchants of British descent could freely engage in activities, using their considerable power to finance.

When importing goods from Japan, they had associated companies in London place the orders to Japan and had the goods shipped to South Africa. Upon doing so, the money order for payment from London took between 90 and 100 days to clear. However, when receiving orders from non-British South African merchants, a Japanese seller had to prepare for a much longer grant of credit. The second problem was that one needed to find a reliable proxy merchant to deal smoothly in Japanese goods, since Japanese people, due to their status as prohibited immigrants in the Union of South Africa, could not engage in business activity. (Nunokawa, 1917: 88-90).

Thus, Nunokawa argued in "Trade conditions" that, given the restrictions on Japanese goods advancing into the South African market, Japan needed to further promote its own industrialization, severely reign in the mass production of inferior goods, and improve the reputation of its goods. The country's manufacturers needed to organize industrial cooperative associations and to select proxy merchants worthy of trust, while it was also necessary to open up a path for developing direct transactions. Nunokawa concluded as follows: "Presumably, in order to develop commercial trade, it will be necessary, on the one hand, to be thoroughly acquainted with the tastes and customs of the people who are our trade partners and to export products matching their preferences and habits; on the other hand, we must observe the industrial position of these countries and import goods that will be of benefit to us, thereby developing trade in both directions. If we are to be thoroughly acquainted with our trading partners, it is surely important for our traders to be allowed free access." (Nunokawa, 1917: 98-99)

In addition to "Conditions of Foreign Trade in South Africa," and also based on his South African survey, Nunokawa wrote "General conditions in South Africa" and "The level of restrictions on Japanese merchants' landfall on South Africa and on their business" (*Naigai Shoko Jiho*, January 1917), as well as "General conditions of imports and exports in the Union of South Africa" (*Naigai Shoko Jiho*, February 1917) and "Tales of a visit to South Africa" (*Tokei Shushi*, No. 434, 1917). Nunokawa also submitted two contributions to *Tokyo Keizai Zasshi*: "General conditions in South Africa (parts one and two)" (Nos. 1886 and 1887, January 1917) and "Tales of a visit to South Africa" (No. 1897, April 1917). The former was a communiqué that Nunokawa, a friend of the Tokyo Keizai Zasshi Company, had sent during his survey, while he was commissioned (as a foreign dispatch agent) by the Ministry of Agriculture and Commerce; the latter was based on notes from a public lecture given at the Tokyo Economics Association.

As shown above, Nunokawa played a major role in spreading knowledge about the South African economy in Taisho-era Japan.

3 Captain Katsue Mori of the Osaka Shosen Kaisha and the two South Africans

Although he was one of many people in prewar Japan who were involved in Africa, we should not overlook Katsue Mori, a captain of the Osaka Shosen Kaisha (OSK). Captain Mori's life came to a close on May 24, 1989, when he was 99 years old. In mourning of his death, the British newspaper *The Times* ran an obituary, opening as follows: "Katsue Mori who died on May 24 at the age of 99, played a role at sea and in the life of Japan which over sixty years evolved from the heroic to the symbolic. He was an almost mythological ancient mariner who had also survived many even greater voyages of events and time than those described in Laurens van der Post's *Yet Being Someone Other*." One can learn just how many friends Captain Mori had from looking at the wide variety of people who submitted pieces for *In Memorial Katsue Mori* (Japan Maritime Public Relations Center), published in May 1990.

Captain Katsue Mori: 70 Stubborn Years at Sea, published in 1975, describes the life of Captain Mori as follows. Katsue Mori was born on April 6, 1890 in an area of the village of Sakurai called Nagaura, within Kamoto County, Kumamoto Prefecture. He graduated from Sakurai Village Middle School in March 1903 and entered Kumamoto Prefectural Seiseiko High School in April. During this period, Japan was finally about to join the ranks of advanced imperialist nations, having secured victories in the Sino-Japanese War, fought from August 1894 to April 1895, and the Russo-Japanese War, fought from February 1904 to September 1905.

In September 1908, Mori enrolled in the maritime program of Tokyo Merchant Marine School, and from July 1912 to October 1913 he sailed across the world in the training sailboat the *Taisei Maru*, overcoming many difficulties. Having graduated from the Tokyo Merchant Marine School in April 1914, he joined the Osaka Shosen Kaisha (OSK) in May, and he sailed the Bombay route as the third officer on the *Marei Maru*. However, after the *Marei Maru* collided with the *Yawata Maru* of Yamashita Kisen Company in May 1915, Mori was forced to stay in Port Said as the director of the moored ship until the marine accident inquiry had been adjudicated. After returning to Japan, he set sail in July 1916 on the North American route as the second officer aboard the *Hawai Maru*. During the World War I, he sailed the Mediterranean route as the first officer aboard the *Roei Maru*. After the war, in May 1923, he became the captain of the *Chosen Maru* on the Java route.

Captain Mori's relationship with Africa began after he assumed the post of captain of the *Kanada Maru*, OSK's first ship on the Southeast Africa route, in March 1926. In total, he spent almost a decade involved with Africa: he sailed on the *Kanada Maru* for three years, became captain of the *Mekishiko Maru* for three years from May 1928, and was also captain of the *Ahurika Maru* on the Africa-South America route for three years from November 1931. He served as captain of the *Shikago Maru* on the Philippine route from January 1935 until he left OSK in September 1938. During World War II, he worked for the Nanyou Souko Company and visited points throughout the South Seas. He was engaged in the construction of wooden ships in Makassar on the island of Celebes when the war ended. He later held numerous positions, including on the board of directors of Ogawa Unyu (September 1949), as vice president of the association Kaiyou-kai (August 1952), and on the board of the Japan Cargo Tally Corporation (May 1965).

Returning to Captain Mori's relationship with Africa, *An Analysis of Export of General Merchandize to Africa: 1939*, published by the Japan Trade Promotion Association in December 1941, states as follows. In the Union of South Africa, Asians had been banned from entering the country since 1913, but Japanese people were "able to enjoy treatment equal to that afforded to whites from October 1931; this was thanks to the efforts of then-Consul Takeshige Yamazaki and Captain Mori, who was involved in OSK's opening of a South Africa-via-East-Africa route and who sailed the same route." In a short piece in OSK's public relations magazine *Nami [Wave]* (April 1929), entitled "The place called East Africa," Mori himself wrote about his efforts as a captain trying to improve the treatment of Japanese people in East Africa and South Africa, which he deemed exclusionary and discriminatory, and looking back from his impending transfer to the Africa-South America route to the six years he had spent making dozens of voyages on the *Kanada Maru* and the *Mekishiko Maru*.

People sometimes discover something extraordinary within themselves during their lives, and sometimes they are able to take something extraordinary and make it their own. For Captain Mori, it would seem that this crucial time came while he was involved in the Southeast Africa route, as the friendships that the captain would make while sailing this route would come to have a great effect on his later life.

In March 1926, Katsue Mori was appointed captain of the *Kanada Maru* (6064 metric tons), the first ship of the Southeast Africa route. He was the tender age of 35 at the time. It is said that this promotion was due to the recommendation of then-sales manager Shozo Murata (later the Minister of Communication). The *Kanada Maru* was a cargo and passenger ship built in 1911 in the Mitsubishi shipyard in Nagasaki, and its coal-fired motor had a speed of 10 knots. When Mori was appointed the ship's captain, the post-World War I Japanese economy was falling into a recession: this was the beginning of a long depressive slump that continued through the 1927 Japanese financial crisis and the worldwide economic crash of 1929. Attempting to respond to this economic situation, in January 1926 the Wakatsuki Government gave 400,000 yen in aid to OSK and appointed it to open an African route, with the aim of gaining new markets in the Balkans, the Middle East, and Africa. Prior to this, OSK had asked Masao Tajima of the Far Seas Division to study mutual economic relations in the East African region, as well as general marine transport routes. The result was a one-ship-per-month line, preparing for a decade in the red. The *Kanada Maru* left Japan on March 23 and reached the port of Mombasa on April 23. Riding on the ship were Ikai Shirakawa of the *Osaka Asahi Shimbun* and Tatsuo Hisatomi of the *Osaka Mainichi Shimbun*, who were there to report on events in Africa. Shirakawa and Hisatomi gathered material over two months while they traveled around Southeast Africa, experiencing discrimination against Japanese people along the way. Shirakawa later published *Jicchi Tosa Higashi Ahurika no Tabi [Field Report: A Trip to East Africa]* (1928). At the time, East African treatment of Asians (Indians) was severely discriminatory, and it seems that Captain Mori appealed for Japanese people to be treated better at every opportunity. For instance, he allowed Kenyan governor Edward Grigg, the governor's wife, and their entourage, to ride with them to Dar es Salaam, using this opportunity to appeal for improvements to the discriminatory treatment that Japanese people received; he also hosted a dinner on the *Kanada Maru*, asking for cooperation from British merchants who belonged to the Mombasa Chamber of Commerce.

For their part, Shirakawa and Hisatomi traveled to Durban in the Union of South Africa, visiting the office of the *Natal Advertiser*. During the trip, the two were rescued from a difficult situation by Laurens van der Post, a reporter with that paper, and they suggested that he meet Captain Mori. In July 1926, the *Kanada Maru* went off on its second voyage, and Captain Mori visited Durban via Mombasa, Zanzibar, Dar es Salaam, Beira, and Lourenço Marques. This was when the captain met the young van der Post (then 19) and William Plomer (then 22). Van der Post would become well known as a writer in Japan through many works he would write later, including *Venture to the Interior* and *The Lost World of the Kalahari*. Plomer had already written a novel decrying racial discrimination in South Africa, *Turbot Wolfe*. This novel portrayed European colonial life, the corruption that comes with such power, its lack of self-awareness, and the blindness seen in attitudes toward other races, non-white races, and, in particular, toward the blacks who live within one's territory. They both also contributed to the literary journal *Voorslag* ("whiplash" in Afrikaans), edited by the South African poet Roy Campbell (then 24), who at this young age was already known for his epic poem "The Flaming Terrapin."

Captain Mori sympathized with van der Post and Plomer, who both challenged racism in South Africa, and, thinking that he would increase their understanding of Japan, he decided to take them back with him. While staying in Durban, Captain Mori had van der Post run an article in the *Natal Advertiser* about the discrimination that he had experienced at a restaurant, and he also submitted a piece of his own. Thus, van der Post went to Japan as a correspondent for the *Natal Advertiser*, and Plomer as a correspondent for the *Natal Witness*, a paper published by Desmond

Young (a friend of van der Post) in Pietermaritzburg, Natal Province. The *Kanada Maru* left Durban on September 2, 1926 and arrived in Kobe on October 19. Van der Post returned to South Africa via the same *Kanada Maru* after a stay of two weeks, and he serialized an article introducing Japan, entitled "To the East," in the *Natal Advertiser*. Later, while staying in Durban in 1927, Captain Mori would give a speech at a Rotary Club meeting on eliminating discrimination, attempting to gain permission to play at golf club that banned the admittance of Asians.

For his part, William Plomer remained in Japan for two years, living in Kaminerima and Higashinakano, and he lectured on *Shakespeare* at the Tokyo School of Foreign Languages (now Tokyo University of Foreign Studies) and Tokyo College (now University of Tokyo College of Arts and Sciences). He serialized a piece on his impressions of Japan, entitled "An Afrikaner in Japan," in eight parts in the *Natal Witness*. One of these parts was published by Masao Tajima in *Nami* (August 1927) under the title "Japan as seen by an up-and-coming writer from South Africa." Afterwards, Plomer returned to the United Kingdom via the Trans-Siberian Railway. He is now known not only for later writing about his life in Japan and Captain Mori in his autobiography, *Double Lives*, but when English composer Benjamin Britten wrote *Curlew River* (based on a Noh play about the Sumida River in Tokyo), he provided the libretto.

So we can see that Captain Mori, as one man, was involved in many aspects of the relationship between prewar Japan and Southeast Africa. Years later, van der Post would write an essay entitled "Fifty years of friendship," which he provided for Captain Mori's autobiography, in which he stated that meeting the captain had great meaning, in that it led to him discovering "not only another country in the world outside, but also a new place in the world inside myself." This sentiment can also be felt in his memoir *Yet Being Someone Other*. One could surely say the same about Captain Mori. Nevertheless, Captain Mori's thoughts and actions in reaction to the discrimination against Japanese people in South and East Africa and his way of relating to the region were primarily aimed at people of European descent, and he did not give consideration to Africans who had been living there since long before white rule, or to his own relationship with them; thus, Captain Mori's thinking was constrained by the era in which he lived and by the relationship between Japan and Africa at that time.

When the OSK started the Africa route and Captain Katsue Mori piloted its first ship, one of the people onboard was the aforementioned *Osaka Asahi Shimbun* reporter, Ikai Shirakawa, who deserves closer scrutiny. Ikai Shirakawa was born in Tokyo in April 1895. After graduating from the First Higher School (a college later absorbed into Tokyo University), he studied at the department of economics at Tokyo Imperial University and then joined the *Asahi Shimbun* in 1921. His book *Jicchi Tosa Higashi Ahurika no Tabi* was published in 1928 as an expanded version of his feature series "East Africa travel diaries," which had run in the *Osaka Asahi Shimbun* and was based on his 1926 observational tour of Africa. Before and after then and since joining the company, Shirakawa was at different times a correspondent in New York and head of the economics department in the Osaka branch. From January 1936, he became chief of the Shanghai bureau, vice-chief of the editing bureau in Osaka, and then, from 1942 to 1945, chief of the editing bureau at the company's western headquarters. Before he published *Jicchi Tosa Higashi Ahurika no Tabi*, he translated various works, including G.D.H. Cole's *Guild Socialism Restated* and G.R.S. Taylor's *Guild Politics: A Practical Programme for the Labour Party and the Co-operators*, and published them through Naigai Publishing Co. Ltd. in 1923. It seems that Shirakawa translated these two works on the recommendation of Kyoson (real name: Tsutomu) Tsuchida, who was then known as a critic of civilization and a thinker. Kyoson Tsuchida was born in Sado in 1891, graduated from Tokyo Higher Normal School in 1914, and then entered Kyoto Imperial University, where he studied philosophy under Kitaro Nishida. Later, Tsuchida lived in Kyoto and edited the magazine *Bunka [Culture]*, which attempted to explain social problems, ideas, and culture. The details of Shirakawa and Tsuchida's meeting and interactions are not known, but one can imagine Shirakawa's ideological background in broad strokes if one considers the connections between the two. Using what is written in Shirakawa's works, let us examine his "understanding of the place of the Japanese in East Africa" and his "view of Africans."

Based on his experiences of discriminatory treatment during his trip to East Africa and South Africa, he wrote as follows in opposition to Asian discrimination and concerning the place of the Japanese:

"In both East Africa and South Africa, we would like to insist to the Europeans loudly, 'Treat us like first-class citizens, not like the other Asians, not like the Indians and the Chinese;' however, if we want Japanese industry to grow, that is, if we want to sell Japanese goods, then we must also cooperate with the Indians, as they have spread throughout the area and hold commercial rights, in fact if not in law. While we cooperate with the Indians, we should demand that the Europeans differentiate us from them. By this, I mean that we should try not to offend the sentiments of the Indians and try to join with the Europeans only when it is advantageous. Could any other stance be as difficult as this? However, I feel that there is one major argument in its favor. As long as the present state of Asia is maintained, or, at least, at the moment, it would seem that if only the Japanese can receive the same status as Westerners, then a similar chance will eventually be afforded to the Indians and Chinese, who mentally and physically differ little from Japanese people, and are even sometimes greatly superior. So our efforts will surely have great value, not only for us as Japanese citizens, but also as leaders of the Asians." (Shirakawa, 1928)

One can also glimpse Shirakawa's extremely interesting "view of Africans" in his argument about "the labor shortage," which, among the various problems in East Africa, was particularly linked to colonial development:

"... [A] nother major cause of the labor shortage is that the natives do not want to work. However, that certainly does not mean that they are natural-born idlers. 'Idlers' implies people who do not work even though it is a situation in which they must work. By contrast, the natives do not want to work because their lives are carefree... The world of East Africa was a heavenly paradise until the Europeans invaded... The measures the European rulers have implemented... the whip of taxation... the stimulation of material greed... have worked as expected to some degree... [but] the gods (the Africans) have taken a leap toward being cultured and fallen... No matter how the rulers try to make them work or to raise their efficiency, they will always struggle with those methods of coercion and seduction." (Shirakawa, 1928)

Here he depicts the Africans as being built into the structure of colonial rule.

In addition, Shirakawa argued as follows about the relationship between the Africans who were being "civilized" under colonial rule and the Japanese:

"Actually, I do not find myself laughing upon seeing the comical acculturation of the natives. After all, even in civilized countries such as our own, such coercion and trickery is quite common, albeit in different forms... How is the idea of capitalists devising various profit-sharing systems and making the workers labor as much as possible any different from what is happening to the African natives? Reconsidering things once more, it is surely ironic to no end that our cotton rags and sundries will sell all because the African natives have had the misfortune of falling so low." (Shirakawa, 1928)

In African studies, the task of looking back at the course of the Japanese understanding of Africa is extremely important. Perhaps Shirakawa's writings can play a significant role in reflecting upon our own understanding of Africa in the present, if nothing else.

4 The Appointment of the Durban Honorary Consul : William Robert Wright

Upon entering Adderley Street in Cape Town, one can see a park ahead (the company garden of the former Dutch East India Company) in which the Iziko South African Museum can be found. In one corner of this park, as well as in a corner of the Durban Botanic Gardens, a stone lantern stands silently, today unnoticed by most. Next to the lantern in Cape Town there is a plaque inscribed as follows: "This stone lantern was presented to Cape Town by the government of Japan as a token of appreciation of the kindness and hospitality shown to Japanese emigrants.

Erected—August 1932." This brings to mind the following cable that Cape Town Consul Tomotsune Ota sent to Foreign Minister Hachiro Arita on June 16, 1936:

"The amended law concerning rights to residence and conducting business was passed by Parliament on the 15th, and all of our side's demands were achieved. Along with expressing my deepest gratitude to both sides involved, and to the Prime Minister, in particular, for their beneficence, I would like to note my hearty congratulations to both Japan and South Africa, as well as my hope that there be further efforts to advance the friendship between our two nations." (Diplomatic Archives of MOFA, File No. K2-6-1-11)

This cable signified that the freedom of Japanese people to live and work in Transvaal Province had been recognized, and that barriers to trade in Johannesburg, the place with the highest demand for Japanese products, had been lifted. Six years earlier, on October 16, 1930, Cape Town Consul Takeshige Yamazaki and Union of South Africa Acting External Affairs Secretary Farrell had exchanged an Agreement between South Africa and Japan concerning entry into residence in South Africa and other matters, recognizing a limited freedom for Japanese people to reside and conduct business in the country.[1] Then, as a result of further negotiations, on June 11, 1932, Japanese people with permanent resident status were given permission to invite assistants to join them from Japan. Permanent residency status had been recognized for Japanese people who had entered the country before the passage of the 1913 immigration law, which was enacted with the purpose of excluding Asians from South Africa, but, a quarter of a century after immigrating, those original migrants had become aged; they needed to be looked after by relatives. It was in this context that the Japanese government of the time presented the stone lanterns to Cape Town and Durban, in response to the South African government's magnanimous treatment.

Prior to this, Foreign Minister Kijuro Shidehara sent a note via Cape Town Consul Tadanao Imai, entitled "Re: Notification of Appointment of Durban Honorary Consul William Robert Wright" and dated April 16, 1926:

"Trade and commerce between Japan and British South Africa is growing ever more frequent. Therefore, upon feeling a need to place an Imperial Honorary Consul in Durban, I have conferred directly with His Imperial Highness and I place confidence in your diligence and faithfulness. As a result, you have been appointed Honorary Consul in Durban. I have sent two letters of appointment and at the same time offer you congratulations. After receiving a letter of approval from the government of Great Britain, Consul Imai should pass on the letter of mandate. No payment or office expenses will be provided on account of your holding this honorary post." (Diplomatic Archives of MOFA, File No. M2-1014-43)

According to a cable from Consul Imai to Foreign Minister Shidehara dated April 20, 1926, the Honorary Consulate in Durban was to be opened on April 26, and its mailing address for inquiries was to be P.O. Box 1021, Durban, South Africa. In addition, parcels were to be sent C/O Wm Cotts & Co. Ltd., 49 Point Road, Durban, Natal, South Africa. On May 21, the Governor-General of the Union of South Africa officially recognized the Durban Honorary Consul. Based on a letter dated May 8, 1942 and sent by Foreign Minister Togo to Chargé d'Affaires Kanda in Sweden, W. R. Wright remained Honorary Consul until diplomatic relations with South Africa were cut off on December 8, 1941.

William Robert Wright was born in London in 1871 as the second son of the late W. M. Wright. After graduating from Hayman's College in London, he moved to Natal in 1889. He worked at W. Dunn & Co. until 1896, then moving to Wm. Cotts & Co., and by the time he was appointed Honorary Consul was a major figure in the management of the latter, a company located in Durban's Point area.

After becoming Honorary Consul, W. R. Wright frequently mailed the *Annual Report of the Durban Chamber of Commerce* to the Japanese Foreign Ministry's Trade Bureau as material that showed the economic trends in Natal in the 1930s. The Durban Chamber of Commerce was founded in 1856, and it was located within the city in Salisbury House on Smith Street. In addition, Honorary Consul Wright also sent reports about trends concerning Japanese goods in the Durban market. According to these reports, it seems that local businesses were growing more concerned about cheap textile goods imported from Japan, including suitcases and silk shirts, as well as rubber boots and drills. South African business owners argued that they could not compete with silk shirts and pajamas that were imported from low-wage countries like Japan and China, and the Association of South African Chambers of Commerce appealed for the introduction of import restrictions.

It was in this environment that, on July 11, 1930, the city of Nagoya and the Nagoya Chamber of Commerce, along with the Trade Association, dispatched a traveling trade fair for Nagoya goods that went throughout South Africa and Eastern Africa. A member of the Nagoya Chamber of Commerce who participated in the trade fair, Yasuji Tamagawa, published a report entitled "The present state of the Union of South Africa and the reality of commercial sales" (*Nagoya Shoko Kaigisho Geppo*, January 1931). Sixteen companies from Nagoya sent goods to the fair. The trade fair was held in the three cities of Johannesburg, Durban, and Mombasa, and the various shops that were involved provided 13 metric tons of merchandise. The Japanese people who participated were Harusuke Takeuchi of the Nagoya City Hall, Yasuji Tamagawa of the Chamber of Commerce, three people from the cotton association, and an interpreter. In Durban, the trade fair was held from August 14 to 15 in Yorkshire House on Smith Street. The two main newspapers in Durban (*The Mercury* and *The Witness*) wrote Japan-friendly articles about it, and the trade fair was well-received (Aoki, 2007; Kitagawa, 1994).

5 Japanese Intellectuals' View to Cecil John Rhodes and the Emerging States in South Africa

Finally, I would like to provide two examples showing how prewar Japanese intellectuals understood Africa and colonialism. The first concerns the evaluation of the founder of the colony, Cecil Rhodes, and the second is a view on the founding of the emerging nations in South Africa (The South African Republic and The Orange Free State).

Cecil John Rhodes died on March 26, 1902. As far as I can tell, his obituary ran in at least 145 newspapers and magazines. *The Times* of London ran an article called "Death of Mr. Rhodes" on March 27, and *The Economist* ran one with the title "The Death of Mr. Rhodes" in its April 5 issue (pp. 523–524). The death of Rhodes was first reported in Japan on March 28, 1902 when the *Osaka Asahi Shimbun* ran a wire report from Reuters under the headline "Cecil Rhodes has finally died." From March 29, the *Osaka Asahi Shimbun* also ran a longer obituary split into five parts (March 29 through April 3), which began as follows:

"The great Cecil Rhodes of South Africa has finally passed away. The Boer War is at last nearing its end, and it should not be so regrettable for him to reach his eternal sleep upon seeing that his long sought for life's work of South African unification is now surely to be achieved. He indeed spent his entire life involved in the South African scheme. Those who sing the praises of imperialism will surely not cease to laud his distinguished service. We would like to mourn the loss of a luminary for Britain and narrate some of his history…"

The *Tokyo Keizai Zasshi* (No. 1126, April 5, 1902) also carried an article with the headline "The extraordinary Cecil Rhodes passes away":

"As the Boers have finally surrendered and the unification of South Africa is now to happen under Great Britain, South Africa's extraordinary Cecil Rhodes has passed away. Though the great achievement of African unification is now to be the success of Mr. Chamberlain, the source of it sprang in truth from Mr. Rhodes…" (p. 38)

Until the Sino-Japanese War, Japanese trade was controlled by Western and Chinese merchants. It was after the Sino-Japanese War that so-called "direct imports" (the switch from foreign to domestic merchants in trade deals) began; in particular, after the Russo-Japanese War large firms traded with Europe, America, Australia, and India, and small traders served Korea and China. However, it was after World War I that Japanese merchants' expansion into foreign trade in Japan's major trading ports became significant. This Japanese expansion required the dangerous task of personally participating in international relations as formed by the Great Powers. Thus, for instance, it was necessary for domestic policy to strongly implement the goals of "a wealthy nation" and "a strong army," based on concern over defending Japan from its neighbors, as well overcoming Japanese weakness in international politics through economic means. Additionally, from a foreign policy perspective, Japan was a late-coming imperialist country and saw Russia as its enemy in East Asia, so strategically it built alliances with the imperialist countries of Western Europe, while studying these nations as "models" of colonial rule.

Therefore, it would seem that interest in the 1899–1902 Anglo-Boer War and founder-of-empire Cecil Rhodes was particularly high. As Terutaro Nishino points out, "If interest in the South African war came from the goal of a strong army, then interest in Cecil Rhodes reflected part of the goal of a wealthy nation." Presumably, "A current of sentiment placing hope in this 'hero' or 'great and unique man', who 'heroically' ventured abroad to gain colonies and achieved success there, arose in response to the demands of a then-flourishing Japanese capitalism". (Nishino, 1964)

It was in this historical context that numerous biographies of Cecil Rhodes were published in Japan immediately following the conclusion of the Boer War and the man's death. The first of these biographies was published in six parts under the title "Cecil Rhodes" in Ukichi Taguchi's *Tokyo Keizai Zasshi* (Nos. 1135, 1136, 1137, 1138, 1139, 1140; June and July 1902). Later, Yasuji Yanagisawa published *Seshiru Rozu (Nan-a Kiketsu)* [*Cecil Rhodes (Colossus in South Africa)*] through Tokyo X Club in September 1902. Yanagisawa originally split the book into "Personal History," "Political and Religious Views," "A Theory of Cecil Rhodes," and "History of South Africa", and it would appear that Taguchi's forward to the book and the section on "Personal History" were serialized in *Tokyo Keizai Zasshi*. Yanagisawa's views on Rhodes are evident in the following passage: "What stimulates our brains is his greatness of character; it is not his being a hero, nor him being a man of virtue, but rather him being a peerlessly great idealist, simply an idealist…" (Yanagisawa, 1902)

One of the next works to be published was a pieced-together semi-translation by Shintaro Mori, titled in Japanese *Seshiru Rozu: Teio-ryu Gofu Dan* (Tokyo Daigakkan, December 1902). Shintaro Mori was born in Osaka in February 1871. He was also known as Gaiho Mori. He was a foreign reporter for *Jiji Shimpo*, and from 1904 to 1905 he published multiple volumes of *Nichi-ro Senso Hihyo* [*A Criticism of the Russo-Japanese War*] through the Jiji Shimpo Company, as well as a translation of Plutarch's *Lives of the Noble Greeks and Romans* through Shoyukan. His *Seshiru Rozu: Teio-ryu Gofu Dan* used then-current research papers on Rhodesian and South African history, as well as periodicals, as references, but he largely relied on Howard Hensman's *Cecil Rhodes: A Study of a Career* (Edinburgh: 1901). The following words by Mori expressed his intentions in writing this book:

"Regardless of whether or not Mr. Rhodes was a hero, and although this book might appear to be nothing more than the biography of a foreigner, the editor believes it to be of vital importance to citizens of this nation, including himself, in regard to today's issues."

Specifically, he stated, this meant that: "The greatness of Mr. Rhodes no longer needs any introduction. Although his exploits seem to have completely polarized South Africa, his consolidation of the diamond mines served as a model for the American Mr. Morgan in formulating the operation plan for the organization of his trust. Today, when the people of this nation have finally begun to notice the issue of trusts, there is surely great value in knowing how he achieved this consolidation. Moreover, what he has done in Rhodesia is the very thing Russia tried to do in invading Manchuria. Will the Qing Chinese really be able to play the role of the Matabele natives? Is the situation of East Asia really equivalent to that of Africa? Will Russia's policies against the Qing succeed? It seems that the answers to all these questions lie within this one point. Knowing the full account of Mr. Rhodes' annexation of Rhodesia will no doubt be of immediate interest to the people of this nation." (Mori, 1902)

One may also understand Mori's view of Cecil Rhodes through the following passages:

"...those who slander him with such accusations as that he committed outrages against humanity are either his political opponents or scoundrels spouting out words without even being able to understand him..." (Mori, 1902)

"It was not in Mr. Rhodes' character to be rough, nor was it to be precise. Rather, he was capable of being rough and precise at the same time. Thus, standing amongst the great unwashed, one may call him such a man... That is, he is capable of combining in one man characteristics that are difficult to combine and completely opposite." (Mori, 1902)

"I now call him the establisher of the British Empire. I believe it is not excessive praise to say so. After all, the British Empire's territory in South Africa was indeed saved thanks to his singular efforts... Bechuanaland, Rhodesia, Transvaal, and Orange were all not possessed by Britain. He saved South Africa from the forces of Dutch misrule. And when schemes by powers to expand their territory grew day by day in strength, he did not doubt that the Cape of Good Hope was in danger and that the decline of Britain hung in the balance. The one who saved all these situations was, namely, Rhodes." (Mori, 1902)

As shown above, Mori's views of Cecil Rhodes were not simply demonstrating a simple interest in a hero who advanced colonial rule, but were also thick with hero worship and heroic expectations. These views and a lack of interest in the African people were two sides of the same coin.

The Japanese had opened their doors to the outside world around the middle of the nineteenth century, and they had come to devote themselves to modeling their society on the advanced nations of the day, copying their systems and cultures. However, they originally had little interest in those countries that had only achieved their independence after the Meiji Restoration. In the first half of the Meiji Period, Japan's intellectuals were greatly interested in the European imperialist powers' processes of colonizing Asia and Africa through invasion, and they took the societies of Asian and African colonies as negative examples, warning against their influence on Japan. This being the case, Japanese intellectuals did not study the newly rising countries in the latter half of the nineteenth century.

One exception, however, would be Makoto (Nichinan) Fukumoto (1857–1921) and his book *New State Building [Shinkenkoku]* (1900). This book is of interest for the following reason: emerging countries of the time, such as the South African Republic (Transvaal) and the Orange Free State, were reliant on the investment of capital from abroad and thus attempted to develop the extraction of gold and diamonds. Fukumoto argued that these two countries had attempted to develop capitalist economies at the end of the nineteenth century, when invasions by imperialist countries were on the ascent, but that they had economic weaknesses. It seems that this book was the first Japanese work to consider emerging nations.

Nichinan Fukumoto, a journalist, politician, and historical essayist, was born on June 14, 1857 and died on September 2, 1921. He was the eldest son of a vassal of the Fukuoka clan, Taifu Fukumoto, and his real name was Makoto Fukumoto. He studied at the clan school, Shuyukan, and later studied under Randen (Chushu) Taniguchi in Nagasaki and then under Senjin Oka in Tokyo, mastering the Chinese classics. In 1876, he entered the Ministry of Justice Law School (now the Faculty of Law at the University of Tokyo), but he was expelled. Afterwards, he was involved in settling Hokkaido and the Philippines, but his plans were cut short. In 1889, he founded the newspaper *Nippon* with Katsunan Kuga, Seigai Kokubu, Kazuo Kojima, and others, and he wrote political pieces. In 1905, he became the main writer and president of the paper *Kyushu Nippo* (the forerunner of *Nishi Nippon Shimbun*), linked to Gen Yo Sha. In 1908, he ran for the House of Representatives as a candidate for Kenseito, and was elected.

While he took a "friendly" stance toward American and British imperialism, Nichinan Fukumoto harshly criticized and denounced Britain's actions in the Boer War. This war was of great interest to the Japanese intellectuals of the day. In 1900, Fukumoto published *Shinkenkoku*. The "newly founded countries" of the title meant emerging nations and referred to the South African Republic (Transvaal) and the Orange Free State in particular. Fukumoto praised the excellence of the Boers, the racial fusion of the Dutch and French. For Fukumoto, who envisioned the settling of Hokkaido and the colonization of the Philippines and other places abroad, and who believed that the only goal of the nation was for Japanese people to settle in unclaimed land, permanently reside there, and build a culture, the Boers at first represented the embodiment of this goal. However, when gold ore and diamonds were discovered in the two countries that the Boers had built, the situation changed. The gold rush brought in many white Europeans, the majority of whom were Anglo-Saxon, and tensions between the Boers (Afrikaners) and foreigners (Uitlanders) became fierce, as Britain attempted to colonize the resource-rich Boer countries. Fukumoto could not conceal his rage at the failure of Cecil Rhodes and Jameson's attempt to overthrow the Boer nation and the slaps on the wrist that they received for carrying out this plot.

Fukumoto again took a critical stance toward Britain's coercion in pressing the South African Republic (Transvaal) to extend its franchise to the resident British, and regarding Britain's treatment of the South African Republic's concessions at the Bloemfontein Conference in 1899.

Fukumoto's pro-Boer stance was derived from his appraisal that it had been the Boers who had colonized a "virgin land" and "occupied it first;" they had "conquered the unconquerable native savages." Any understanding or consideration of the indigenous Africans was left out of this evaluation. However, as he considered the British Empire's initiation of the Boer War merely to represent it veering off track from British "imperialism as it ought to be," or from the "righteousness" of British imperialism, his basic approval of British imperialism was no different from that of other writers (Hirose, 2004).

Notes

1   Union of South Africa, *NOTES exchange between the Union Government and the Japanese Consul in the Union concerning Japanese Immigration into South Africa* (Laid upon the Table of the House of Assembly on the 13th February, 1931) (Document No. A. 1-'31 Japanese Consul on Japanese immigration into Union).

References

Aoki, Sumio, (1993), *Ahurika ni watatta Nipponjin [Japanese emigrated to Africa]*, Jiji Tsushin Sha.
Aoki, Sumio, (2007), "Showa Senzenki ni okeru Nagoya Keizaijin no Ahurika e no Kansin, Nagoya Shoko Kaigisho no Katsudou wo Chushin ni [Nagoya business leaders' interest in Africa in the Showa prewar period: Centered on the Activities of the Nagoya Chamber of Commerce]" Chubu University Institute of Global Humanics, *Arena* (No. 4).
Ano, "Eiryo Minami Ahurika" ["British South Africa"] (1903). *Tokyo Keizai Zasshi [Tokyo Economics Magazine]* (Nos. 1196, 1197, 1199, 1200, 1201; August, September 1903).
Anon., "Seshiru Rōzu" ["Cecil Rhodes"], *Tokyo Keizai Zasshi [Tokyo Economics Magazine]* Nos. 1135, 1136, 1137, 1138, 1139, 1140; June, July 1902.
Fukumoto, Makoto (Nichinan), (1900), *New State Building [Shinkenkoku]*, Hakubunkan.
Furuya, Komahei, (1916), "Nan-a Boeki ni Oyoboseru Jikyoku no Eikyo narabini Yushutsu Yubohin" ["The impact of current affairs on South African trade and goods with hopeful prospects for export"]., *Boeki Zasshi [Trade Magazine]* (Vol. 3, No. 2, February).
Hirose, Reiko, (2004), *Kokusuishugisha no Kokusai Ninshiki to Kokka Koso, Fukumoto Nichinan wo Chushin toshite [The International Understanding of Nationalists and Their Plans for Nations:*

Focusing on Nichinan Fukumoto], Fuyoshobo Shuppan.

Japan Trade Promotion Association, (1941), *Ahurikashu-muke Honpo Zakka Yushutu Boeki no Bunseki, Showa 14-nen [An Analysis of export of General Merchandize to Africa: 1939*], Japan Trade Promotion Association.

Jeppe, Julius, (1911), "Nan-a Senkyuhyakujunen Gaikyo" ["General outlook on South Africa: 1910"], (June 1, 1911) *Tusho Isan [Journal of Commercial Report]* (No. 62).

Kitagawa, Katsuhiko, (1997), *Nihon, Minami Ahurika Tsusho Kankeishi Kenkyu [A Study in the History of Japanese Commercial Relations with South Africa]*. International Research Center for Japanese Studies.

Kitagawa, Katsuhiko, (1994), "Nanbu Ahurika wo Tabi shite" ["Traveling to Southern Africa"] Gendai Sekai to Bunka no Kai, *Griot* (No. 7), Heibonsha, pp. 156-157.

Ministry of Foreign Affairs Trade Bureau, "Nan-a Shisatsu Fukumeisho" ["Report of the mission to South Africa"], *Tsusho Isan [Journal of Commercial Report]*, No. 22, 1903.

Mori, Katsue, (1929), "Minami Ahurika to iu Tokoro" ["The place called East Africa"], Osaka Shosen Kaisha, *Nami [Wave]*, April 1929.

Mori, Shintaro, trans., (1902), *Seshiru Rozu Teioryu Gofudan [Cecil Rhodes: Story of an Imperialist Magnate]*, Tokyo Daigakkan.

Nagoya Chamber of Commerce, (1931), "Nan-a Renpo no Genjo to Sho Torihiki no Jissai" ["The present state of the Union of South Africa and the reality of commercial sales"], Nagoya Shoko Kaigisho [Nagoya Chamber of Commerce], *Geppo [Monthly Report]* (January).

Nippon Kaiji Public Relations Association, (1990), *Tsuito Mori Katsue [In Memorial Katsue Mori]*, Nippon Kaiji Public Relations Association.

Nippon Kaiji Public Relations Association, (1975), *Kyaputen Mori Katsue: Umi no Mokkosu 70-nen [Captain Katsue Mori: 70 Stubborn Years at Sea]*, Nippon Kaiji Public Relations Association.

Nishino, Terutaro, (1964), "Meijiki ni okeru Nihonjin no Ahurikakan" ["Japanese view of Africa in the Meiji period"], Tokyo University Institute for Advanced Studies of Asia, *Toyo Bunka Kenkyusho Kiyo [Memoirs of the Institute of Oriental Culture]*, No. 32.

Nunokawa, Magoichi, (1916), "Taguchi Hakase to Meiji no Keizaigakkai" ["Professor Taguchi and the Meiji economics academia"], *Tokyo Keizai Zasshi [Tokyo Economics Magazine]*, No. 1845, January 1916.

Nunokawa, Magoichi, (1911), "Teiken Sensei no Koto domo" ["Matters related to Mr. Teiken"], *Tokyo Keizai Zasshi [Tokyo Economics Magazine]*, No. 1591, April 1911.

Nunokawa, Magoichi, (1906), "Sengo no Ninki ni tsuite" ["Popular sentiment after the war"], *Tokyo Keizai Zasshi [Tokyo Economics Magazine]*, No. 1334, April 1906.

Nunokawa, Magoichi, (1907), "Zaikai Hendo ni Tomonau Eikyo" ["The effects of financial fluctuations"], *Tokyo Keizai Zasshi [Tokyo Economics Magazine]*, No. 1373, 1907.

Nunokawa, Magoichi, (1906), "Chibetto Mondai no Kaiketsu" ["Solving the Tibet Problem"], *Tokyo Keizai Zasshi [Tokyo Economics Magazine]*, No. 1335, May 1906.

Nunokawa, Magoichi, (1907), "Tozai Bunmei no Yuka, Jyo, Ge" ["The fusion of Eastern and Western civilization (parts one and two)"], *Tokyo Keizai Zasshi [Tokyo Economics Magazine]*, Nos. 1404, 1405; September 1907.

Nunokawa, Magoichi, (1914), "Nihonjin wa Shina no Chishiki ni Toboshi" ["The Japanese have poor knowledge of China"], *Tokyo Keizai Zasshi [Tokyo Economics Magazine]*, Nos. 1751, 1752; May, June 1914.

Nunokawa, Magoichi, (1907), "Keizai to Dotoku" ["Economics and morality"]. *Tokyo Keizai Zasshi [Tokyo Economics Magazine]*, No. 1375, February 1907.

Nunokawa, Magoichi, (1915), "Honpo Jinko Mondai no Ichi Kansatsu" ["An observation on this nation's population problem"], *Tokyo Keizai Zasshi [Tokyo Economics Magazine]*, No. 1809, July

1915.

Nunokawa, Magoichi, (1915), "Tokyo Shokko Jokyo no Ichi Kansatsu, Jo, Chu, Ge" ["Observations on the conditions of manual laborers in Tokyo (parts one, two, and three)"], *Tokyo Keizai Zasshi* [*Tokyo Economics Magazine*], Nos. 1811, 1912, 1913; July, August 1915.

Nunokawa, Magoichi, (1916), "Marusasu Tanjo 150-nen Kinen, Jo, Chu, Ge" ["The 150th anniversary of Malthus' birth (parts one, two, and three)"], *Tokyo Keizai Zasshi* [*Tokyo Economics Magazine*], Nos. 1838, 1839, 1841; February, March 1916.

Nunokawa, Magoichi, (1916), "Taguchi Hakase to Meiji no Keizaigakkai, 1, 2, 3" ["Professor Taguchi and the Meiji economic academia (1) (2) (3)"], *Tokyo Keizai Zasshi* [*Tokyo Economics Magazine*], Nos. 1835, 1836, 1837; January, February 1916.

Nunokawa, Magoichi, (1917), "Minami Ahurika Boeki Jijo" ["Conditions of Foreign Trade in South Africa"], Ministry of Agriculture and Commerce, Commerce Bureau, *Shoko Isan* [*Journal of Commerce and Industry*], No. 48, March 1917.

Nunokawa, Magoichi, (1918), "Roshia Saikin Jijo" ["Current Affairs in Russia"], *Tokyo Keizai Zasshi* [*Tokyo Economics Magazine*], No. 1950, April 1918.

Nunokawa, Magoichi, (1918), "Urajiostoku no Shokyo" ["Commercial conditions in Vladivostok"], *Tokyo Keizai Zasshi* [*Tokyo Economics Magazine*], No. 1937, January 1918.

Nunokawa, Magoichi, (1918), "Nichiro Boeki no Kinkyo to Shorai, Jo, Ge" ["Recent conditions of Russo-Japanese trade and its future (parts one and two)"], *Tokyo Keizai Zasshi* [*Tokyo Economics Magazine*], Nos. 1979, 1980; November 1918.

Nunokawa, Magoichi, (1917), "Nihon Shonin no Nan-a Joriku oyobi Eigyo ni kan suru Seigen no Teido" ["The level of restrictions on Japanese merchants' landfall on South Africa and on their business"], *Naigai Shoko Jiho* [*Naigai Commerce Times*], January 1917.

Nunokawa, Magoichi, (1917), "Nan-a Renpo Yushutsunyu Boeki no Gaikyo" ["General conditions of imports and exports in the Union of South Africa"], *Naigai Shoko Jiho* [*Naigai Times of Commerce and Industry*], February 1917.

Nunokawa, Magoichi, (1917), "Minami Ahurika Shisatsu Dan" ["Tales of a visit to South Africa"], *Tokei Shukei Zasshi* [*Statistics Collection Magazine*], No. 434, 1917.

Nunokawa, Magoichi, (1917), "Minami Ahurika no Gaikyo, Jo, Ge" ["General conditions in South Africa (parts one and two)"], *Tokyo Keizai Zasshi* [*Tokyo Economics Magazine*], Nos. 1886, 1887; January 1917.

Nunokawa, Magoichi, (1917), "Minami Ahurika Shisatsu Dan" ["Tales of a visit to South Africa"], *Tokyo Keizai Zasshi* [*Tokyo Economics Magazine*], No. 1897, April 1917.

Okakura, Takashi and Katsuhiko Kitagawa, (1993), *Nihon, Ahurika Koryu Shi: Meiji-ki kara Dai-ni-ji Sekai Taisen-ki made* [*A History of Japan-Africa Exchange: From the Meiji Era until World War II*], Dobunkan.

Shirakawa, Ikai (1928), *Jicchi Tosa Higashi Ahurika no Tabi* [*Field Report: A Trip to East Africa*], Hubunkan.

Tajima, Masao, (1927), "Nan-a no Shinshin Sakka no Mita Nihon" ["Japan as seen by an up-and-coming writer from South Africa"], Osaka Shosen Kaisha, *Nami* [*Wave*], August 1927.

Yanagisawa, Taiji, (1902), *Seshiru Rozu (Nan-a Kiketsu)* [*Cecil Rhodes (Colossus in South Africa)*], Introduction by Ukichi Taguchi, Tokyo X Club.

(1902) "Death of Mr. Rhodes", *The Times* (London), March 27.

(1902) "The Death of Mr. Rhodes", *The Economist*, April 5.

(1902) "Seshiru Rozu Shi wa Tsui ni Shikyo Shitari" ["Cecil Rhodes has finally died"], *Osaka Mainichi Shimbun*, March 28.

(1902) "Seshiru Rozu Shi wa Tsui ni Shikyo Shitari" ["Cecil Rhodes has finally died"], *Osaka Asahi Shimbun*, March 29–April 3.

(1902) "Kaiketsu Seshiru Rozu Yuku" ["The extraordinary Cecil Rhodes passes away"], *Tokyo Keizai Zasshi* [*Tokyo Economics Magazine*], No. 1126, April 5, 1902.

Diplomatic Archives of MOFA, "Nan-a Tokosha Jinmei Ikken" ["South African Travelers' Names"], (December 1916) (File No. 3-8-8-20).

Diplomatic Archives of MOFA, "Nan-a oyobi Zanjibaru ni okeru Honpojin Taigu-buri ni kan suru Zakken" ["Various matters relating to treatment of this nation's citizens in South Africa and Zanzibar"], (1905–1920) (File No. 3-8-2-219).

Ch 6
Japan's Trade with East Africa

In the first half of the 1930s, starting with India and China, low-priced and efficiently sold Japanese textiles had spread throughout Southeast Asia, the Middle East, and the Balkans, then into Europe, the United Kingdom, and throughout tropical African colonies under British rule, causing several trade frictions with Britain and her colonies by capturing new markets in these regions. (Kitagawa, 1990; Austin and Sugihara, 2013)

This chapter will focus on East Africa and consider the following points. First, it will show Japan's economic interest in East Africa. Secondly it will provide an overview of trade of Japanese cotton goods in East Africa. Thirdly it will consider East Africa as Japan's source of raw cotton. Fourthly, it will explain how Japanese trading firms provided an important role in facilitating trade between Japan and these regions. Lastly, it will examine the issues that emerged in Japan's delicate relations with other nations because of Japan's advances into East Africa.

1 Japan's Economic Interests in East Africa
Oyama Mission
In 1927, the Japanese government wanted to encourage the development of trade with East Africa and sent an investigating mission headed by Ujiro Oyama. The Oyama team, which included two engineers from Taiwan colonial government, Hakusai Yamada and Eitaro Kishimoto, and Kanae Irie of the Trade Association of Japanese Cotton Yarn and Cloth, conducted research in Kenya, Uganda, Tanganyika, Zanzibar, Madagascar, Abysinnia, and Portuguese East Africa from September 1927 to February 1928. Their three volume report, *Conditions in British East Africa* and *Conditions in Abysinnia, Madagascar and Portuguese East Africa* which were written by Oyama, and *A Research Report of the Economic Conditions in East Africa* written by Irie, were published by the Ministry of Foreign Affairs' Bureau of Trade and Commerce. Irie argued that in order to encourage the development of Japan's trade with East Africa it was necessary to shorten the time of voyage between Japan and East Africa, to establish Japanese Consulate, and to open local branch offices of commercial banks for trading.[1]

The Osaka Merchants' Trade Mission to East Africa

In 1929 the industrial research division of the Osaka city government planned sending a trade mission to East Africa. Osaka city and various trade associations wanted to launch a sales campaign for cotton piece and general merchandize manufactured in the Osaka district. The participants included Masaaki Oba (Industrial Research Division of Osaka City), Ryoichi Okuno (Hamaguchi & Co. Ltd.), Shinkichi Yamazoe (Kuwahara & Co.), Kozo Nikawa (Nikawa & Co.), Shizuo Miyaji (Fukushima Yoko & Co.), and Hikozo Sueoka (Shimada Glassware Co.). The places of inspection and the trade fair were to cover the whole of East Africa, notably Mombasa, Nairobi, Kisumu, Jinja, Kampala, Entebe, Mwanza, Tabora, Kigoma, Dar es Salaam, Zanzibar, and Beira. The Exhibiters were Hamaguchi & Co. (handkerchiefs), Nihon Paints Co. (paints), Yoshizaki & Co. (towels and sheets), Dai Nihon Jochugiku Co. (peppermint oil, insect powder and mosquito repellent), Kuwahara & Co. (rubber shoes), Nikawa & Co. (umbrella), Suzuki & Co. (blankets, towels and sheets).[2]

"1930 Africa Exhibition" in Osaka

In December 1930 'Africa Exhibition' was held at Osaka Commercial Museum under the cosponsorship of the Ministry of Foreign Affairs and the Ministry of Agriculture and Commerce. During the Exhibition people who were involved in trading activities in East Africa and who were experienced in making voyage to Africa met to hold a roundtable talk about the promotion of Japanese trade with Africa, and also held lectures and film projections about general affairs in East Africa. The members of the roundtable talk were Ujiro Oyama (consul), Satoru Nakame (president of the Osaka Foreign Language School), Kunitatsu Oshima (Osaka Shosen Kaisha, OSK), Enjiro Yamahigashi, Sengo Shibata, Keizo Fukui, Hiroshi Tsuge (Nihon Menka Co.), Shinkichi Yamazoe (Kuwahara & Co.), Ryoichi Okuro (Hamaguchi &Co.), Kozo Nikawa (Nikawa & Co.), and Shizuo Miyaji (Fukushima Yoko & Co.). Masao Tajima (Osaka Shosen Kaisha, OSK) delivered a lecture of "General Affairs in Africa", Junichi Tabuchi (Toyo Menka Co.) on "the Story of Kenya and Uganda", and Tsuge on "A Short History of Tangaryika".[3]

2 Japanese Goods in East African Market

East Africa's (Kenya, Uganda, Tanganyika, and Zanzibar) main imports from overseas countries were cotton piece goods, motor cars and lorries, gasoline, machinery (agricultural, electrical and industrial machines) and iron and steel manufactures. Imports from Japan consisted of beer, pottery and chinaware, glassware, tableware, plates and mirrors, cement, tin plates, enameled hollowware, iron and steel manufactures (cutler's ware, implements and tools, locks, knives), cotton piece goods, cotton blanket, knitware, clothes, and matches. (Oishi, 2015) Japan's exports to East Africa consisted of cotton piece goods and miscellaneous merchandise. In contrast to exports from Europe and the United States, Japan exported the necessities of life for the Africans, Indians and Arabians living there. The value of the Japanese goods in East Africa's cotton piece goods imports increased rapidly from 1931, and in 1936 her share rose 80%. Considering that cotton piece goods from Britain, India, and the Netherlands held the main share in 1920s, it is impressive that in 1930s, on the average, Japanese goods accounted for 65% of East Africa's imports of cotton piece goods. (Table 6-1, 6-2)

What kind of cotton piece goods were imported into the East African market? Japanese cotton goods imported into East Africa consisted mostly of unbleached grey cloth in terms of both volume and value between 1926 and 1939, but starting from 1932 imports of printed cloth, dyed cloth and dyed yarn also increased steadily.

First, in the case of unbleached grey cloth, the Japanese share made up 90% in the latter half of 1930s in spite of the sharp decline in the period of the Great Crash of 1929-1933; in the years between 1926 and 1939, on the average, the Japanese market share for this category was 67%. This grey cloth was manufactured in such companies as Toyo Boseki Company, Nihon Boseki Company, Senshu Textile Company, and Naigai Cotton Company. Demand depended on and fluctuated according to the income of the indigenous consumers, and fluctuations in the seasonal harvest of cotton and other agricultural crops. Japanese grey cloth was mainly used for making such African clothes as kanzu and shuka.

Secondly, in the case of bleached cloth, from the latter half of the 1920s to the early 1930s, British and Dutch goods were overwhelming, and the Japanese share of imported bleached cloth was around 20%. In the middle of 1930s, owing to the innovations in bleaching technology in Japan, her share rose to about 80%. From 1926 to 1939, the Japanese share of bleached cloth was, on the average, 41% and these were used for kanzu, shuka, and the underwear of Africans.

Thirdly, in the case of printed cloth, British goods occupied the major share in the East African market and after 1934 Japanese goods were gradually imported. Japanese goods mostly consisted of printed jeans. Japan was no match for Britain in khanga. Imports of Japanese dyed cloth increased in the 1930s so that in the latter half of the 1930s the Japanese share of dyed-in-the-piece exceeded 75%. This reverse of position in the colour manufactures market between Japan and Great Britain in East African market bred a trade conflict. These dyed-in-the-piece goods were kaniki, black cloth for female hoods (buibui) and shuka, hodorunk (dyed dark brown cloth, kanzu for males), bleached calico, khaki-coloured drill (clothes for Africans living in urban areas), and crepe (kanzu for middle class Africans, clothes for European children).

Finally, in the case of yarn-dyed cloth, Japan accounted for over 70% of the total value of imports. Yarn-dyed cloth includes striped cloth (underware for Africans,

Indians, and Arabians), striped drills, kikoi for African men, kunguru (checked underware for Africans), kisuwa (headkerchief for African women and turbans for Arab men). (Table 6-3)

These Japanese cotton piece goods were transported to the East African market via Bombay and Aden before 1926. Thereafter, ships of the OSK's East African Line such as the Kanada Maru, the Mekishiko Maru, the Shikago Maru, and Panama Maru transported Japanese goods from Kobe to Mombasa. From there these goods were handled by and distributed into the hinterlands by Nihon Menka Company or Indian Commercial houses. Japanese cotton piece goods penetrated African areas along the Kenyan coast and the urban areas of Nairobi, Kisumu, Kampala and Jinja and their rural vicinities along Ugandan railway line. It should be added that these goods were manufactured by not only large-scale cotton factories like those of Toyo Boseki Company, Kanebo Company, Dai Nihon Boseki Company, Hattori Company, but also by small scale local weavers. Large scale producers exported their goods through large scale commercial houses. On the contrary, the smaller ones exported their goods through small commercial houses supported by financial aid from the Federated Association of the Japanese Cotton Manufacturers and the Federated Association of Japanese Cotton exporters. In Osaka, the Osaka Trade Association of Exporters to Africa was founded to promote trade with Africa. (Abe, 1989; Sugiyama and Brown, 1990; Sugiyama and Grove, 1999)

3 East Africa as a Source of Raw Cotton

East African exports consisted mostly of cotton, coffee, maize, sisal and carbonate of soda. Japan imported carbonate of natural soda, cotton and wattle bark; of these, cotton was by far the major commodity; almost all of the cotton was exported from Uganda. Japanese consular reports do not allow identification the precise time sequence of fluctuations in the quantity and value of cotton imports. However, it is observable that Japan's cotton imports fluctuated considerably depending on whether the harvest of Ugandan cotton was good or bad. In spite of the sharp decline of trade in Ugandan cotton during the 1930s Great Crash, the value of Japanese cotton imports rose from 614,000 pounds in 1934, to 1,241,000 pounds in 1936 and then fell to 802,000 pounds in 1938.

It was significant that consular reports researching the conditions of cotton cropping and its price fluctuation in Uganda were sent one after another to the Ministry of Foreign Affairs' Bureau of Trade and Commerce. On the one hand, good and poor harvests of raw cotton had a profound effect on steadying the supply of raw materials for cotton cloth weavers in Japan, and on the other hand, the income and purchasing power of the African peasants who were much involved in cotton growing in the East African colonial economy also affected the sales of Japanese cotton textiles and general merchandise goods among the African people

Table 6-1 East African Trade toward Japan, 1926-1939 (1000 pound)

Year	Export	to Japan	Import	from Japan
1926	9,035	475	9,754	618
1927	8,692	632	10,532	553
1928	10,712	542	11,310	638
1929	11,009	869	12,135	693
1930	8,380	252	10,244	723
1931	6,212	143	7,036	754
1932	6,861	151	6,746	842
1933	8,254	450	6,844	1,049
1934	8,920	759	8,818	1,461
1935	10,709	141	10,604	1,791
1936	13,671	1,439	11,604	2,017
1937	15,289	1,239	15,986	2,692
1938	12,875	323	14,109	1,763
1939	13,397	960	12,864	1,655

Note : East Africa includes Kenya, Uganda, Tanganyika, and Zanzibar. 1926-1933 : Total of Kenya, Uganda, and Tanganyika, 1934-1939 : Kenya, Uganda, Tanganyika, and Zanzibar

Source : Consular Reports regarding East Africa in *Overseas Economic Conditions*

in East Africa. Therefore, it is noteworthy that the daily life of Ugandan cotton cultivators was linked to the life of the ordinary Japanese people working every day in large scale spinning and weaving factories near large cities and small scale local weavers in the countryside.

In Uganda, cotton cultivation developed because the colonial government allocated cotton seeds to Ugandan peasants and forced them to cultivate cotton under leadership of the chiefs who mobilized the traditional and personal networks. In the latter half of 1920s, there were 176 cotton ginneries: two thirds of them were owned and managed by Europeans and the rest by Indians. Under the supervision of the colonial government the time and place of cotton buying was limited to the cotton ginneries or the 32 specified local stores where African cotton growers could sell their crop directly. (Aman, 1927)

In East Africa Nihon Menka Company bought some Indian cotton ginneries and began direct buying. Toyo Menka Company and Gosho bought cotton through the hands of Indian cotton dealers. The main cotton growing areas were Buganda, which was situated in the lake Victoria basin and Kyoga, the East Province on both sides of the Nile, and the Busoga Province (Yoshida, 1974; Nichimen Jitsugyo Kabushiki Kaisha, 1962).

Table 6-2 Imports of Cotton Cloth to East Africa by Countries, 1926-1939 (1000 pound)

Year	Total Import	Japan	United Kingdom	India	Netherlands
1926	1,797 (31,475)	438 (-)	543 (-)	335 (-)	375 (-)
1927	1,958 (41,051)	436 (-)	592 (-)	335 (-)	462 (-)
1928	1,050 *(41,920)	- (-)	- (-)	- (-)	- (-)
1929	1,176 *(50,041)	- (-)	- (-)	- (-)	- (-)
1930	1,436 (38,322)	253 *(-)	227 *(-)	81 *(-)	178 *(-)
1931	1,183 (75,288)	503 (15,523)	237 (3,548)	196 (8,000)	204 (2,848)
1932	1,151 (77,180)	527 (21,884)	258 (4,616)	116 (4,621)	114 (1,558)
1933	1,188 (87,744)	675 (28,551)	220 (3,299)	77 (2,010)	114 (1,208)
1934	1,258 (90,543)	891 (74,978)	240 (925)	60 (1,558)	45 (1,238)
1935	1,478 (110,159)	1,109 (93,445)	263 (11,121)	57 (2,285)	38 (2,121)
1936	1,530 (120,731)	1,225 (107,597)	190 (7,538)	57 (2,930)	32 (2,027)
1937	2,026 (134,281)	1,612 (115,543)	195 (7,005)	103 (5,733)	78 (4,660)
1938	1,562 (109,620)	1,168 (919,790)	186 (6,462)	81 (4,138)	99 (5,944)
1939	1,457 (117,999)	1,087 (92,612)	146 (5,004)	63 (3,163)	63 (3,877)

Note : East Africa includes Kenya, Uganda, Tanganyika, and Zanzibar. 1926-1933 : Total of Kenya, Uganda, and Tanganyika, 1934-1939 : Kenya, Uganda, Tanganyika, and Zanzibar
( ) : square yard, * : not include Tangayika
Source : Consular Reports regarding East Africa in *Overseas Economic Conditions*

Table 6-3 Imports of Cotton Cloth to East Africa by Kinds, 1926-1939 (1000 pound)

Year	unbleached	bleached	khanga	printed	dyed in piece	yarn dyed
1926	669(403)	149(11)	-	233(5)	397(6)	349(37)
1927	669(390)	881(20)	-	261(16)	431(9)	427(78)
1928	265(143)	96(10)	-	135(51)	266(10)	288(15)
1929	390(346)	78(17)	-	157(61)	248(11)	303(87)
1930	423(142)	93(16)	-	124(44)	181(9)	186(54)
1931	393(163)	100(22)	-	143(65)*	282(14)	143(68)
1932	272(96)	86(18)	-	150(30)*	269(54)	213(21)
1933	295(86)	76(22)	-	133(39)*	303(112)	229(32)
1934	284(261)	90(59)	102(6)	184(163)	339(207)	253(187)
1935	362(343)	115(87)	141(6)	245(215)	376(270)	241(184)
1936	393(374)	149(124)	106(13)	254(233)	379(285)	240(188)
1937	426(395)	195(168)	155(21)	284(54)	581(464)	376(302)
1938	393(384)	108(82)	191(51)	226(196)	371(262)	267(193)
1939	374(275)	121(92)	112(22)	225(196)	452(359)	191(137)

Note : East Africa includes Kenya, Uganda, Tanganyika, and Zanzibar. 1926-1933 : Total of Kenya, Uganda, and Tanganyika, 1934-1939 : Kenya, Uganda, Tanganyika, and Zanzibar
( ) : Import of Japanese Goods, * : include Khanga
Source : Consular Reports regarding East Africa in *Overseas Economic Conditions*

4 Japanese Trading Firms in East Africa

Progress in the technology for mixing cottons made it possible to use almost any kind of cotton from abroad to produce high-quality cotton yarn. This is one reason why increasing attention was paid to East African cotton as well as to American and Indian cotton. Particularly in Uganda, cotton cultivation developed extensively since it was introduced in 1903. By the mid-1920s, the number of Indian cotton ginneries increased to the point that the colonial government tried to enforce a Cotton Ordinance aimed at regulating their number. Ugandan cotton was originally imported into Japan through the Bombay cotton market via Indian and British commercial houses. Therefore, it was inevitable that the Japanese industrialists, in their efforts to reduce costs, would attempt to purchase cotton directly from East Africa, especially since a shipping route to this area was opened.

In the pre-war period, 80% of Japan's raw cotton was imported by three large companies: Nihon Menka (Nichimen), Toyo Menka (Tomen), and Gosho. Nichimen opened a branch office in Mombasa in 1919 and in Dar es Salaam in 1927. Tomen opened an office in Jinja in 1920 and Gosho opened an office in Kampala in 1928. These Japanese trading houses, together with British and Indian merchant houses such as the Liverpool Uganda Company and Baili Brothers played an active role in expanding the export of Ugandan cotton to China, Europe and Japan. Japanese trading companies not only offered financial credit to small and middle-sized Indian cotton ginneries but also entered into direct management of cotton ginneries themselves.

Of the three companies buying cotton, Nichimen was the most involved in the cotton trade in East Africa. As early as 1917, Nichimen sent a team of investigators from Bombay branch office to East Africa in order to survey general economic conditions in Kenya, Uganda, Tanganyika, the Belgian Congo, Ethiopia, and Italian Somaliland. In 1926, as soon as the OSK line from Japan to East Africa was opened, Nichimen not only bought six cotton ginneries in Uganda (in Kamuli, Namaganda, Namirumba, Naminaga, Namawenda, and Irapa) but also expanded the cotton-buying area to Mikese in Tanganyika.

However, the colonial government prohibited Japanese management of local cotton ginneries and the sale of their ginned cotton abroad in 1933. After that Nichimen exercised self-control and limited its activities in this region to just buying cotton. On the other hand, Nichimen made great efforts to sell cotton piece goods, artificial silk, and general merchandise in East African markets. Thus, these trading companies played a significant role in the pre-war period in developing the Japanese cotton industry as well as in promoting Japan's trade with East Africa.[4] (Nichimen Jitsugyo Kabushiki Kaisha, 1962, Japanese Association for Trade Promotion, 1941)

5 Trade Issues in East Africa

There were various difficulties caused by Japan's advance into East African market. The most grave was the Anti-Asian sentiment and movement. Japanese being Asians were among its victims.

In East Africa, Indians immigrated from the Northwestern coast of the Indian subcontinent and from generation to generation lived in such urban areas as Mombasa, Nairobi, Kampala, and Dar es Salaam and spread their commercial influence to the people in all strata of society. In particular, they formed a firm commercial network system over all of East Africa as middlemen who sold cotton cloth, daily necessities, and general merchandise to Africans and bought cotton from African peasant cultivators.

"The Indian problems" in Kenya dated from the introduction of a discrimination policy between Europeans and Non-Europeans in African colonies under the British rule. Specifically after World War I the British Imperial government encouraged its ex-servicemen to immigrate to Kenyan Highlands as settler farmers and farm managers. At the same time many European middlemen and businessmen flowed into this area. These white invasions brought about commercial conflicts with Indian merchants who had hitherto enjoyed a dominant commercial position there. In 1908 the British attempted to evict Indians to make room for white settlers in the Kenyan Highlands and in 1913 segregated Indians from European areas.[5]

Given this historical background, a compromise agreement between them was hard to reach. In addition, after World War I, plans for "Union of East Africa" were brewing among the British settlers. Kenya, Uganda and Tanganyika had a close economic relations with each other and by the January 1924 Agreement, the tariff rates in Tanganyika conformed to the rates in Kenya and Uganda, and the East African shilling became the official currency of the whole region.[6]

The time was ripe for a closer union of the East African territories because Germany had become a member of the League of Nations as a result of Locarno Pact in 1925; Germans began to resettle in Tanganyika where equal opportunity was assured as a mandate of the League of Nations. As a result, the British settlers became restive. The British settlers who wanted to possess this area exclusively appealed for a closer union in East Africa in tandem with their movement for the return of the Mt. Kilimanjaro area to Kenya under British rule. This movement brought acute anxiety to the Indians in East Africa and made them worry about their position, should the plans for the Union of East Africa materialize. They were aware of what was likely to happen in the light of the fundamental change of their constitutional position after the formation of the Union of South Africa.[7]

The Japanese, as Asians, also were faced with various kinds of discrimination in East Africa. Several cases can be found in diplomatic documents. For example, when Consul Tadanao Imai of Cape Town started to investigate into economic conditions in East Africa, he was also confronted with discrimination. Arriving at Mombasa, he asked the manager of Magadi Soda Company to reserve a room for him in Metropole Hotel, but this hotel refused to accommodate him. The manager of Magadi Soda Company negotiated with the Commissioner of this province. Regrettably, the Commissioner replied that the authorities could not intervene directly in the business of privately managed hotels. Therefore, Imai had to stay overnight in the Magadi Soda company house, thanks to the kind offer of the company's manager. The Manor Hotel in Mombasa also refused to take in the Japanese Consul. On the way back to Cape Town, Imai was treated in the same way by the Savoy Hotel in Portuguese Beira. This case came to light because a correspondent of an Indian newspaper reported it to his Bombay office and the news got to an Indian merchant residing in Japan, who appealed to the Ministry of Foreign Affairs to take measures to cope with this situation.[8]

Because of such experiences, the Japanese in East Africa were justifiably wary of any moves by the British to restrict Asians in immigration and trade. This determined their attitude toward the movement for the Union of East Africa. Immediately after the formation of the Union of South Africa, Japanese immigration and trading activities were curtailed by the Immigration Act of 1913. Japanese traders faced many difficulties when dealing with their South African counterparts because the 1913 Act handicapped Japanese immigration and therefore Japanese businessmen inconveniently had to settle their accounts through confirming houses in London instead of through the usual payment by a letter of credit. The Japanese therefore had misgivings about the Union of East Africa fearing that the same treatment would be meted to them in East Africa as had previously happened in South Africa. Moreover, because Japanese cotton piece goods usually flowed into East African market through Indian middlemen, the Japanese were in a very delicate position. On the one hand, the Japanese wanted to be treated more favourably than other Non-Europeans in East Africa and yet, on the other, had to act in concert with Indian middlemen in order to strengthen the marketing of Japanese goods. (Shirakawa, 1928)

Notes

1 In detail see Diplomatic Archives of the Ministry of Foreign Affairs, File K210-4-1-1, "Miscellaneous Matter on a Tour Overseas Inspection : Division of Inspective Mission, Inspective Mission for the Condition of East African Economy and Immigration". The news of Oyama Team was carried in such local news papers as *Kenya Daily Mail* ("Japanese Mission: Mr. Oyama in its subjects and Hopes" and "Japanese Investigators" 30 September 1927) and *Mombasa Times* ("Japan and Kenya" 30 September 1927, "Welcome to Japanese Mission : Pleasant Function at Manor Hotel" 1 October 1927).

2 This trade mission was to leave Japan on 20 August 1928 and to return on 24 December. *A Study of East Asian Trade [To-A Boeki Kenkyu]*, Vol. 8, No. 8, 1929. The report on "Economic Conditions in East Africa" by this trade mission was inserted in *A Study of East Asian Trade*, Vol. 9, No. 3, 1930.

3   Kitagawa, "Africa Exhibition : Pre-war Japan's Economic Interests in African Market", The Japan Society of Africa, *Africa Monthly [Gekkan Ahurika]*, Vol. 30, No. 6, 1990, pp. 14-15. Other exhibitors were Osaka Association for Export to Africa, Osaka Branch of Nihon Yusen Shipping Company, and Association of Cotton Yarns and Piece Goods Exporters. Investigative reports sent by Nagahito Yagi, news writer of Asahi Newspaper, were inserted under the title of "An Account of Traveling African Continent" from 15 June to 9 July in 1930 and his other reports were again carried under the title of "Africa : New Overseas Market" from 21 August to 4 September in 1930. These showed the rise of Japanese interests in Africa.

4   The oldest Japanese store in the African continent was Mikado & Co. which was opened by Komahei Furuya in Cape Town at the end of 19th century and Nanbu Trading Company in Port Said, whose main activity was to sell foodstuffs to Japanese ships and sell general merchandize in local area. In Alexandria Yokohama Specie Bank opened a branch office in 1926 and Mitsui, Mitsubishi and Nichimen had offices there as well. Moreover, office agents of Yamamoto Hiroshi & Co. (Kobe), Yamamoto Koyata & Co. (Osaka) and Mataichi & Co. (Osaka) were stationed in Casablanca in addition to the branch office of Mitsui and Mitsubishi. In Mombasa in East Africa additional to the three large trading companies, Daido Trading Co., Kokita & Co., and Koide & Co. engaged in selling Japanese general merchandize. Those goods were also brought into East African markets by the Indian merchant houses there, and by Indian and British traders residing in Japan.

5   Joint Committee on Closer Union in East Africa, vol. 1 together with the proceeding of the Committee, HSMO, London, 1931, pp. 4-5.

6   Department of Overseas Trade, *Report on Economic and Commercial Conditions in British East Africa*, by A.E. Pollard, July 1937-July 1938, London, HMSO, 1939, p. 55. "For many years the idea of economic unification of the three mainland territories (eventually including Zanzibar) has animated the commercial community. In its political implications the subject has formed the basis of a number of enquiries. During recent years there have appeared the 'Hilton Young ' report and the 'Wilson ' report ; the joint Parliamentary Committee of Enquiry sat in England in 1931 and more recently an expert enquiry was undertaken by Roger Gibb into the administration of the East African Railways" (Department of Overseas Trade, *Economic Conditions in East Africa*, by C. Kemp, April 1932~March 1934, London, HSMO, 1934, p. 25.) See below. *Report of the Commission on Closer Union of the Dependencies in Eastern and Central Africa*, London, HMSO, 1929. *Report of Sir Samuel Wilson on his Visit to East Africa*, 1929, London, HMSO, 1929. Statement of the Conditions of His Majesty's Government in the United Kingdom as regards Closer Union in East Africa, London, HMSO, 1927.

7   See *Report of the East Africa Commission*, London, HMSO, 1925 and Future Policy in regard to Eastern Africa, London, HMSO, 1927.

8   "On the rejection of hotel staying in Mombasa" (Letter on 8 August 1924 from Tadanao Imai to the Ministry of Foreign Affairs), Diplomatic Archives of MOFA, File No. 3-8-2-314. ("Problem of Asian People in South Africa and Treating Japanese in Zanzibar")

References

Abe, Takeshi, (1989), *Development of Local Cotton Weaving in Japan [Nihon ni okeru Sanchi Menorimonogyo no Tenkai]*, Tokyo University Press.

Aman, W.C., (1927), *Cotton in South and East Africa, South and East Africa Cotton Year-Book, 1926 : An Annual Book of Reference for the Cotton Merchants, Ginners, Planters, and Prospective Settlers*, Longman Green & Co., R.L. Esson & Co.

Ampiah, Kweku, (1990), "British Commercial Policies Against Japanese Expansionism in East and West Africa, 1932-1935", *The International Journal of African Historical Studies*, Vol. 23, No. 4, 1990, pp. 619-641.

Anon., (1927), "Japanese Mission : Mr. Oyama in its subjects and Hopes", *Kenya Daily Mail*, 30 September.

Anon., (1927), "Japanese Investigators", *Kenya Daily Mail*, 30 September.

Anon., (1927), "Japan in Kenya", *Mombasa Times*, 30 September.

Anon., (1927), "Welcome to Japanese Mission : Pleasant Function at Manor Hotel", *Mombasa Times*, 30 September.

Austin, Gareth and Sugihara, Kaoru eds., (2013), *Labour-Intensive Industrialization in Global History*, Routledge.

Bradshaw, R.A., (1992), "Japan and Colonialism in Africa, 1800-1039", Ph.D. Thesis, Ohio University.

Cabinet, (1934), "Committee on Japanese Trade Competition", 19 March, 27 March, 11 April, CAB/27/568.

Department of Overseas Trade, (1939), *Report on Economic and Commercial Conditions in British East Africa* by A.E. Pollard, July 1937-July 1938, HMSO, London.

Goey, Ferry de (2014), *Consuls and the Institutions of Global Capitalism, 1783-1914*, Pickering and Chatto, London.

Japanese Trade Promotion Association [Nihon Boeki Shiko Kyokai], (1941), *An Analysis of Export Trade of General Merchandize to Africa 1934 [Ahurika muke Zakkahin Yushutu Boeki no Bunseki]*, Research Report, No. 6.

HMSO, (1931), Joint Committee of Closer Union in East Africa, Vol. 1, together with the proceedings of the committee, London.

Iwai Shoten, (1963), *Iwai Shoten : One Hundred Years. [Iwai Shoten 100 Nenshi]*.

Kanematsu, (1934), *Kanematsu : A History of 60 Years [Kanematsu 60 Nenshi]*.

Kennedy, C.S., (1990), *The American Consul : A Study of the United States Consular Service, 1775-1914*, New York.

Kitagawa, K., (1990), "Japan's Economic Relations with Africa between the Wars : A Study of Japanese Consular Reports", Kyoto University, *African Study Monograph*, Vol. 11, No. 3, 1990, pp. 125-141.

Kitagawa, K., (1990), "Africa Exhibition : Pre-war Japan's Economic Interests in African Market [Ahurika Kokujo Tenrankai : Senzenki Nihon no Ahurika Shijo e no Kanshin]", The Africa Society of Japan, *Africa Monthly*, Vol. 30, No. 6, pp. 14-16.

Kitagawa, K. (2006), "Japanese Competition in the Congo Basin in the 1930s", in A.J.H. Latham and Heita Kawakatsu eds., *Intra-Asian Trade and the World Market*, London, Routledge, pp. 135-167.

Kitagawa, K. (2016), "Revision of the Congo Basin Treaty and Japan in the 1930s : Examining the Narratives of Consular Reports", *The Economic Review of Kansai University*, Vol. 65, No. 4, pp. 61-71.

Mitsui Trading Company (1951), *A Short History of Mitsui Trading Company before the World War I* [Mitsui Bussan Sho-Shi], Tokyo.

Mitsui Trading Company, (1986), *A History of Mitsui Trading Company [Mitsui Bussan no Rekishi]*, Vol. 1, Tokyo.

Nichimen Jitsugyo Kabushiki Kaisha, (1962), *A 70 Year History of Nichimen*, Osaka.

"On the rejection of hotel staying in Mombasa" Imai to the Ministry of Foreign Affairs, 8, 9 August 1924, Diplomatic Archives of MOFA, File No. 3-8-2-314.

Oishi, Takashi, (2015), "Traded Goods and the Socio-Economic/Cultural Transformations in Asian Intra-regional Context : The case of Ornaments and Matches in Modern India", Paper presented International Workshop on "Complexity of Innovative Colonial Milieu : Socio-Economic Transformation in the Colonial Ports and their Hinterlands in Modern Asia, 1850s-1940s" Kyoto University, 10 August.

Osaka Shosen Kaisha (OSK), (1956), *History of African Shipping Lines*, OSK, Osaka.

Padayachee, Vishnu and Robert Morell (1991), "Indian Merchants and Dukawalas in Natal Economy,

1889~1914", *Journal of Southern African Studies*, Vol. 19, No. 1, pp. 71-102.

Platt, D.C. M., (1971), *The Cinderella Service : British Consul since 1825*, London.

Shirakawa, Ikai, (1928), *Field Report : A Trip to East Africa [Jicchi Tosa Higashi Ahurika no Tabi]*, Hakubunkan.

Sugiyama, Shinya and Ian Brown eds. (1990), *Economic Conflicts in South East Asia during the Inter-War Period [Senkanki ni okeru Tounan Asia no Keizai Masatsu]*, Dobukan, Tokyo.

Sugiyama, Shinya and Linda Grove eds. (1999), *Commercial Networks in Modern Asia [Kindai Asia no Ryutu Nettowaku]*, Sobunsha, Tokyo.

Tajima, Masao, (1924), *Report of Economic Conditions in East Africa [Higashi Ahurika Keizai Jijo Hokokusho]*, Osaka Shosen Kaisha (OSK), Osaka.

Takashimaya 135th Commemorative Publication (1968), *Takashimaya : A History of 135 Years [Takashimaya 135 Nen-Shi]*.

The Ministry of Foreign Affairs, (1932), *A General View of Economic Conditions in Africa [Ahurika Keizai Jijo Tenbo]*, Tokyo.

The Ministry of Foreign Affairs, (1903), "Report of the Mission to South Africa [Nan-A Shisatsu Fukumeisho]", *The Journal of Commercial Reports*, No. 22.

Yoshida, Masao, (1974), "Japanese Merchant House and Cotton Ginnery in East Africa before the World War II [Dai 2 ji Sekai Taisen izen no Higashi Ahurika ni okeru Nihon no Shosha to Kuriwata Kojo]", *Africa Monthly*, Vol. 14, No. 9.

Ch 7
Japan's Trade with West Africa

This chapter will focus on West Africa and consider the following points. Firstly, it shall introduce surveys of economic conditions in inter-war West Africa undertaken by private firms. Secondly, it shall provide an overview of this trade development. Thirdly, it shall examine the disputes that emerged in Japan's relations with other nations because of its advances into West Africa.

1 Economic Surveys of West Africa by Private Firms : The Osaka Shosen Kaisha (OSK) and the Yokohama Specie Bank (YSB)
Tajima's Report of the Osaka Shosen Kaisha (OSK)
There is *Report of the Economic Conditions in West Africa [Nishi Ahurika Keizai Chosa Hokokusho]* (December 1934) published by the Osaka Shosen Kaisha (OSK hereafter). This report was written based on a survey of West Africa's trade and transport network by OSK's Cape Town representative, Masao Tajima, who on company orders had joined the voyage of the Arasuka-Maru to West Africa, which left Cape Town on January 13, 1934, and lasted until March 1. The survey included detailed investigations of ports, such as Lagos in Nigeria, Accra in the Gold Coast (both British), Dakar in Senegal (French), and Lobito in Angola (Portuguese).

The incentive for this survey was that "our Empire's commercial supremacy already extends to the northern, eastern, and southern areas of the African continent, and our Imperial nation has no little interest in West Africa as the one remaining new market" (OSK 1934 : 1).

Additionally, the extension of Japanese commercial shipping to West Africa would have the following significance:

"Although during the war Japan's regular shipping to Europe was diverted to Dakar via Cape of Good Hope to avoid the ravages of war in the Mediterranean, Japanese vessels have not been seen in the region of West Africa since. The voyage of our Arasuka-Maru to West Africa aroused great attention and interest in Accra and Lagos, it being the first time a Japanese ship was seen, while we received an enthusiastic welcome in Dakar that recalled the former call at the port by Japanese vessels. Today, when the recent growth of our commercial influence has already drawn East and

South Africa into the orbit of our supremacy in commerce and shipping, surely the time has come to establish regular shipping routes between Japan and West Africa." (OSK, 1934 : 23)

Furthermore, Tajima outlined the prospects for Japanese trade with West Africa based on his survey:

"If one surveys the current system of trade, relations with the various European nations like Britain, France, Germany, Holland and Belgium are closest on the basis of imports and exports, with the United States next ... trade with the East consists of things like rice from Saigon and Rangoon and sacking from Calcutta, but the volumes are not large, and while Japanese goods have been making inroads into the West African market in recent years, such trade has occurred via European ports like Liverpool and Marseilles because of the lack of a direct sea route between Japan and West Africa until now. ... It is obvious that trade between Japan and West Africa has only just begun and there is tremendous scope for future development, with various areas in West Africa offering exceedingly good prospects as new markets for Japanese commodities in particular. ... I believe that with the establishment of a direct sea route, through the cooperation of the entire nation, and specifically closely regulating and deepening cooperation between traders and exporters, our commercial supremacy can be established in West Africa in the face of European and American competition. ... These are places in which the buying power of the native consumer is ideal for Japanese imports, which they would warmly welcome, and they would strongly oppose any artificial efforts at their limitation. ... Moreover, there was great interest in trading Japanese goods shown by European merchants resident in Africa. ... While Japan must raise trust in its business dealing and the quality of its products in order to maintain cooperation and coordination with those involved in trade in West Africa, it must also urgently plan to develop a smooth reciprocal commerce by closely investigating which of the natural resources from the various areas of West Africa shall serve as raw material for our factories and clear the way to their importation, which will remedy the dangers of one-sided trade." (OSK, 1934 : 7-8; OSK, 1956, 1966)

Ouchi's Report of the Yokohama Specie Bank (YSB)

There is the *Report on Survey of the West African Coast [Ahurika Seibu Kaigan Shisatsu Hokokuhso]* (Report no. 83, January 1932) by the chief investigations officer of the Yokohama Specie Bank (hereafter YSB).

West Africa was unknown, virgin land, and still an undeveloped market for Japanese overseas trade. Japanese goods were already available in northern, eastern, and southern Africa; only the push into West African markets remained. Taking advantage of a three-man inspection party dispatched by the Japan Association for Export Promotion of Cotton Textiles to investigate the cotton market in western Africa, the report's author, Ouchi Hirohito, departed Marseilles for West Africa on November 12, 1931 in order to investigate the economic situation in West Africa with the inspection team and the Consul of Bombay.

Ouchi went via Casablanca in Morocco, and entered West Africa at Dakar in Senegal. He travelled through Freetown in Sierra Leone, Ivory Coast, Gold Coast, and Slave Coast (around the port of Guinea), and was in Cameroon and Equatorial Guinea in January 1932 before reaching Matadi in Belgian Congo on February 1. He then travelled up the Congo River, south through central Africa, approached the Union of South Africa via Rhodesia and arrived in Cape Town on March 10. On March 21, he arrived in Kobe via Mombasa and Zanzibar on the OSK liner Shikago-Maru.

Ouchi made the following points in his report. Firstly, the following differences were pointed between East and South Africa, and West Africa: "West Africa means the blacks. Economically, the agricultural production of the blacks is the lifeblood of economic development in these colonies, for the price of these products is reflected in the buying power of the natives, influencing increases or decreases in the demand for imports, and normally demand for imports is in direct proportion to state of the agricultural export trade", (YSB, 1932 : 457)

Furthermore, Ouchi was conducting his survey during the Great Crash, which was reflected in the following comment:

"Above all, the current world economic crisis has spread to every part of West Africa, and the slump in prices for those West African commodities produced through the blood and sweat of the natives—of cocoa, palm kernels, palm oil, peanuts, coffee, and rubber—threatens the lifestyle of the native and can only cause feelings of despair for the black man under current conditions. This resentment is visible in the "cocoa hold-up" that recently broke out in Gold Coast, and the general economy is atrophying because as the collapse in native buying power caused by low commodity prices, the volume of imports declines and their stock dramatically rises, doing enormous damage to importers and exporters in West Africa." (YSB, 1932 : 476)

Colonial policies in West Africa were the following: "As the chief source of revenue for all of the colonial governments was customs revenue, the governments invest their energy in promoting the export trade that is the lifeblood of these colonies, throwing themselves into the development and improvement of agricultural commodities, native education, moral guidance, and welfare advances". (YSB, 1932 : 475)

West Africa here largely refers to British Africa and French Africa. What's more, Ouchi points out that West Africa had an enormous demand for textiles, with the level of cotton imports into British Africa and French Africa surpassing the level of imports in the Union of South Africa, British East Africa, the Belgian Congo, Morocco, or any other territory.

Therefore, Ouchi focused on West Africa as a new market for Japanese products and advocated the following:

"The import of our nation's products into West Africa began several years ago, I believe. However, this was through the offices of European firms, and the amounts are yet trifling, as there are almost no direct transactions between our nation and West Africa. ... Recession in West Africa provides the ideal opportunity to expand the market for our nation's cheap commodities in West Africa...it should be thought of as the ideal chance to raise the reputation of Japanese products and open new markets. ...While flexible approaches tend to be made subservient to plans for the large-scale export of our nation's mass-produced commodities and it is difficult to envisage such large-scale exports to West Africa, this is not a market which should be discarded by our small and medium manufacturers and export firms, and we in the presently strangled business, trade, and maritime sectors eagerly anticipate the future development of the West African market." (YSB, 1932 : 483)

Ouchi further noted that "in our nation's current situation, the dispatch of travelling merchant, the residence of trade representatives in regions of importance, and the introduction of measures to gain accurate knowledge regarding the other party should all be considered as methods of promoting trade". (YSB, 1932 : 485)

2 Japan's Trade with West Africa

During the First World War Japanese goods had shown strong sales at one point, spreading into African markets as substitutes for European goods, but after the war, they had been driven out by European countries resuming economic activity and returning their goods to Africa. The textile and sundry-goods industries that had developed in Japan during the war experienced slowdown or losses. Furthermore, Japanese goods were affected by postwar depression in the world market, strengthened links between metropoles and colonies, and autarchic block economic policies by European states. Capturing new export markets became a pressing need for the Japanese economy.

In such circumstances, new markets that had potential for development were given attention in Africa, Near East, Balkans, and Central and South America, and, particularly in the aftermath of the Great Crash during the early 1930s, interest switched to East and West African market. The abiding theme of the era was the search for a constructive commercial strategy.

Except for a brief period when exports exceeded imports during the First World War, Japanese trade with Africa ran a deficit until 1923, before becoming a surplus due to policy changes. Exports to Africa as a proportion of Japan's total exports increased from 2.5% in the 1920s to around 6-7% in the 1930s. Furthermore, while Africa's proportion of total Japanese imports was 2% in the 1920s, it was 3-5% in the 1930s. Below, based on contemporary surveys and consular reports, Japan's trade with British and French West Africa shall be considered, with a focus on the first half of the 1930s.

(1) British West Africa

Information about the economy of British West Africa began to be collected from the mid-1920s. For example, the Ministry of Foreign Affair's Trade Bureau published an introductory summary based on parts of the British government's *Colonial Report* in its *Overseas Economic Conditions [Kaigai Keizai Jijo]*, and an edited translation of an article on that economy in *Times* published on March 4, 1929 was published as "The Situation in British West Africa [Eiryo Nishi Ahurika Jijo]." Furthermore, an abbreviated translation of an article on December 8, 1928 from *l'Europe Naval* was published as "The Ports of the West African Coastline [Nishi Ahurika Engan Shoko]," providing additional information on the West African economic situation.

In addition, on November 22, 1928, the consul general in London, Kikuji Yonezawa, gave a presentation on "The Nigerian Economic Situation [Naijeria Keizai Jijo] (1928)," while details of Gold Coast's colonial economy were communicated based on a survey performed and published by the Empire Marketing Board in Great Britain.

However, in 1929, Ouchi of the YSB analyzed colonial markets in British West Africa and recommended which commodities had good prospects in the following manner:

"The primary import into British West Africa is textiles. Such imports run to 6,000,000 pounds annually. This makes up over 20% of total imports. The patterns and colors of cloth demanded differ by region and by the customs and habits of the blacks. Those thought to be desirable include grey bafta, blue bafta, salempores, cheap shirting, Croydon, twill, brocade, prints, domestics, real and imitation madras, and handkerchiefs. Nigeria has the greatest demand, importing 3,500,000 pounds worth annually. As there are many Muslims, the demand for bleached cotton is high. Dyed cloth is about 30% of the total imported cloth, and demand for checked and striped cloth is high. Sales of imitation Madras cloth, which replicates real Indian Madras, are good. There are prospects for printed material. The Yoruba around Lagos like white, ash, slate, brown, green, and blue, while the Hausa in the north prefer red, white, yellow, orange, and green. The people of the Niger River delta in South Nigeria like unpatterned gaudy colors. In Gold Coast, the market for cloth depends upon whether the price of cocoa is low or high, but generally a type of printed material known as wax block prints are popular. African women here use rayon and silk in place of the cotton handkerchiefs found in other places. There is demand for both black and white brocade, and sales of both blue bafta and salempore are good. In Sierra Leone, there is no obvious demand shown for any particular item, but demand for "fancy cotton" (patterned cloth) is comparatively high, and handkerchiefs and head ties are of silk. Gambia has large population of Muslim and thus receives lots of bleached muslin and white brocade. 75% of cotton imports into British West Africa are from Britain, while 90% of bleached cotton and grey bafta are British-made. Elsewhere in the market, the Dutch export raw and bleached cloth, while Germany, Italy, Czechslovakia, Belgium, and Switzerland all export their particular materials. It is essential for expansion into the West African market that the preferences of Africans regarding colors and materials are investigated. West Africa, and in particular Nigeria and Gold Coast, are markets that Japan should focus on." (YSB, 1932 : 237-241)

In addition, Ouchi noted the following regarding other sundry goods: "Currently the focus is on items from Britain, like dress shirts, vests, shirts, underwear, and other items of Western dress. The popularity of canvas and rubber shoes has increased dramatically. African homes generally have two to three items of enamel wear, with the greatest demand in vases, kettles and soup dishes, and we have hopes for these items." (YSB, 1932 : 241)

However, by the beginning of the 1930s, the Consul Yamazaki in Cape Town was collecting materials for "Business in Nigeria" (In *Overseas Economic Conditions [Kaigai Keizai Jijo]* December 13, 1935), with information on that country and its trade provided by Mr. Matsuyama, the commercial chargé d'affaires in London. Particular attention was paid to "packaging and labeling exported textiles" and "custom regimes and tariffs" (*Overseas Economic Conditions [Kaigai Keizai Jijo]* April 6, 1934). Additionally, the spread of British fabric in West Africa was noted in detailed surveys, which explored possible openings for Japanese goods. The areas surveyed spread out from Nigeria to Sierra Leone and Gold Coast.[1] A survey of the various British territories is offered below.

Gambia

It is difficult to learn anything detailed from consular reports. However, the YSB's Ouchi noted the following.

In 1929, 90% of exports consisted of peanuts, with the only other goods being small volumes of palm kernels and hides. Imports were centered on cloth, textiles, rice, kola nuts, yarn, sugar, and flour from Britain and France. Most cloth imports were also from Britain and France, and largely consisted of bleached, yarn-dyed, or patterned fabrics. (YSB, 1932 : 61-66)

However, Japanese textiles and rubber boots began to make their appearance in Gambia in the early 1930s. In 1932, 4,329,000 square yards of the former and 4,700 pairs of the latter were British-made, while 24,500 square yards and 4,900 pairs came from Japan. By 1933, 5,390,000 square yards and 1,400 pairs were from Britain, while 1,271,000 square yards and 12,250 pairs were from Japan. Japanese competition in the Gambian market had rapidly become fierce. British authorities were initially skeptical about placing restrictions on Japanese products, but introduced a quota system on June 30, 1934.[2]

Sierra Leone

According to Ouchi of the YSB, foreign trade contracted in 1929 because of reductions in import expenditure that accompanied the collapses of export prices and purchasing power of Africans. Sierra Leone's most important exports were palm kernels and kola nuts. The main buyers were Britain and France, and the price of palm kernels was driven by trends in Europe. The primary imports were cloth, textiles, clothing, tobacco, beer, rice, wheat flour, indigo, and lumber. These were primarily imported from Britain, Germany, France, and the Netherlands. Dyed cloth, bleached cloth, yarn-dyed, and patterned fabrics, in that order, made up the largest amount of cloth imports. Ouchi wrote the following regarding Japan's trade with Sierra Leone (YSB 1932 : 87-96):

"Trade between Sierra Leone and Our Empire remains insignificant, with exports from Sierra Leone to Our Empire essentially at zero, and imports from Our Empire do not exceed the following, according to government statistics:

	1928	1929
Clothing and textiles	166 pounds	535 pounds
Sundry goods	-	69 pounds
Totals	166 pounds	604 pounds

However, it is noteworthy that the volume of Our Nation's commodities traded in West Africa by British, French, and German firms is gradually increasing." (YSB 1932 : 97)

However, competition of Japanese goods with British goods became fierce in Sierra Leone at the beginning of the 1930s. The volume of imported Japanese textiles increased seven-fold between 1932 and 1933, shocking the British merchant community. Over the same period, imports from Britain fell by 50%.[3]

Nigeria

Ouchi of the YSB gave the following presentation on trade with Nigeria in 1929.

Nigerian imported from Britain, Germany, the USA, the Netherlands, and France, in that order, while its exports went to Britain, Germany, the USA, France, and the Netherlands. Its primary exports were palm kernels, palm oil, peanuts, cocoa, raw cotton, and tin, while its primary imports were cloth and textiles. In order, the largest shares of imported cloth were in bleached cotton, dyed cloth, patterned fabrics, grey cloth (unbleached), and yarn-dyed fabric. The largest supplier was Britain, followed by Germany, Italy, France, and the Netherlands.[4] (YSB, 1932 : 192-203)

Ouchi noted the following about trade with Japan:

"According to government statistics on the trade between Nigeria and Our Empire, Nigeria imported 1,931 pounds of goods from Our Nation in 1929, while their exports to Our Empire were negligible. The imports were as follows:

Ceramics and glassware	31 pounds
Glass bottles and lamps	8
Knitted cotton products	1,762
Wooden goods	45
Stationary	39
Others	46
Total	1,931 pounds

As can be seen, trade with Our Empire is as yet insignificant, as can be imagined when we consider that in the example of knitted products, Our Nation's commodities are initially taken to Britain, Germany, the Netherlands, Italy, or France and only then imported into Nigeria from Europe. Direct trade with Our Empire remains a totally undeveloped in this market that Our Empire's traders increasingly desire to advance to." (YSB, 1932 : 218-219)

However, Tajima of the OSK noted the following about trade between Nigeria and Japan based on 1932's trading statistics.

"Imports from Japan, primarily cloth, rayon, and canvas shoes, totaled 28 items with a value of 121,678 pounds, and are welcomed for their low prices and good quality. In the absence of artificial barriers, we anticipate high possibilities for further increase. In contrast to the promise demonstrated above for import trade in Japanese goods, exports of Nigeria's natural resources to Japan have not yet been seen and is labeled as nothing in trade statistics, yet the Arasuka-Maru on the occasion of its West African voyage loaded 700 tons of scrap metal from the government's railway department in Lagos, and perhaps in the future we shall be able to record Nigerian exports to Japan. The bulk of Nigeria's exported natural resources ... include palm kernels, peanuts, palm oil, cocoa, hides, and tin, and I believe that, taking into account recent development of Our Nation's manufacturing sector, research should be undertaken into the utilization of the above commodities as resources, and, in cooperation with manufacturers and traders, an export market with Japan be opened. This is vital for balanced trade between Japan and Nigeria that will clearly aid the development of Our Empire's export market." (OSK, 1934 : 83)

The spread of Japanese commodities in the early 1930s was a threat to the British in Nigeria too. The Nigerian governor proposed adopting more vigorous measures than merely raising tariffs in February 1934. By the end of 1934, British-manufactured textile imports totaled 37,799,409 square yards, but imports of inferior Japanese-manufactured textiles had reached 15,925,075 square yards.[5]

Gold Coast

Ouchi of the YSB noted the following regarding trade with Gold Coast in 1929. Gold Coast was essentially a mono-crop colony, with its cocoa exported to the United States, Germany, Britain, and the Netherlands making up half of the world's supply and over 80% of exports. Its primary imports were cloth, textiles, foodstuffs, beer, alcohol, and tobacco. Patterned fabric held the largest share of imported cloth, followed by yarn-dyed fabric, dyed cloth, and bleached cotton. The suppliers of this cloth were Britain in the case of bleached cotton, and Britain, Germany, and Belgium for yarn-dyed fabric. Dyed cloth was from Britain, Nigeria, Germany, and Belgium. Grey Cloth was from Britain, and patterned fabric was from Britain, Germany, and Sweden. (YSB, 1932 : 120-129) The following note can be found on Japanese trade with the Gold Coast:

"Trade between Our Empire and Gold Coast are, according to the government's statistics for 1929, as follows:

1929	Exports to Japan		88 pounds
	Imports from Japan		41,361 pounds
	Exports	Cocoa (2 tons)	88 pounds
	Imports	Clothing	7,328 pounds
		Grey Cloth	178
		Other textiles	2,046
		Silk	1,689
		Rayon	418 "

However, Tajima of the OSK noted the following regarding Japanese cloth[6] (YSB, 1932 : 128-129):

"It is significant that Our Empire, along with Germany and the Netherlands, is competing to gain a strong position in the market for eleven types of cloth that are dominated by Britain, and it seems that the reason for Our Nation's weakness in the calicos particularly favored by Gold Coast natives is a lack of market research, which could well be an area with scope for further development."

"The imports of Our Empire's commodities, as shown in the trade statistics, had seen a significant increase by the end of 1932, with good reason to think that such an increase will accelerate in 1933. While we can assume that as the government's statistics are collected on the basis of the country in which the cargo is loaded, in reality the correct figure for Japan's cotton imports is likely to be higher, although to what degree cannot be established. In spite of this however, across all of the various cotton goods—sewing cotton, towels, knitted cotton, clothing and so forth—there was an increase in imports in 1932. Across imports of all cotton goods, 1932 displayed an increase over previous years due to decline in prices, reduction in tariffs (which changed from 15% to 12% in 1932) and a depletion of stock towards the end of 1931." (OSK, 1934 : 127-128)

Finally, Tajima summarized trade relations and policies between Japan and Gold Coast in the following terms:

"Imports from Japan consisted of a total of 39 items, primarily various cotton cloths, rayon, clothing, and canvas shoes, and topped 71,131 pounds, and were the other, indirectly imported Japanese commodities not captured in these trade figures recorded, the total amount would not be any smaller, making the Gold Coast second only to Nigeria as the most favorable and important market for Our Nation's goods. Regarding the increase in imports of Japanese canvas shoes, the following point should be made in the trade statistics. Notwithstanding the fact that the large-scale imports of cheap Japanese canvas shoes shown in the trade figures for this year are unlikely to show the full value of Japanese imports, for the reasons noted above, it is the case that for the years 1928 and 1929, imports of Japanese shoes were zero, in 1930 we see 6,504 pairs and 33,104 pairs in 1931, which increases rapidly to 194,000 pairs in 1932. Were the bulk of these shoes sold at about a shilling a pair, this would be favorable and increase sales. In contrast to this development of imports from Japan outlined above, exports to Japan remain nonexistent, and the need for Our Empire to examine policies that would stimulate Japanese purchases of Gold Coast's main export of cocoa so that its growth mirrors that in imports must be thought a matter of great importance." (OSK, 1934 : 143)

Thus in 1932, Japan contributed 1.3% of Gold Coasts imports, but this figure increased to 3.3% by 1933. Imports of Japanese textiles increased from 0.5% in 1932 to 2.9% in 1933. In Gold Coast, the issue was not these figures as such; rather the issue was that, despite improvements in the quality of Japanese goods, their prices remained 25-40% cheaper in comparison with British goods. Somewhat before this, on June 7, 1932, commercial counsellor Matsuyama in London had explained and reviewed the spread of British textiles in West African markets in the following manner.

"In British West Africa, textiles from Lancashire overwhelmed those of other countries and had tremendous scope for future growth. Furthermore, because the British had left the gold standard, exchange rates had fallen and the spread of textiles and woolen goods into African markets had become easier. However, while a taste for Lancashire textiles could generally be seen across British West Africa, consideration must be taken for different demands and tastes in the various colonies. British merchants had come to consider West Africans as conservative and uninterested in novelty or fashion, but, in truth, arousing demand for new products is a vital task."[7]

Although it began late, Japanese trade expansion into British West Africa was rapid. In 1932, Japanese textile exports to West Africa were 4,400,000 square yards, whereas Britain's exports were 160,000,000 square yards. Japan's exports to the region showed remarkable progress in the early 1930s, with the Japanese share of the region's imports reaching 11% in 1933. This was the beginning of Britain losing its overwhelming market share. In the British West African market, Japanese exports had reached 21,830,000 yen by 1937, though they were not in a dominant position. This level of penetration into the West African market was clearly a threat to the British. (Bradshaw, 1992 : 380-381)

Britain was restricted by its treaty obligations to not introduce discriminatory measures regarding foreign commodities in its West African markets. The Anglo-Dutch Gold Coast Treaty of 1871 and the Anglo-French Convention of 1898 both specified this point. However, there was no such treaty binding its actions in Sierra Leone or Gambia, making discriminatory measures against Japanese imports there possible. In 1932, tariffs were applied to Sierra Leone and Gambia, restricting imports of Japanese goods. When the British understood those to be insufficient, they sought to introduce a more effective quota system to halt Japanese imports. In order to counter this, the Japanese sought to diversify its exports to West Africa. (Bradshaw, 1992 : 382)

(2) French West Africa

We can use Japanese consular reports to determine the situation in French West Africa from the latter half of the 1920s. For example, there are the reports from the extraordinary chargés d'affaires to the French Empire, Hiroyuki Kawai, based on surveys of monthly reports and statistics published by the French government-general undertaken by the Embassy Clerk Maruo,[8] and those of the Ambassador Extraordinary and Plenipotentiary to the French Empire, Mineichiro Adachi, based on the research of Consular Representative Tomoda of Marseilles.[9] Furthermore, during the Great Crash, Tomoda published reports on the demand for knitted cotton, the Ambassador to France, Kenkichi Yoshizawa, published reports that relied on the investigations of various consuls, and Consul Munemura put together reports on the state of exports to French West Africa.[10] Tomoda noted the following in his report:

"Given that, to date, the minimal trading of Our Empire's commodities has not been sufficient to find expression in the statistics collected by the customs houses, it is significant that, in 1929, we leapt into third on the list of suppliers of knitted cotton. …This advanced position compared to other nations was not the result of superior quality, but the sale of great numbers of goods of not particularly high quality. However, recognizing that these types of Our Empire's commodities fulfill the demands of many natives in these colonies should allow us to survey our future prospects with satisfaction." ("Demand for Knitted Cotton (in French West Africa) [Men Meriyasu Juyo Jokyo (Futsu Ryo Seibu Ahurika)]," Report of Consular Representative Tomoda of Marseilles, August 29, 1930)

Additionally, Tajima of the OSK noted the following about Japan's trade with French West Africa in 1932.

"There is nothing reported of Japanese commodities in trade statistics because the goods are officially calculated as French or British exports due to being transshipped via Marseilles or Liverpool. Although, in reality, the quantity of Japanese imports such as textiles and canvas goods is increasing, it is difficult to know its quantity or value. As the import tariff on all goods coming into Morocco was set at 12.5% with all countries except the Soviet Union by the Algeciras Conference of 1906, there has been a gradual increase in the import of Japanese commodities into West Africa that have initially been imported into Morocco, where they become eligible for a preferential tariff rate by being shipped onward from there as French cargo. In short, there is no way to separate out Japanese commodities that are recorded as British or French cargo in the trade statistics." (OSK, 1934 : 181-182)

Tajima noted the following about exports: "Unlike with imports, the recording of exports to Japan as zero is because, in reality, until today there are no indirect exports to Japan either." (OSK, 1934 : 187)

At the beginning of the 1930s, Japanese commodities began to be exported to French West Africa in large quantities. For example, in March 1934, the consul-general of Dakar noted the increase of Japanese exports to French West Africa, showing the rivalry being provided in French West Africa by Japanese goods.[11] Between 1931 and 1933, textile exports from France to its West African colonies doubled, while British exports also expanded considerably, but textile exports from the "other countries" category, which presumably includes Japan, also doubled. This increase was particularly marked for knitted cotton, rayon, and rubber goods. In March 1924, import quotas were imposed on various foreign textiles, and in November 1935, this quota system was extended to a number of commodities, including alcohol, knitwear, incense, soap, rayon, clothes, bicycles, cars, and tires. Additionally, beginning on January 1937, foreign-produced cotton cloth was incorporated in French West Africa's quota system.[12]

During this period, Japanese consular reports on French West Africa had become much more detailed. For example, around the time import quotas were being introduced, the Consulate in Marseilles was dispatching reports on the trade situation and customs revenue in French West Africa, drawn from the likes of Le Petit Marseillaise.[13] Additionally, from 1935 on, there are collections of reports detailing the foreign trade situation in the West African mandates and the trade picture in the various neighbor colonies of French West Africa.[14]

3 Japan and Britain in the West African market

Japanese firms that had temporarily entered their commodities in the African market during the First World War had lost that market after the war, with the return of European goods to the African market. The textile and sundry-goods industries that had developed in Japan during the war urgently sought to capture new export markets because of postwar depression, the strengthening of metropole–colonial relations, and autarchic block economic policies pursued by the European states. In such circumstances, the focus shifted to new markets that could be developed in Africa, Near East, Balkans, and Central and South America. In particular, the Great Crash during the 1930s saw a notable increase in interest in the West African market, which rivaled interest in the East African market.

However, how important were these new African markets to Japan? Between 1930 and 1934, Japanese exports to Africa increased by 219.8%, while trade surplus rose by 470%. Africa's share of Japan's total exports rose during the same five-year period, from 3.9% to 8.4%. The primary destination for exports was Egypt, followed by the Union of South Africa, but next came the new markets in East and West Africa. The fact that from 1937 onwards, the value of exports to these new markets had surpassed the value of exports to Egypt and South Africa, is particularly significant. (Bradshaw, 1992 : 365-366)

About half of all Japanese exports to Africa were textiles. In the first half of the 1930s, starting with India and China, low-priced and efficiently sold Japanese textiles had spread throughout Southeast Asia, the Middle East, and the Balkans, then into Europe, the United Kingdom, and throughout Britain's colonies, inducing trade friction with Britain by capturing new export markets in these regions. (Sugiyama and Brown, 1990 : 365-366)

In the 1930s, the two biggest textile exporters were Britain and Japan, who together accounted for 60% of the global textile trade. However, Britain's share declined from 33% at the beginning of the 1930s to 27% at the end of the decade, while Japan's share increased from 31% to 38% during that time. Moreover, as already noted, in 1932 Japanese textile exports to British West Africa, at 4,400,000 square yards, accounted for 3% of the region's total, but by 1937, Japanese exports accounted for 11% of the region's total; the 1937 figure was itself only half the level of Japanese textile exports to East Africa. With this spread of Japanese products into the West African market and the retreat of British textile exports, Manchester was seized with fear and a sense of crisis. (Bradshaw, 1992 : 380; Sugiyama and Brown 1990 : 88; Ampiah 1990)

In December 1932, the Manchester Chamber of Commerce established the "Special Committee on Japanese Competition," which called for the abrogation of the 1911 Anglo-Japanese Treaty of Commerce and Navigation. Commercial Counselor Matsuyama in London reported that the Directors of the Liverpool Chamber of Commerce had adopted the following resolution from this movement at the end of November, with the same resolution being adopted by the Manchester Chamber of Commerce at an Extraordinary General Meeting, attended by 400 members, on December 2: "In the face of a situation in which Japanese commodities are seeking to infiltrate the British West African market through outrageously low prices and disturb the proper conduct of trade in this area, we urgently recommend the immediate abrogation of the most-favored nation clause with Japan in order that the British Empire might protect its own market as others have"[15].

According to a report by Consul Noda of Liverpool in January 1934, the British government proposed in April 1933 to hold a conference of British and Japanese textile manufacturers in London in response to these actions, and announced the repeal of those terms from both the 1911 Anglo-Japanese Treaty of Commerce and the Navigation and Supplementary Treaty of 1925 that applied to British West Africa. At the same time, the Manchester Chamber of Commerce submitted a memorandum to the President of the Board of Trade about the basic framework of Anglo-Japanese textile negotiations. At the negotiations, the Japanese side asked questions about the steps undertaken by the British. According to a report by Consul Noda of Liverpool on February 26, 1936, Conservative MP J. R. Remer spoke about the Anglo-Japanese textile competition issue at a meeting of the House of Commons on January 31, 1934. He pointed out that members of the Manchester Chamber of Commerce included those involved with selling Japanese commodities and questioned their qualifications as representatives at the Anglo-Japanese textile negotiations.[16]

The Anglo-Japanese textile negotiations were ultimately held in London in February and March of 1934. The negotiations reflected the differing positions of Japan and Britain in the world economy, and were doomed from the start. Following the breakdown in negotiations, the Manchester Chamber of Commerce's "Special Committee on Japanese Competition" recommended that the government introduce a quota system in Britain's colonies. At a meeting on March 19, 1934, the Cabinet organized "the Committee on Japanese Trade Competition," on the advice of the Board of Trade. The committee's members were drawn from the Home Office, the Foreign Office, the Dominion Office, and the Colonial Office, and the President of the Board of Trade chaired it. Its first meeting, on March 27, 1934, considered introducing import quotas. The second meeting, on April 11, explored imposing quotas on Japanese goods in British colonies, introducing an import quota system in West Africa, and, in a move that recognized the importance of the East African market to Britain, investigating the possibility of amending the Treaty of Saint-Germain and either amending or abolishing the Anglo-Japanese Treaty of Commerce and Navigation. On May 7, Walter Runciman, the President of the Board of Trade, announced that import restrictions on foreign textiles and rayon had been imposed in British colonies and protectorates. However, Runciman announced to the committee on June 6 that the idea that only Japan would be discriminated against in East Africa based on the Treaty of Saint-Germain was dispiriting.[17]

In Sierra Leone and Gambia during this time, where Japanese goods had been spreading as fast as British goods had sharply decreased from 1932, import regulations were imposed, and when adjudged insufficient, quota impositions were investigated. Japanese industrialists opposed to this sought to diversify their exports to West Africa. Britain, which had become nervous about inroads made by Japanese commodities, sought to introduce measures against Japanese exports to British West Africa because it was "unfair." Implementing a quota system in British West Africa caused discussion within Britain as well, but as previously noted, quota systems were introduced in Sierra Leone, the Gold Coast, and Nigeria on May 17, 1934 and in the Gambia on June 30.

The result was that in the Gambia, where the sharp increase in Japanese rubber boot and textile imports had alarmed the British governor, Japanese goods were clearly hit by the quota system's imposition. However, what replaced them were not British goods, but in fact Soviet goods. Furthermore, in the Gold Coast, Japan contributed 1.3% of imports in 1932, which had increased to 3.3% by 1933, but the problem was that Japanese prices were 25-40% cheaper relative to their share of the market, which was dealt with by the import quota. While the British situation did improve, Japanese goods were largely replaced by goods from India, Italy, Hong Kong, the USA, and the Soviet Union. Meanwhile, the efficacy of the quota system introduced into Nigeria remained unclear.[18]

Notes

1   On this see "Naijeria Boeki Jokyo Fu Ippan Kokujo [The Condition of Nigeria's Trade; with a supplement on the state of the country]," *Kaigai Keizai Jijo [Overseas Economic Conditions],* Showa 5 nen (1930), Vol. 24 ; "Honpo Yushutsu Hosho Seido to Naijeria no Torihiki Jijo [The compensation system for Our Nation's exports and business conditions in Nigeria]," *Kaigai Keizai Jijo [Overseas Economic Conditions],* Showa 5-nen (1930), Vol. 7; and "Sei-A Muke Yushutsu Orimono Hyoki oyobi Hoso ni kansuru Zeikan Kisoku [Concerning the export of textiles to West Africa and customs regulations regarding their packing]," *Kaigai Keizai Jijo [Overseas Economic Conditions],* Showa 9-nen (1934), Vol. 30.

2   "Japanese Trade Competition in the Colonies," 22 February 1934, FO 371/18170.

3   "Written Answers, House of Commons," 30 May 1934, FO 371/18179.

4   For clothing and accessories, the largest importers in order were Britain, Germany, and France. Textile products imported into Nigeria included the following: grey bafta, croydons, shirting, domestics, mules, dhooties, twill, brocade, drill, tussores, shantung, damasks, satin, sheets, mosquito nets, muslin, flannel, handkerchiefs, dress shirts, knitwear, silk handkerchiefs, velvet, and velvet goods.

5   "Japanese Trade Competition in the Colonies," 22 February 1934, FO 371/18170.

6   In addition, Tajima of the OSK, based on 1932 statistics, noted the following about trade between Japan and Gold Coast. Britain made up 60% of Gold Coast imports, a figure that had recently contracted. Following Britain were countries like the USA, Germany, France, Belgium, and Japan. Although imports from most of these countries were decreasing, imports from Japan were increasing. In addition, to be included in Japanese goods are those items re-exported from Western nations and thus not officially recorded as Japanese commodities. Cotton and textiles constituted the largest volume of goods imported, followed by gasoline, tobacco, rayon, iron and steel, and cloth for sacking. (OSK, 1934 : 121, 122)

7   See "Eikoku Menpu no Nishi-Ahurika Shinshutsu Jokyo [The Spread of British Textiles into West Africa]," *Kaigai Keizai Jijo [Overseas Economic Conditions],* Showa 6-nen (1931), Vol. 30.

8   See "Futsuryo Sei-A Boeki Jokyo [The trade situation in French West Africa] —The report of the extraordinary chargés d'affaires to the French Empire Hiroyuki Kawai dated March 13, 1928," *Kaigai Keizai Jijo [Overseas Economic Conditions],* Showa 3-nen (1928), Vol. 4; "Futsuryo Seibu Ahurika Boeki Jokyo [The trade situation in French West Africa] —The report of the extraordinary chargés d'affaires to the French Empire Hiroyuki Kawai dated December 12, 1928," *Kaigai Keizai Jijo [Overseas Economic Conditions],* Showa 3-nen (1928), Vol. 53; and so on.

9   See "Futsuryo Kamerun Keizai Jokyo [The economic conditions in French Cameroon] —The report of the Ambassador Extraordinary and Plenipotentiary to the French Empire Mineichiro Adachi dated February 7, 1929," *Kaigai Keizai Jijo [Overseas Economic Conditions],* Showa 4-nen (1929), Vol. 2; "Futsuryo Seibu Ahurika Yunyu Jokyo (1927-nen) [The import situation in French West Africa (1927)] —The report of the Ambassador Extraordinary and Plenipotentiary to the French Empire Mineichiro Adachi dated March 18, 1929," *Kaigai Keizai Jijo [Overseas Economic Conditions],* Showa 4-nen (1929), Vol. 6; and so on.

10 "Men Meriyasu Juyo Jokyo (Futsuryo Seibu Ahurika) [The demand for knitted cotton (in French West Africa)] —The report of Consular Representative Tomoda of Marseilles dated August 29, 1930," *Kaigai Keizai Jijo [Overseas Economic Conditions],* Showa 5-nen (1930), Vol. 44; "Futsuryo Seibu Ahurika Gaikoku Boeki (1929-nen) [Foreign trade in French Western Africa (1929)] —The report of French Consul Munemura dated March 31 and April 28, 1931," *Kaigai Keizai Jijo [Overseas Economic Conditons],* Showa 6-nen (1931), Vol. 33.

11 Consul-General Cusden (Dakar) to Secretary of State, 30 May 1934, FO 371/18172.

12 Gaimusho Tsushokyoku Hensan [Compiled by the Ministry of Foreign Affairs' Trade Bureau], *Showa 12-nenban Kakkoku Tsusho no Doko to Nihon [Trends in trade between Japan and Other Nations—1937 Edition]*, Nihon Kokusai Kyokai, 1938, p 378.

13 Examples include "Futsuryo Sei-A no Kanzei Shunyugaku (1934-nendo) [Customs Revenue in French West Africa (For 1934)] —The report of Imperial Consular Representative of Marseilles Yoshiro Yamashita dated May 7, 1935," *Kaigai Keizai Jijo [Overseas Economic Conditions]*, Showa 10-nen (1935), Vol. 14; and "Futsuryo Sei-A Boeki Jokyo (1934-nen) [The trade situation in French West Africa (1934)] —The report of Imperial Consular Representative of Marseilles Yoshiro Yamashita dated September 23, 1935," *Kaigai Keizai Jijo [Overseas Economic Conditions]*, Showa 10-nen (1935), Vol. 22.

14 Among many reports, the following should be consulted: "Sei-A Inintochi Chiiki Gaikoku Boeki Jokyo (1935-nen) [The Foreign Trade Situation in the West African Mandate Regions (1935)] — The report of the Ambassador Extraordinary and Plenipotentiary to the French Empire Naotake Sato dated May 11, 1936" *Kaigai Keizai Jijo [Overseas Economic Conditions]*, Showa 11-nen (1936), Vol. 13; "Futsuryo Sei-A Boeki Tokei (1936-nen) [Trade Statistics for French West Africa (1936)] —The report of Imperial Consular Representative of Marseilles Yoshiro Yamashita dated May 18, 1937," *Kaigai Keizai Jijo [Overseas Economic Conditions]*, Showa 12-nen (1937), Vol. 14; and "Futsuryo Sei-A Keizai Jijo [The Economic Situation in French West Africa] —The report of the Imperial Consul of Casablanca Naokichi Katsuta dated February 22, 1938," *Kaigai Keizai Jijo [Overseas EconomicConditions]*, Showa 13-nen (1938), Vol. 8.

15 See "Honpo Menseihin no Eiryo Nishi-Ahurika Shijo Shinshutsu to Eikoku Togyosha no Tokkei Hogo Undo [The spread of Our Empire's textiles into the British West African market and the protectionist movement amongst British merchants] —The report of Commercial Counsellor of Britain Matsuyama dated December 16, 1932," *Kaigai Keizai Jijo [Overseas Economic Conditions]*, Showa 8-nen (1933), Vol. 15; and A. Redford, *Manchester Merchant and Foreign Trade*, Vol. 2, Manchester, 1956, pp. 249-262. "Japanese Competition and the British Cotton and Artificial Silk Export Trade," 22 December 1932, Manchester Chamber of Commerce Archives, M 8/5/18.

16 See "Rankashia Tai Sei-A Shokuminchi Boeki Fushin to Nihon Kyoso Mondai [Depression in the Lancashire trade with West Africa and the problem of Japanese competition] —The report of Liverpool Consul Noda dated January 13, 1934," *Kaigai Keizai Jijo [Overseas Economic Conditions]*, Showa 9-nen (1934), Vol. 11; "Eikoku Kain Giin no Manchester Shogisho Kogeki to Sono Hankyo [The Censure by Member of the House of Commons to the Manchester Chamber of Commerce and its effects] —The report of Liverpool Consul Noda dated February 2, 1934," *Kaigai Keizai Jijo [Overseas Economic Conditions]*, Showa 9-nen (1934), Vol. 12; "Sei-A no Nichi-Ei Tai Kyoso ni Koseinaru Iken [Public Opinion regarding Anglo-Japanese competition in West Africa] —The report of Liverpool Consul Noda dated January 9, 1934," *Kaigai Keizai Jijo [Overseas Economic Conditions]*, Showa 9-nen (1934), Vol. 10; and Joint Committee of Cotton Trade Organization, "Japanese Competition," 12 May 1933 Manchester Chamber of Commerce Archive, M 8/5/18.

17 The *Osaka Asahi Shimbun* provided successive reports on the Anglo-Japanese textile negotiations at the time. See the reports dated February 13, 15, 22, and 28, and March 9, 14, and 15, 1934. In addition, see Cabinet minutes, "Committee on Japanese Trade Competition," 19 March 1934, 27 March 1934, and 11 April 1934, CAB 27/568. British East Africa was the market within which Japanese goods made the largest inroads, after Egypt and South Africa. The peak of this surge occurred in 1937, particularly in Kenya, Uganda, and Tanganyika. In 1933, Britain had halted spun cotton exports from Japanese firms into East Africa. However, despite the end of the Anglo-Japanese Alliance in 1923, the 1911 Anglo-Japanese Treaty of Commerce and Navigation remained

in effect, and as the 1919 Treaty of Saint-Germain recognized Japan as a member of the League of Nations, Britain was unable to undertake tough restrictive measures against Japan. In 1934, as Japan pulled out of the League of Nations, Britain explored the possibility of expelling Japan from the East African market, but nothing was done. In West Africa, Britain was unable to take effective measures against Japanese imports because of the Congo Basin Treaties, and consequently lost their market.

18 Consult the following about the results from introducing the import quota system in British West Africa: "Textile Import Quotas: West Africa" (CO 852/17/14), "Quota on Japanese Cotton and Rayon Textiles" (1 February 1935), "Memorandum on the Working and Effect of Quotas on Cotton and Artificial Silk Piece Goods up to 31 December 1934" (26 February 1935) (CO 852/17/14).

References

Bradshaw, Richard, (1992), "Japan and European Colonialism in Africa, 1800-1939," Ph.D. Thesis, Ohio University.

Gaimusho Tsushokyoku [Compiled by the Ministry of Foreign Affairs' Bureau of Trade and Commerce], (1938), *Showa 12-nenpan Kakkoku Tsusho no Doko to Nihon [Trends in trade between Japan and Other Nations—1937 Edition],* Nihon Kokusai Kyokai.

Kitagawa, Katsuhiko, (2003), "Japan's Trade with South Africa in the Inter-War Period: A Study in the Japanese Consular Reports" in *Japan and South Africa in a Globalizing World: A Distant Mirror,* ed. by Katsumi Hirano and Chris Alden, Ashgate, pp. 25-44.

Kitagawa, Katsuhiko (2006), "Japanese Competition in the Congo Basin in the 1930s: A Study of Japanese Consular Reports" in *Intra-Asian Trade and the World Market* ed. by A. J. H. Latham and Heita Kawakatsu, London, Routledge, pp. 135-167.

Muroi, Yoshio, (1992), *Rengo Ahurika Kaisha no Rekishi 1879-1979—Naijeria Shakai-keizaishi Josetsu [History of the United Africa Company 1879-1979; an introduction to Nigeria's socio-economic history],* Dobunkan.

Osaka Shosen Kaisha, (1956), *Ahurika Koro-shi [A History of African Lines].*

Osaka Shosen Kaisha, (1966), *Osaka Shosen Mitsui Senpaku Kabu-shiki Gaisha 80-nenshi [80 years of the Osaka Mercantile Steamship Co. Ltd.]*

Redford, R., (1956), *Manchester Merchant and Foreign Trade*, Vol. 2, Manchester.

Sugiyama, Shinya & Ian Brown (eds), (1990), *Senkanki Tonan Ajia no Keizai Masatsu—Nihon no Nanshin to Ajia/Obei [Trade friction in Inter-war South-East Asia: The Japanese southern advance and Asia and the West],* Dobunkan.

Yokohama Shokin Ginko Todori-seki Chosaka [Chief Investigations Office of the Yokohama Specie Bank], (1932), *Ahurika Seibu Kaigan Shisatsu Hokokusho [Survey of the West African Coast],* Report no. 83, Showa 7-nen.

FO/CO/CAB

"Japanese Trade Competition in the Colonies," 22 February 1934, FO 371/18170.

"Written Answers, House of Commons," 30 May 1934, FO 371/18179.

Consul-General Cusden (Dakar) to Secretary of State, 30 May 1934, FO 371/18172.

"Textile Import Quotas: West Africa", CO 852/17/14.

"Quota on Japanese Cotton and Rayon Textiles" (1 February 1935), CO 852/17/14.

"Memorandum on the Working and Effect of Quotas on Cotton and Artificial Silk Piece Goods up to 31 December 1934" (26 February 1935), CO 852/17/14.

Cabinet minutes, "Committee on Japanese Trade Competition," 19 March 1934, 27 March 1934, and 11 April 1934, CAB 27/568.

Manchester Chamber of Commerce Archives

"Japanese Competition and the British Cotton and Artificial Silk Export Trade," 22 December 1932,

Manchester Chamber of Commerce Archives, M 8/5/18.

Joint Committee of Cotton Trade Organization, "Japanese Competition," 12 May 1933, Manchester Chamber of Commerce Archives, M 8/5/18.

Japanese Gonsular Reports

"Futsuryo Sei-A Boeki Jokyo [The trade situation in French West Africa] —The report of the extraordinary chargés d'affaires to the French Empire Hiroyuki Kawai dated March 13, 1928," *Kaigai Keizai Jijo [Overseas Economic Conditions]*, Showa 3-nen (1928), Vol. 4.

"Futsuryo Seibu Ahurika Boeki Jokyo [The trade situation in French Western Africa] —The report of the extraordinary chargés d'affaires to the French Empire Hiroyuki Kawai dated December 12, 1928," *Kaigai Keizai Jijo [Overseas Economic Conditions]*, Showa 3-nen (1928), Vol. 53.

"Futsuryo Kamerun Keizai Jokyo [The economy in French Cameroon] —The report of the Ambassador Extraordinary and Plenipotentiary to the French Empire Mineichiro Adachi dated February 7, 1929," *Kaigai Keizai Jijo [Overseas Economic Conditions]*, Showa 4-nen (1929), Vol. 2.

"Futsuryo Seibu Ahurika Yunyu Jokyo (1927-nen) [The import situation in French West Africa (1927)] —The report of the Ambassador Extraordinary and Plenipotentiary to the French Empire Mineichiro Adachi dated March 18, 1929," *Kaigai Keizai Jijo [Overseas Economic Conditions]*, Showa 4-nen (1929), Vol. 6.

"Honpo Yushutsu Hosho Seido to Naijeria no Torihiki Jijo [The compensation system for Our Nation's exports and business conditions in Nigeria]," *Kaigai Keizai Jijo [Overseas Economic Conditions]*, Showa 5-nen (1930), Vol. 7.

"Naijeria Boeki Jokyo Fu Ippan Kokujo [The Condition of Nigeria's Trade; with a supplement on the state of the country]," *Kaigai Keizai Jijo [Overseas Economic Conditions]*, Showa 5-nen (1930), Vol. 24.

"Men Meriyasu Juyo Jokyo (Futsuryo Seibu Ahurika) [The demand for knitted cotton (in French West Africa)] —The report of Consular Representative Tomoda of Marseilles dated August 29, 1930," *Kaigai Keizai Jijo [Overseas Economic Conditions]*, Showa 5-nen (1930), Vol. 44.

"Sei-A Muke Yushutsu Orimono Hyoki oyobi Hoso ni kansuru Zeikan Kisoku [Concerning the export of textiles to West Africa and customs regulations regarding their packing]," *Kaigai Keizai Jijo [Overseas Economic Conditions]*, Showa 9-nen (1934), Vol. 30.

"Eikoku Menpu no Nishi-Ahurika Shinshutsu Jokyo [The Spread of British Textiles into West Africa]," *Kaigai Keizai Jijo [Overseas Economic Conditions]*, Showa 6-nen (1931), Vol. 30

"Futsuryo Seibu Ahurika Gaikoku Boeki (1929-nen) [International trade in French Western Africa (1929)] —The report of French Consul Munemura dated March 31 and April 28, 1931," *Kaigai Keizai Jijo [Overseas Economic Conditions]*, Showa 6-nen (1931), Vol. 33.

"Honpo Menseihin no Eiryo Nishi-Ahurika Shijo Shinshutsu to Eikoku Togyosha no Tokkei Hogo Undo [The spread of Our Empire's textiles into the British West African market and the protectionist movement amongst British merchants] —The report of Commercial Counsellor of Britain Matsuyama dated December 16, 1932," *Kaigai Keizai Jijō [Overseas Economic Conditions]*, Showa 8-nen (1933), Vol. 15.

"Sei-A no Nichi-Ei Tai Kyoso ni Koseinaru Iken [Public Opinion regarding Anglo-Japanese competition in West Africa] —The report of Liverpool Consul Noda dated January 9, 1934," *Kaigai Keizai Jijo [Overseas Economic Conditions]*, Showa 9-nen (1934), Vol. 10.

"Rankashia Tai Sei-A Shokuminchi Boeki Fushin to Nihon Kyoso Mondai [Depression in the Lancashire trade with West Africa and the problem of Japanese competition] —The report of Liverpool Consul Noda dated January 13, 1934," *Kaigai Keizai Jijo [Overseas Economic Conditions]*, Showa 9-nen (1934), Vol. 11.

"Eikoku Kain Giin no Manchester Shogisho Kogeki to Sono Hankyo [The Censure by Member of the House of Commons to the Manchester Chamber of Commerce and its effects] —The report of Liverpool Consul Noda dated February 2, 1934," *Kaigai Keizai Jijo [Overseas Economic Conditions]*, Showa 9-nen (1934), Vol. 12.

"Futsuryo Sei-A no Kanzei Shunyugaku (1934-nendo) [Customs Revenue in French West Africa (For 1934)] —The report of Imperial Consular Representative of Marseilles Yoshiro Yamashita dated May 7, 1935," *Kaigai Keizai Jijo [Overseas Economic Conditions]*, Showa 10-nen (1935), Vol. 14.

"Futsuryo Sei-A Boeki Jokyo (1934-nen) [The trade situation in French West Africa (1934)] —The report of Imperial Consular Representative of Marseilles Yoshiro Yamashita dated September 23, 1935," *Kaigai Keizai Jijo [Overseas Economic Conditions]*, Showa 10-nen (1935), Vol. 22.

"Sei-A Inintochi Chiiki Gaikoku Boeki Jokyo (1935-nen) [The Foreign Trade Situation in the West African Mandate Regions (1935)] —The report of the Ambassador Extraordinary and Plenipotentiary to the French Empire Naotake Sato dated May 11, 1936", *Kaigai Keizai Jijo [Overseas Economic Conditions]*, Showa 11-nen (1936), Vol. 13.

"Futsuryo Sei-A Boeki Tokei (1936-nen) [Trade Statistics for French West Africa (1936)] —The report of Imperial Consular Representative of Marseilles Yoshiro Yamashita dated May 18, 1937," *Kaigai Keizai Jijo [Overseas Economic Conditions]*, Showa 12-nen (1937), Vol. 14.

"Futsuryo Sei-A Keizai Jijo [The Economic Situation in French West Africa] —The report of the Imperial Consul of Casablanca Naokichi Katsuta dated February 22, 1938," *Kaigai Keizai Jijo [Overseas Economic Conditions]*, Showa 13-nen (1938), Vol. 8.

Ch 8
Japan's Trade with Central Africa

After the Great Crash in the late 1920s, Britain took measures to protect its colonial market, whilst simultaneously Japan tried to increase her exports to Africa where it had found new markets. In the mid-1930s, attention was concentrated in British East Africa, the Belgian Congo and nearby areas as new markets for Japanese exports. Because the Congo Basin is in the center of the continent, it was recognized as being a commercially strategic area. Diplomatic moves by Britain and Japan involved an amendment to the Peace Treaty in Saint-Germain-en-Laye in 1919. This was based on the general protocol of the Berlin Conference of 1885, which gave free and equal opportunity of development, residence and trade to citizens of all countries in tropical Africa, including the Congo Basin area.

This chapter will consider the role of the Congo Basin Treaty as the framework which enabled Japan to advance in African markets in the mid-1930s and Anglo-Japanese rivalries over its revision and abolition. To begin with, the commercial agreement between Japan and Belgium as historical background of the Congo Basin Treaty is considered. Then the Congo Basin Treaty as the international framework of Japan's advance to Central Africa is examined and competition between British and Japanese textiles in Belgian Congo market is discussed. Lastly Japan's diplomacy to the move to revise and abolish the Congo Basin Treaty is considered.

1 The Commercial Agreement between Japan and Belgium

Before examining the Congo Basin Treaty, it is necessary to discuss relations between Japan and Belgium prior to the Japanese economic advance into the Belgian Congo. On August 1, 1866 Japan concluded a treaty of amity and commerce with Belgium, based largely on the Tax Revision Agreement (Kai Zei Yakusho) of June 25, 1866. (Isomi, Kurosawa and Sakurai, 1989 : 209) In this the 20 percent tariff rate fixed in the Five Countries Agreement of the Ansei period (November 1855~March 1860) was reduced to 5 percent. So Japan had to accept what amounted to Free Trade and was afraid that the absence of an import barrier would prevent the rise of modern industry in Japan. So from 1871 the Meiji government sought to revise the treaty.

In 1894 there were negotiations with Britain by Foreign Minister, Munemitsu Mutsu, to revise the Treaty and it was agreed that some tariffs could be increased Imports from Britain, France, Germany and the United States of more than ¥50,000 annually were listed as agreed items on which tariffs could be placed. On June 22, 1896, a new treaty of commerce and navigation with an attached protocol was signed between Japan and Belgium. This revised treaty came into action on July 17, 1899.[1] (Isomi, Kurosawa and Sakurai 1989 : 210) On January 17, 1900, a declaration of amity and residence between Imperial Japan and the Congo Free State was signed by Ichiro Motono, the Japanese Minister Extraordinary and the Belgian Ministry of Foreign Affairs.[2] In this, freedom of trade and navigation was agreed and the subjects of both countries were allowed equal rights to travel and reside, and buy and sell property. The agreement as revised by Foreign Minister, Munemitsu Mutsu, was for 12 years and was to end on July 16, 1911. The second Katsura Taro Cabinet (July 1908~August 1911) hoped to regain complete tariff autonomy and went to the negotiations to try to revise the treaty and obtain equality and reciprocity. These negotiations with Belgium was unsuccessful, but both Japan and Belgium thought that an interim agreement should be made on July 8 1911, rather than no agreement be reached.[3] (Isomi, Kurosawa and Sakurai, 1989 : 211-213)

After the end of the First World War, the Japanese government began negotiation to conclude a new treaty, hoping to gain both a tariff and residence agreement. A new treaty was signed on June 27, 1924 by Mineichiro Adachi, the Ambassador to Belgium, and the Belgium Minister of Foreign Affairs. Japan went ahead with reciprocal trade liberation. The trade and navigation agreement with Belgium of 1924 was the first to be concluded under this policy. It introduced the mutual opening of coastal trade, and the treat was applied to the dependencies of both countries (Korea and Belgian Congo).[4] (Isomi, Kurosawa and Sakurai, 1989 : 214-215) The Agreement was reached easily because equal opportunities to all in Belgian Congo had been declared in the Berlin protocol in 1885 and the Brussel protocol of 1890, and Japan had signed the Congo Basin Treaty (Saint-Germain-en-Laye) of September 10, 1919.

2 The Congo Basin Treaty : International Framework for Japan's Advance to Central Africa

It was a general Protocol of the Berlin Conference of February 16, 1885 which established the principle of free trade and equal opportunity to foreigners in Central Africa in order to expand the spheres of influence of the European power there. On April 26, 1884, an Anglo-Portuguese Treaty had been made to prevent France and Belgium from advancing into this region.[5] France, Belgium, Germany and other nations had protested vehemently against this move, which was why the

Berlin Conference was held under the auspices of the Prime Minister of Imperial Germany. The resulting protocol secured freedom of trade and navigation in the Congo River Basin and its adjoining lands to all interested countries. The signatory nations included Germany, Austria, Belgium, Denmark, Spain, the United States of America, France, Britain, Italy, the Netherlands, Portugal, Russia, Sweden and Turkey.

At the Brussel Conference on July 2, 1890 this protocol was supplemented with a general protocol and declaration. It was amended by the Treaty concluded in Saint-German-en-Laye on September 10, 1919 at the end of the First World War, but the principle of equal opportunity trade was confirmed. The Congo Basin Treaty was signed by the ministers of Japan, the United States, France, Belgium, Portugal, Britain and Italy. It was ratified Italy and the United States respectively on October 14, 1931 and October 29, 1934.[6]

Although both Germany and Austria were involved directly with the Berlin and Brussel Protocols, they did not become members of the Congo Basin Treaty. However it was interpreted that the protocol also applied to them in spirit. Turkey was allowed to join the Congo Basin Treaty and ratify it in the Turkish Peace Agreement. The difference between the Congo Basin Treaty and the Protocol of the Berlin Conference was that although the protocol allowed complete freedom to trade, the treaty prohibited only discriminatory tariffs in the Congo Basin. In the case of the Berlin Protocol, all nations were treated equally but only the member countries benefited from the Congo Basin Treaty.[7] (MOFA, 1938 : 117-118)

Article I of the treaty established equal trading rights to those countries which signed. It applied to the basin of the Congo River and its tributaries, the attached coastal zone from latitude South 2'30" to the mouth of the Loge River and the Congo Basin to the Indian Ocean coast from latitude 5' North to the mouth of Zambezi River. In other words it applied to part of French Equatorial Africa and French Cameroon, the Belgian Congo, Belgian Luanda and Ulundi, part of British Northern Rhodesia, Nyasaland, Uganda, Zanzibar, British Kenya, British Tanganyika, part of British Somaliland, Southern Ethiopia, and part of Anglo-Egyptian Sudan.[8] (MOFA, 1938 : 119-120)

In the region listed in Article 1 member nations could trade freely, both importing and exporting. There were no taxes, extra commissions or additional charges other than commission charges. (Article 2 Clause 1) Citizens of member nations and their properties were protected in all areas. In their business activities the citizens of the member nations were treated likely citizens of the regions, subject to the need to maintain public order and safety in the provinces in question. (Article 3) Although each country could dispose of state-owned assets and exploit natural resources in the provinces in question, the right to do this was given to all member nations equally. (Article 4)

Article 1 also allowed the ships of member nations to pass freely along the coast and call at ports and harbors without discriminatory treatment. The navigation of the Congo, without excluding any of its branches or outlets, remained, free for the merchant-ships of all nations equally, whether carrying cargo or ballast, for the transport of goods or passengers. In the exercise of this navigation the subjects and flags of all nations were to be in all respects treated on a footing of perfect equality, not only for direct navigation from the open sea to the inland ports of the Congo and vice versa, but also the great and small coasting trade, and for boat traffic on the course of the river. Consequently, on all courses and mouths of the Congo there would be no distinction made between the subjects of Riverain States and those of not-Riverain States, and no exclusive privilege of navigation would be conceded to companies, corporations, or private persons whatsoever. The navigation of the Congo would not be subject to any restriction or obligation which was not expressly stipulated by the Act. It would not be exposed to any landing dues, to any station or depot tax, or to any charge for breaking bulk, or for compulsory entry into port. In all the extent of the Congo, the ships and goods in process of transit on the river would be submitted to no transit dues, whatever their starting-place or destination. This free navigation also applied to the river Niger and its tributaries. (Article 5 and 9) The roads, railways or lateral canals which may be constructed with the special object of obviating the in-navigability or correcting the imperfection of the river route on certain sections of the course of the Congo, its affluents, and other waterways placed under a similar system would be considered in their quality of means of communication as dependencies of this river, and as equally open to the traffic of all nations. And on the river itself, so tolls would be collected on these roads, railways and canals calculated on the cost of construction, maintenance and management and on the profits due to the prompters. As regards the tariff of these tolls, strangers and the natives of the respective territories would be treated on a footing of perfect equality. (Article 7) Article 15 stated that ten years after the protocol was signed and passed, member nations were to have a conference to amend its provisions in the light of their experience. In this way the Treaty became a framework which made possible Japanese commercial advance in the Congo Basin in the 1920s and 1930s. (MOFA, 1938 : 120-124)

3 The Japanese Textiles in Belgian Congo Market

In 1927 Yoshitaro Kato, embassy clerk at Cape Town, was sent to the Belgian Congo to investigate economic conditions. This is known from a letter of June 27 from Tadanao Imai, consul of Cape Town to Giichi Tanaka, Minister of Foreign Affair. Kato returned to the Consulate at Cape Town on June 3, 1927 and submitted his report, which was later printed and published by the Ministry of Foreign Affairs' Bureau of Trade and Commerce.[9] (MOFA, 1927)

This report outlined the future of the Belgian Congo for Japanese exports. The market in general was not likely to expand rapidly because there were few European there, but commodities like silk manufactures, cotton goods, fancy goods, earthenware, glassware, and bulky goods (enameled ware for example) and canned fish seemed promising for Africans to buy. There were African workers in the mining towns, and small farmers in rural area who grew raw cotton and coffee. The mine workers had incomes and purchasing power and the farmers would buy more if they could earn cash by collecting palm produce and growing cotton. In the towns, Africans wanted khaki shirts and shorts and cotton cloth for women (white pattern on blue cloth, red headkerchiefs with a white pattern or indigo with polka dots) Farmers in the rural areas also wanted cutlery, knives with handles, enameled ware, candles, matches, chinaware and aluminum ware.[10] (MOFA, 1927 : 61-64)

A trade strategy was suggested operating from Dar es Salaam in Tanganyika. There seemed to be three routes by which Japanese merchandize could flow into the Belgian Congo. There was the route from Beira to Elizabethville by the Rhodesian railway, the route from Dar es Salaam to Kigoma on the East Coast of Lake Tanganyika and on to Albertville in Katanga by waterways, and the route from Mombasa via Uganda to the Northeast Congo. It was thought that the second route was most important as without a base in East Africa, the Congo could never be a market for Japanese goods. The Japan-East African shipping line had opened in 1926 and Mombasa was well known in the Japanese business world, but the importance of Dar es Salaam was not yet recognized. Tanganyika, where sisal, groundnuts, coffee, cotton and other agricultural products were cultivated, was of critical importance as a source of raw materials and an area for investment. Special attention was to be paid to cotton cultivation, and Japanese trading companies were encouraged to participate in the cotton market and Japanese investors to seek production estates and contribute to the development of East Africa. Tanganyika was an area classified as a "B" mandate territory of the League of Nations, that is, an area to be developed. (MOFA, 1927 : 64-71) Thus the Export Promotion Association and the Chamber of Commerce and Industry were to plan o advance into East and Central Africa. Japanese traders interested in business with Africa were advised to study the aims, organization and activities of the British Cotton Growing Association and organize a Business Association for Africa to devise measures to encourage investment. Exports were to be sent to investing opportunities in Tanganyika and the eastern Congo.[11] (MOFA, 1927 : 72-75)

According to the Consular Report by Chosaku Mogaki, resident at Mombasa, in Belgian Congo the main items for indigenous Africans were cotton cloth and in various districts of Stanleyville Province 60-80 percent of commodities in the shops for Africans were cotton textiles.[12] In the retailer outlets printed cloth was favored followed by dyed-in-the piece, gray cloth, yarn dyed cloth and bleached cloth.

Printed cloth consisted of *Kitenge*, a plain-weave printed cloth with a large pattern used for loincloths by Africans and *Mombasa Rordi* for women's clothes. *Kitenge* was classified into superior and inferior according to the quality of printing. The superior was a wax-block print made in Britain with beautiful colors and patterns and Africans found it expensive. It was similar to the *Khanga* of the British East African market. The inferior imitated wax-block print stuffs was cheap enough for Africans. These stuffs were imported from Britain, Belgium, and the Netherlands. Japanese traders tentatively sent *chinz* from Java to this market, but its price was similar to the products of other countries and the pattern was unpopular among the Africans. The *Kitenge* market included the Belgian Congo and West Africa. Consul Mogaki in Mombasa reported that Japanese traders ought to study the framework weaving patterns of Africans and sent expert designers to the region, and cooperated with local middlemen. Consul Mogaki's reports suggested that printed cloth of red and deep blue was popular in Stanleyville and blue cloth with a large pattern like the Japanese *Yukata* sold well.[13] (MOFA, 1927 ; 61-64) But ordinary printed cloth was cheap Japanese merchandize like those clothes exported to British East Africa. These were used for loincloths and women's clothes usually made of *Kitenge*. This kind of cloth sold well, but attention had to be paid to change in fashions. Cheap

Table 8-1 Imports of Cotton Cloth to the Belgian Congo by Countries, 1932-1936 (£1000)

Year	Imports	Japan(%)	UK	Belgium
1932	49,578	3,082(6)	25,316	16,381
1933	52,174	10,225(19)	27,277	10,477
1934	53,367	18,183(34)	22,857	6,565
1935	96,836	43,025(44)		
1936	125,296	83,473(66)		

Source : Consular Reports in *Overseas Economic Conditions.*

Table 8-2 Imports of Cotton Cloth to Belgian Congo by Kinds, 1932-1936 (£1000)

Year	Bleached	Unbleached	Printed	Dyed in	Yarn dyed
1932	988(52)	5,081(1,434)	23,507(504)	19,392(1,075)	-
1933	1,146(192)	5,017(3,464)	28,180(3,318)	17,407(3,208)	-
1934	2,473(880)	6,040(4,960)	25,222(5,139)	12,620(3,038)	6,876(4,128)
1935	3,619(1,339)	8,037(7,238)	54,185(18,289)	17,535(6,245)	13,462(9,917)
1936	5,426(3,371)	16,855(15,662)	60,123(34,176)	23,659(15,329)	19,237(14,937)

Source : Consular Reports in *Overseas Economic Conditions.*
Note : Figures in parentheses represent import of Japanese goods.

printed striped cloth for underwear among Africans and printed cloth with stripes was welcomed for loincloths by the indigenous people of Luanda and Ulundi.[14] In the case of dyed-in-piece cloths only indigo drill and khaki drill was found in the Congo market. Indigo drill was mostly in demand for deep blue jeans, and was also used for men's and women's loincloths. Standard goods manufactured by Texaf (Societe Textile Africaine) for the Belgian Congo was rough to touch. Japanese cloth made by Sugimoto & Co. in Nagoya entered this market and was imported via Mombasa. African men usually put on khaki shorts or long trousers. The supplies of this cloth were Japan, Britain, Belgium and the Netherlands, but Japanese cloth was predominant in Stanleyville market. Unbleached cotton cloth, the coarse quality, was called *Americani*. This was mainly used for loincloths. In British East Africa unbleached cloth was imported mostly, but in Congo more printed cloth than bleached was imported. Eighty percent of unbleached cloth was imported from Japan and Japanese cloth competed with Texaf in Belgian Congo. Yarn dyed cloth was used for men's underwear. Gingham had not yet been introduced here. Besides the above, loincloths woven in red, yellow and white yarn were welcomed. Yarn dyed cloth from Japan took 64 percent of the market and those made in Belgium 24 percent.[15] (Table 8-1, 8-2)

4 The Japan's Diplomatic Move to the Revision of the Congo Basin Treaty

The year 1930 was the tenth year after the Treaty of Saint-German-en-Lay had been signed, and member nations held a conference to revise the treaty in the light of their experiences. In July 1930 the British Ambassador in Japan proposed that the Japanese government convene a conference to revise the treaty five years later on 31 July 1935. The Japanese Government in its official letter to the British Embassy replied it found no reason to object to this proposal unless other signatory countries objected. However, subsequently, the Japanese Government worried about the intentions of the other signatory nations. In particular attention was paid to the Great Britain's position, because desires to revise or abolish the treaty was witnessed in the British Empire and its Colonies. Given this backdrop, Japan who attached a great importance to Africa as a new export market, moved towards retaining the treaty.[16] (MOFA, 1938)

After 1930 Japan started to examine the attitudes of European countries toward the revision and application of the Congo Basin Treaty. In particular the views of organizations in Britain and her colonies were investigated with scrupulous care. These included official policy making organizations such as the Ministry of Foreign Affairs and the Colonial Office and unofficial business organizations such as the Manchester Chamber of Commerce, the Mombasa Chamber of Commerce, the Nairobi Chamber of Commerce, the Association of Chambers of Commerce of East Africa, and the British Empire Federation of Chambers of Commerce.

On 19 February 1930, the Japanese Ambassador Extraordinary and Plenipotentiary to Britain, Tsuneo Matsudaira asked the British Foreign Minister, Arthur Henderson, whether revision of the Congo Basin Treaty was to be discussed in the British Parliament. Henderson replied that it had not been decided yet but was still under consideration. Matsudaira sent this report to the Minister of Foreign Affairs of Japan, Kijuro Shidehara. (Letter on 27 February 1930 from Matudaira Tsuneo, the Ambassador Extraordinary and Plenipotentiary of Britain to Kijuro Shidehara, the Minister of Foreign Affairs, Diplomatic Archives of MOFA, File B-10-5-0-8)

Then in November 1933 and October 1934, the Minister of Foreign Affairs in Japan, Koki Hirota, sent the official notice to the Japanese Embassies in Britain, France, Belgium, Italy, Portugal, and the United States. And also the Japanese Consulates in Alexandria, Cape Town and Mombasa instructed them to investigate and report the actions of the signatory countries of the Congo Basin Treaty. (Letter on 7 November 1933, from Koki Hirota, the Ministry of Foreign Affairs to Matsudaira Tsuneo, the Ambassador Extraordinary and Plenipotentiary of Britain, Diplomatic Archives of MOFA, File B-10-5-0-8)

In October 1934, the Acting Ambassador to Portugal, Kumabe, investigated into the operation of the Congo Basin Treaty in Mozambique, Angola, Italian Somaliland, French Equatorial Africa, and the Cameroon and sent his report to the Minister of Foreign Affairs, Koki Hirota. Then in December 1934, the Japanese Embassy in Belgium sent this report to the Ministry of Foreign Affairs:

"The Belgian Foreign Ministry says that this issue is so complicated that close communication among the countries concerned is necessary. An official in charge of the Belgian Foreign Ministry had said that he expected the Conference to be convened under the initiative of Britain and Japan." (Letter on 31 October 1934, Kumabe, the Ambassador of Portugal to Hirota, the Minister of Foreign Affairs, Letter on 11 December 1934, Hachiro Arita, the Ambassador Extraordinary and Plenipotentiary of Belgium to Koki Hirota, the Minister of Foreign Affairs, Diplomatic Archives of MOFA, File B-10-5-0-8)

In January 1930, a report was sent from the Japanese Consulate in Cape Town to the Ministry of Foreign Affairs:

"On 25 January, the East African Federation of Chambers of Commerce in the Colony of Kenya discussed the revision of the Congo Basin Treaty and as a result objected to the Bill establishing the British Imperial Preferential Tariff System in East Africa."

"In the meeting of the Federation of Chambers of Commerce of the British Empire, to be held in London at the end of May, delegates of the Chambers of Commerce from the African colonies under the British rule will discuss the revision of the Congo Basin Treaty." (Letter on 24 January 1930, Letter on 27 January 1930 from Yamazaki Takeshige, the Consul of Cape Town to Kijuro Shidehara, the

Minister of Foreign Affairs, Diplomatic Archives of MOFA, File B-10-5-0-8)

Subsequently, in May and June 1932, the Japanese Consulate in Mombasa reported to the Ministry of Foreign Affairs :

"Some members of Parliament in Britain with economic interests in East Africa called for a revision of the Congo Basin Treaty, but the Mombasa Chamber of Commerce rejected this motion because abolition of the treaty would not profit the trade of the British Empire."

"The Nairobi Chamber of Commerce preferred the abolition of the Congo Basin Treaty, and the formation of a Customs Union of Kenya, Uganda, and Tanganyika and a revision of the mandate articles."[17] (Letter on 14 May 1932, from Kuga, the Consul of Mombasa to Yoshizawa, the Minister of Foreign Affairs, Letter on 21 June 1932, from Kuga, the consul of Mombasa to Saito, the Minister of Foreign Affairs, Diplomatic Archives of MOFA, File B-10-5-0-8)

In addition, Consul Kuga, in the Mombasa consulate, sent the statement by the Chairperson of the Mombasa Chamber of Commerce, John Seidman Allen, in September 1933:

"An extraordinary Assembly of the Mombasa Chamber of Commerce shelved a judgement of revision of the Congo Basin Treaty as difficult, because it intertwined with articles of the Tanganyika mandate and other treaties. Besides, East Africa itself exports to Japan." (Letter on 5 September 1933, from Kuga, the Consul of Mombasa to Uchida, the Minister of Foreign Affairs, Diplomatic Archives of MOFA, File B-10-5-0-8)

In Tanganyika, free trade was secured by the article of the mandate of the League of Nations and unanimous acceptance by members of the League of Nations was an essential condition to revise it. In addition, signatory countries that had political and economic interests in this region had signed Saint-German-en-Lay Treaty. This was incorporated in more than 30 international treaties, including the Zanzibar Treaty. So even if the Congo Basin Treaty was abolished, it would be difficult to exclude Japan as one of these treaties contained a most favoured nation trade clause by which benefits must be extended to all.

In June 1935, the Japanese Embassy in Belgium reported by quoting the magazine, *Soir* :

"The British government will not convene Parliament to discuss a revision of the Congo Basin Treaty. This issue was examined by the relevant ministries but was so complicated that they could not arrive at a conclusion. However, fear of competition from Japanese goods in Central Africa was felt seriously among industrialists in Britain, and the Manchester Chamber of Commerce appealed for an urgent investigation into the state of affairs." (Letter on 29 June 1935, from Hachiro Arita, the Minister Extraordinary and Plenipotentiary of Belgium to Hirota, the Ministry of Foreign Affairs, Diplomatic Archives of MOFA, File B-10-5-0-8)

In the mid-1930s "cotton diplomacy" or "primary products purchasing strategy" was proposed in Japan to prevent revision of the Congo Basin Treaty. In February and March 1934, Anglo-Japanese cotton negotiations were held in London, but finally broken down. In May 1934, Walter Runciman, the President of the Board of Trade announced that an import quota system would be placed on foreign manufactures such as cotton piece goods and artificial silk in colonies and protectorates under British rule. Consequently, the import quota system was introduced in the British colonies of West Africa. Recognizing that East Africa was an important market for British cotton textiles, revision or abolition of the Congo Basin Treaty was discussed as a way to prevent sales of Japanese cotton goods from increasing there. (Kitagawa, 1997, 2006, 2015)

The Japanese Consul in Mombasa, Chosaku Mogaki, expressed his understanding of the impending crisis as follows:

"It is thought that the British Government sees the Congo Basin Treaty as a barrier to making Runciman's announcement effective as it would deprive the validity of the Congo Basin Treaty without an article of abrogation. Our Empire should encourage other concerned signatories to prevent the British manoeuvres and put up stubborn resistance in order to retain this treaty. Recognizing that a variety of diplomatic measures have been already taken, abolition of this international treaty would mean an irreparable loss to the future of our Empire." (Letter on 22 August 1934, Chosaku Mogaki, the Consul of Mombasa to Koki Hirota, the Minister of Foreign Affairs, Diplomatic Archives of MOFA, File B-10-5-0-8)

Against this backdrop, Consul Mogaki made the following suggestion :

"As a provisional measure regarding this matter, our Empire should adjust the balance of trade on a reciprocal base and construct close relations with this region. If necessary, our Empire should strategically buy raw cotton in Uganda and natural soda in Kenya to improve the balance of trade and in the same way encourage the selling of cotton cloth, cotton piece goods, artificial silk, and general merchandise in this market. However, such local products as coffee, sisal, wattle, and maize, with the exception of raw cotton, should only be traded as samples. Believing it would take some time to develop substantial imports of these products, our Empire should focus on the strategic buying of raw cotton and natural soda to prevent the abolition of the Congo Basin Treaty." (Letter on 22 August 1934, Chosaku Mogaki, the Consul of Mombasa to Koki Hirota, the Minister of Foreign Affairs, Diplomatic Archives of MOFA, File B-10-5-0-8)

In a later communication Consul Mogaki continued:

"Considering diplomatic move against those who wish to prevent the sale of Japanese goods from increasing in East Africa is a matter of the utmost urgency compared with South Africa, as this area is at a critically significant transitional period. In this regard, Japan needs more powerful measures of national policy in East Africa than in buying wool in South Africa. The rise and fall of Japan's export trade with East and Central Africa depends heavily on the fate of the Congo Basin Treaty. Although alternative policies might possibly be drafted in order to retain this treaty, it is expected that the improvement in the balance of trade can be achieved by buying raw cotton, the only commodity that East Africa hopes to export to Japan. This is an essential manoeuver because serious attention should be paid to the most important exports from Japan, cotton cloth and cotton piece goods, which are linked to the import of cotton. But Japanese exports to South Africa are not so closely connected to South African wool. Business interests in Japan feel some difficulty in promoting wool buying. However, interested traders and manufacturers in Japan think that promotion of cotton buying in East Africa is easier to achieve than promoting wool buying in South Africa." (Letter on 18 February 1935, Chosaku Mogaki, the Consul of Mombasa to Koki Hirota, the Minister of Foreign Affairs, Diplomatic Archives of MOFA, File B-10-5-0-8)

The period from the Versailles Conference in 1919 to the Greater East Asian Conference in 1943 was only a quarter of a century. However, this period was one of substantial ups and downs for Japanese economic growth. In 1919 Japan had already become one of the Imperial powers in the world and achieved outstanding success in economic and political development. In the following 25 years, Japan continued further economic growth and established the quasi-colony of Manchukuo under the rule of the Japanese Empire. The prosperity of the Japanese Imperial economy depended substantially on its exports to overseas countries. Business leaders in Imperial Japan maintained high industrial productivity by employing low wage workers and exploiting low raw material prices, and hoped to increase exports. (Nish, 2002)

The "Report of Research on the Congo Basin Treaty" circulated within the Ministry of Foreign Affairs in 1938, recorded the reasons why Japan stood in a good position to retain this treaty as follows:

"It is needless to say that Japan, which is limited in area and whose population is increasing year by year has more than 70 million people, depends heavily for her survival and development on the promotion of imports and exports. So, Japan has always insisted over the years on freedom to acquire natural resources and to expand markets overseas for manufactured goods. In the A mandate and the B mandate, the Covenant of the League of Nations and the articles of each mandate prescribe the principle of open-door and free trade policy, and the Congo Basin Treaty provides free and equal opportunities for development, residence and trade in Central Africa to signatory countries. These principles are in full accord with the Empire's position over the years even though application of the Treaty has been limited. The Empire supported and retained these principles and at the same time made a substantial efforts to extend them to uncivilized areas. However,

Japan, after withdraw from the League of Nations, there was discussion among member countries to exclude Japan from equal opportunities to trade, while there was discussion in Great Britain and signatories to repeal the Congo Basin Treaty. Naturally Japan had to pay serious attention to these developments". (MOFA, 1938; Diplomatic Archives of MOFA, File B-10-5-0-8)

Notes

1   This new Japanese-Belgian treaty was signed by the Minister Plenipotentiary, Shuzo Aoki and Paul de Favereau.

2   Letter on August 2, 1899 from the Minister Plenipotentiary at Belgium, Katsunosuke Inoue to the Minister of Foreign Affairs, Shigenobu Okuma, "Congo State and Treaty of Amity", Letter on March 9, 1900 from the Minister Plenipotentiary at Belgium, Ichiro Motono to the Minister of Foreign Affairs, Shuzo Aoki, "Exchange of the Declaration with Congo Free State", Letter on October 7, 1900 from Prime Minister, Aritomo Yamagata to Minister of Foreign Affairs, Shuzo Aoki, "Draft to the Declaration between Imperial Japan and Congo Free State", in Diplomatic Archives of MOFA, File 2-5-1-59, Belgium, Congo Commercial Treaty.

3   Letter on April 18, 1911 from the Minister of Foreign Affairs, Jutaro Komura to the Minister at Belgium, Keijiro Nabeshima : Instruction on September 23, 1911 from the Minister of Foreign Affairs, Kaoru Hayashi to the Minister at Belgium, Nabeshima.

4   "Revision of Japanese-Belgian Commercial Treaty", Diplomatic Archives of MOFA, File 2-5-1-43, 90, 111.

5   Ministry of Foreign Affairs, "An Outline of the General Protocol of the Berlin Conference (February 26, 1885) and the General Protocol and Declaration of the Brussel Conference (July 2, 1890)", p. 1. Diplomatic Archives of MOFA, File B-10-5-0-8 ; "International Treaty on the Revision of the General Protocol of the Berlin Conference and the General Protocol and Declaration of the Brussel Conference."

6   Ministry of Foreign Affairs, "An Outline of the General Protocol", *ibid.*, pp. 1-2.

7   The Ministry of Foreign Affairs' Bureau of Trade and Commerce, "A Study of Equal Treatment in the Mandate Territories and the Congo Basin Treaty" (1938), pp. 117-118, Diplomatic Archives of MOFA, File B-10-5-0-8 ; "International Treaty on the Revision of the General Protocol of the Berlin Conference and the General Protocol and Declaration of the Brussel Conference".

8   See also "Protocols and General Act of the West African Conference", presented to both Houses of Parliament by Command of Her Majesty, March 1885.

9   Letter on June 27, 1927 form Consul Tadanao Imai at Cape Town to the Minister of Foreign Affairs, Giichi Tanaka "Dispatch of the Embassy Staff to the Belgian Congo", Diplomatic Archives of MOFA, File E-1-2-0-X1-BE2 ; "Miscellaneous Matter on Fiscal, Economic and Financial Issues in Several Countries : A Part of Congo". See Also The Ministry of Foreign Affairs Bureau of Trade and Commerce, *Economic Conditions in Belgian Congo*, 1927.

10   See also "The General Conditions in the Belgian Congo", *Overseas Economic Conditions [Kaigai Keizai Jijo]*, No. 7, 1937, pp. 219-243.

11   "Economic Conditions of the Belgian Congo" (October 11, 1927) from Ambassador Extraordinary and Plenipotentiary of Belgium, Mineichiro Adachi to the Ministry of Foreign Affairs' Bureau of Trade and Commerce, *Overseas Economics Conditions [Kaigai Keizai Jijo]*, No. 1062, January 1928, pp. 1424-1526.

12   "The Belgian Congo as Japanese Merchandize Market" (March 26, 1936, Chosaku Mogaki to the Ministry of Foreign Affairs' Bureau of Trade and Commerce), *Overseas Economic Conditions*, No. 15, August 10 1936.

13 "The Belgian Congo as Japanese Merchandize Market" (March 26, 1936, Chosaku Mogaki to the Ministry of Foreign Affairs' Bureau of Trade and Commerce) *Overseas Economic Conditions [Kaigai Keizai Jijo]*, No. 15, August 10 1936, pp. 128-129.

14 "The Belgian Congo as Japanese Merchandize Market" (March 26, 1936, Chosaku Mogaki to the Ministry of Foreign Affairs' Bureau of Trade and Commerce), *Overseas Economic Conditions [Kaigai Keizai Jijo]*, No. 15, August 10 1936, p. 130.

15 "The Belgian Congo as Japanese Merchandize Market" (March 26, 1936, Chosaku Mogaki to the Ministry of Foreign Affairs' Bureau of Trade and Commerce), *Overseas Economic Conditions [Kaigai Keizai Jijo]*, No. 15, August 10 1936, pp. 132-135.

16 The Ministry of Foreign Affairs' Bureau of Trade and Commerce (1938) "A Study of Equal Trade Treatment in the Mandate Territories and the Congo Basin Treaty (The Congo Basin Treaty)" (1919-1937), Diplomatic Archives of MOFA, File B-10-5-0-8.

17 The League of Nations mandate was a legal status for certain territories transferred from the control of one country to another following World War I, or the legal instruments that contained the internationally agreed upon terms for administering the territory on behalf of the League of Nations. The mandate system was established under Article 22 of the Covenant of the League of Nations, entered into on 28 June 1919. The League of Nations decided the exact level of control by the mandatory power over each mandate on an individual basis. The first group of class A mandates were territories formerly controlled by the Ottoman Empire, the second group of Class B mandate were all former German territories in West and Central Africa, and Class C mandate, including West Africa and certain of the South Pacific Islands. Anghie, A., *Imperialism, Sovereignty and the Making International Law*, Cambridge University Press, 2005. Callaghan, M.D., *A Sacred Trust : The League of Nations and Africa, 1929-1946*, Sussex Academic Press, 2004.

References

Anghie, Antony, (2005), *Imperialism, Sovereignty and the Making of International Law,* Cambridge University Press.

Ampiah, Kweku, (1990), "British Commercial Policies against Japanese Expansionism in East and West Africa, 1932-1935", *International Journal of African Historical Studies*, Vol. 23, No. 4, pp. 619-641.

Cabinet, (1934), "Committee of Japanese Trade Competition", March 19, March 27, April 11, CAB/27/568, PRO (London).

Callahan, Michael D., (2004), *A Sacred Trust : The League of Nations and Africa, 1929-1946*, Sussex Academic Press.

Department of Overseas Trade, (1934), *Economic Condition in East Africa,* HMSO, London.

"Decision of the Revision of the Congo Basin Treaty by the Association of Chamber of Commerce of British East Africa" (Telegraph on July 27, 1933 from Consul Kuga at Mombasa) *Overseas Economic Conditions [Kaigai Keizai Jijo]*, No. 30, July 1933.

Forster, S., W.J. Mommsen and R. Robinson, (1988), *Bismarck, Europe, and Africa : The Berlin Africa Conference 1884-1885 and the Onset of Partition,* Oxford, Oxford University Press.

Isomi, Tatsunori, et. al., (1989), *A History of Japanese-Belgian Relations [Nihon-Berugi Kankeishi]*, Hakusuisha, Tokyo.

"Issue of the Revision of the Congo Basin Treaty and the Opinions of the Settlers in British East Africa", *Overseas Economic Conditions [Kaigai Keizai Jijo]*, No. 35, September 1932.

Kitagawa, K., (1990), "Japan's Economic Relations with Africa between the Wars ; A Study of Japanese Consular Reports", Kyoto University, *African Study Monograph*, Vol. 11, No. 3, pp. 124-141.

Kitagawa, K., (1997), *A Study in the History of Japanese Commercial Relations with South Africa [Nihon-Minami Africa Tsusho Kankeishi]*, International Research Centre for Japanese Studies,

Monograph Series, No. 13.

Kitagawa, K, (2003), "Japan's Trade with South Africa in the Inter-War Period", in Chris Aden and Katsumi Hirano eds., *Japan and South Africa in a Globalizing World : A Distant Mirror*, Hampshire, Ashgate, pp. 25-44.

Kitagawa, K., (2006), "Japanese Competition in the Congo Basin in the 1930s", in A.J.H. Latham and Keita Kawakatsu eds., *Intra-Asian Trade and the World Market*, London, Routledge, pp. 135-167.

Kitagawa, K., (2012), "Retrospective and Prospective for Japanese Policy on Africa : Focusing on the Tokyo International Conference on African Development (TICAD) Process", *Kansai University Review of Economics*, No. 15, pp. 1-28.

Kitagawa, K., (2015), "Japan's Trade with West Africa in the Inter-War Period : A Study of Japanese Consular Reports", *Kansai University Review of Economics*, No. 17, pp. 1-28.

Kitagawa, K. ed., (2016), *Africa and Asia Entanglements in Past and Present : Bridging History and Development Studies*, Asian and African Studies Group, Faculty of Economics, Kansai University.

Ministry of Foreign Affairs, "An Outline of the General Protocol of the Berlin Conference (February 26, 1885) and the General Protocol and Declaration of the Brussel Conference July 2, 1890)", Diplomatic Archives of MOFA, File B-10-5-0-8 ; "International Treaty on the Revision of the General Protocol of the Berlin Conference and the General Protocol and Declaration of the Brussel Conference".

Ministry of Foreign Affairs Bureau of Trade and Commerce, (1938), "A Study of Equal Trade Treatment in the Mandate Territories and the Congo Basin Treaty", Diplomatic Archives of MOFA, File B-10-5-0-8.

Ministry of Foreign Affairs' Bureau of Trade and Commerce, (1927), *Economic Conditions in the Belgian Congo [Berugi-Ryo Kongo Keizai Jijo]*.

Nish, Ian (2002), *Japanese Foreign Policy in the Inter-War Period*, Praeger.

Osaka Shosen Kaisha (OSK), (1924), *Report of Economic Conditions in East Africa [Higashi Africa Keizai Jijo Hokokusho]*, Osaka.

Osaka Shosen Kaisha (OSK), (1956), *History of African Shipping Lines [Africa Koro Shi]*, Osaka.

Tanaka, Giichi, "Dispatch of the Embassy Staff to the Belgian Congo", Diplomatic Archives of MOFA File E-1-20X1-BE2 : "Miscellaneous Matter on Fiscal, Economic and Financial Issues in Several Countries : A Part of Congo".

"The Belgian Congo as Japanese Merchandize Market" (March 26, 1936, Chosaku Mogaki to the Ministry of Foreign Affairs' Bureau trade and commerce), *Overseas Economic Conditions [Kaigai Keizai Jijo]*, No. 14 August 10, 1936.

"The Issue of the Congo Basin Treaty" (July 24, 1939, From Mamoru Shigemtsu, the Minister Extraordinary and Plenipotentiary of Britain to the Ministry of Foreign Affairs), *Overseas Economic Conditions [Kaigai Keizai Jijo]*, No. 19, October, 1939.

Ch 9

Post-War Japan and
New Independent Africa
in the Late 1950s and the Early 1960s

Interdependence of all the world peoples and the collective endeavour for global peace and security are obligations on all of us, if we are to ensure our survival as the human species. And this obligation is proportionately heavier on Japan, as an economic power, in order to positively contribute to the reconstruction of an international framework to facilitate the rightful and equitable participation of the non-western world in the global political economy. Africa is an essential part in this non-western world. It is the aim of this chapter to historically delineate the political movement towards independence in Africa and to examine the stance that Japan has taken in relation to the decolonization process in the continent.

Presumably, owing to the relatively low level of political and economic interactions between the African continent and Japan, which are, in turn, a consequence of the physical barriers of geographical distance and the fact that Africa was partitioned with executive colonial spheres of influence between European powers the continent has remained a relative blind spot in the Japanese consciousness. However, it is imperative for Japan to consciously relocate Africa in its world scenario, in this period of global crisis and the thoroughly reassess its perspective vis-à-vis the economic dynamism within African countries. (Aden and Hirano, 2003)

In this regard, it is meaningful that the Meetings of Tokyo International Conference on African Development (TICAD) has taken place since 1993. It is of critical importance for Japan and Japanese people to be properly aware of the role to play and the position to hold in globalizing world in general and Asia-African context in particular. Looking at striking trends that recently Japan has played an important and active role in the construction of an elaborate and highly sophisticated system of international relations, it is an essential requirement to extend the state of our knowledge in order to put this international scheme into effect.

This chapter forms a part of wider study on the issue of how Japan and Japanese people faced with Africa and African people from the partition of Africa to the age of decolonization. This work is only indirectly about international relations in the sense of relations between the states. Rather, it is about the image of foreign societies that shapes our attitudes and policies toward them. Specifically this is an exploration of attempts by opinion makers in Japan to construe the meaning and implications of African independence for their readers. At one level, foreign policy making may consist of setting general goals and asserting broad principles, but in application such goals and principles have to be related to conceptions of foreign reality. In recent time, works on international relations have been stressing the importance of perception and cognition as well as the connections between domestic politics and foreign policy. The domestic connection is usually interpreted as referring to political and economic pressure groups, while the cultural and intellectual strand is ignored. This chapter is about Japanese intellectuals and about Africa and an attempt is to show their views of foreign societies as an approach not only to understanding the cognitive undergrowth of foreign policies but also illuminating rival views about what is valuable and basic in the domestic society. (Staniland, 1991; Hunt 1989; Kitagawa and Hirata, 1999) The main purpose of this chapter is to examine how Japan and Japanese people reacted and responded towards the independence movement or the building of new states on the African continent in the period of the late 1950s and the early 1960s since the Afro-Asian Conference held at Bandung in Indonesia in 1955. (Okakura, 1986; Miyagi 2001) This chapter is mainly based on the contemporary documents published within Japan. The order of discussion in this chapter will be as follows.

Firstly various issues existent between the post-war Japan and Asia and Japan's position in the context of post-war world politics are to be investigated briefly. The second thing attempted is a survey of main articles which appeared in the leading Japanese newspapers such as *Asahi* and *Mainichi* in order to know how the Japanese press reported African affairs. Thirdly, official and unofficial recognition of the political upheavals on the African continent will be examined. Special attention will be paid on the *Diplomatic Blue Books* of MOFA (Ministry of Foreign Affairs), the *White Paper on International Trade* of METI (Ministry of Economy and Industry) and reports which appeared in the periodicals published by business organizations. The fourth to be considered was the views held by those Japanese intellectuals who were interested in the development of African affairs and tried to disseminate their knowledge of Africa into the ordinary people in Japan.

1 Post-War Japan in Asian-African Relations

Post-War Japanese diplomacy is discussed centering on the relations with the United States. Negotiation between occupied Japan and the United States concerning peace and security constructed the political, economic and international framework of post-war Japan. Thereafter discussion on the Japanese foreign policy, either cooperation with or autonomy to the United States was developed primarily centering on relations with the United States. Under the Cold War system, Japanese behavior was defined by the Japanese alliance with the United States. (Morikawa, 1979)

It is frequently pointed that post-war Japanese policy toward Asia has consistently toed the United States line. For instance the most important issue for the post-war Japanese foreign policy toward Asia was Chinese issues but Japan could not move until reconciliation between the United States and China in 1970s. During the World War II Japan invaded and occupied Asia under the reckless strategy of the Greater East Asian Co-prosperity but her defeat excluded Japan from this area. Only after the San Francisco Peace Treaty Japan regained her independence and it was in Bandung Conference in 1955 that Japan faced with Asian and African countries directly. Invitation of Japan to the Bandung Conference was a product of international political dynamism in Asia. This Conference is widely known as the arena of the union of newly independent Asian and African countries that hoisted the flag of anti-colonialism. In reality this conference was strongly coloured by the Cold War system in which Asian countries of liberal camp defended against offensive move by communist or neutral countries like India and China. India tries to call China to the conference. On the contrary Pakistan, who was in the liberal camp and opposed to India, schemed to invite Japan, an important figure as anti-communist, in order to put a check on the India-China leadership in this conference. Japan tries to survive this difficult situation by the passive political stance but her existence itself had already become an important part of international politics regardless her intentions.

Japan's return to Asia was confined to South-East Asia because of being shut out of Japan-China relations under the Cold War. The beginning of Japan's return to Asia coincided with the final settlement of the negotiation of war reparations in the latter half of 1950s. Among others special attention should be paid on Japanese reparations to Indonesia in 1957. Because the reparation to Scarno had a significant political meanings for the United States, who secretly intervened with the civil war in Indonesia in order to plot to overthrow the Scarno government. However, in the end the United States approved Japan's reparation even though it meant to support the Scarno government, because the United States was afraid about such development in which Soviet Russia and China went into the vacancy which appeared after the collapse of the Nederland's power in the decolonization process. Therefore, Japan's reparation to Indonesia was situated in the political crossroad of the Cold War, decolonization and Japan's Return to Asia. (Ampiah, 1997 : 34-35)

It was in the mediation process of an outbreak of Malaysian dispute in the first half of 1960s when Japan stepped into the political affairs. Great Britain, who could no longer sustain her colonies, integrated former Malaya and Singapore into new state, Malaysia. Scarno blamed this development for Britain's conspiring an encircling net toward Indonesia and militarily conflicted against Malaysia and Britain. Japan tried to mediate in several ways as the only state of the liberal camp which had close relations with Indonesia. Eventually it proved to be difficult to conclude this mediation itself successfully. However, it might be thought that this happened in the process which British influence was reversed by the rise of Japanese presence in this area even though Britain as an empire mainly based on Singapore still kept prominent position in South East Asia. (Miyagi, 2001 : 20-57)

Britain, who had been annoyed by the nightmarish memory of Japanese southward movement in the pre-war and during the war, was unpleasant to Japan who stood on Scarno side and intervened into this dispute. Nevertheless Britain was no longer influential toward Japan. Then Britain tried to put pressure upon Japan in collaboration with the United States as the most effective way. Britain reluctantly realized that the United States expected Japan, who had two faces both as a member of liberal camp and as a member of Asian and African countries, had played a significant role in order to mediate radical communism and socialism into moderate one rather than took risks to keep pace with Britain who was criticized as imperialist and colonialist. Thus the United States stood behind Japanese active mediation. Finally Britain found the way out of this dispute by entrusting the leadership to Japan. South East Asia shifted to the period of "economic development" under the political stability or suffocation as a result of collapse of Scarno rule owing to the coup in fall of 1965.

"The Age of Economy" in Asia which emerged since the latter half of 1960s might be called as the phenomenon like "Japanization of Asia". Newly independent Asian countries after the World War II did hope both political independence and economic prosperity. And as the means to materialize these purposes rightist and leftist ideologies and political systems had great relevancy. Japan, who was once completely destroyed during the War, advanced the way to "high economic growth" which was expected to cope with class struggle. Another means against this line was "revolution". In Asia the representative state which challenged to construct its polity by means of revolution was the People's Republic of China. Revolution in China was very much influential to all over South East Asia because of the existence of extensively scattered Chinese diaspora. (Sugihara, 2003: 13-36)

Japan's mediation to Malaysian dispute strongly aimed at detaining Scarno's rapid rapprochement to Chine in order to construct Beijing-Jakarta axis. The communist party in Indonesia had been gaining its influence and at the beginning of 1965 schemed to withdraw from the United Nations and construct "the Second United Nations" in corporation with China. Although Scarno was leaning toward accepting the proposal by Shojiro Kawashima, vice president of Liberal Democratic Party, Chou En-lai persuaded him to reconsider Japanese proposal. In the post-war Asia, Indonesia was one of the typical state building cases where there was no common ground except for the former Netherlands' colony. It was symbolic fact that, Japan and China that tried to materialize the two different ways of state building in the post-war Asia played at tug-of-war. (Miyagi, 2001 : 157-163)

In due time in the first half of 1970s China steered to the dramatic US-China reconciliation. Recently diplomatic documents of US-China Talks toward Nixon's visit in 1972 was opened to the public. It is very impressive that in those days political leaders in China were strongly conscious of the pressure of Japan. Political leaders of China recognized the US-China rapprochement as the effective means to put a check on the Soviet Russia and at the same time was remarkably precautious against Japan who attained high economic growth and emerged as a prominent economic power because they had suffered bitter memory during the World War II.

On considering the post-war China-Japan relations, China consistently situated this relation as a factor of her world strategy but Japan recognized it in the framework of bilateral relations. From the Chinese point of view its peace offensive to Japan in the 1950s and thereafter was a strong measure which reflected both her world strategy and domestic and overseas political struggles. In contrast in the post-war international politics Japan considered its foreign policy solely based on bilateral relations, in particular witnessed in the US-Japan alliance. Looking at US's prominent position in the post-war world, it might be thoughtful that it was an inevitable preference for Japan. However, thinking exclusively from such a framework, one may lose sight of the reality of the post-war Japan. It is necessary to acquire the view point of Japan within multi-lateral relations and the recognition of its position in the international political arena.

In the post-war international politics Japan was drawn as if it were silent and absent except for Japan-US relations because it unconsciously reflected the feelings of Japanese people who burned their countries and neighborhood to the ground during the World War II and kept a distance from the reality of international politics. When Japan was extremely small country in terms of population and economic viability, her absence and silence was likely to be. However, the state which has more than one hundred million people and the worldly prominent industrial and economic power inevitably became an essential factor of the international politics in Asia. It is no doubt that economic and political behavior by Japan in terms of bilateral relations substantially influenced the dynamism of international order in Asia. (Miyagi, 2003)

2 News of Independent Africa in the Leading Japanese Newspapers

As it is generally thought that newspapers play a significant role in forming public opinion and ordinary peoples' imaginations about the contemporary African affairs, it is worthwhile to examine the way Japanese newspapers treated the independence of Africa. At present in this chapter a survey is given only on the reports of African affairs which appeared in the two leading Japanese newspapers —*Asahi* and *Mainichi*— and some features will be indicated. It was during the decade of 1950s when Libya, Sudan, Morocco and Tunisia achieved their independence, the war broke out in Algeria, and the wave of political independence in North Africa lapped the shore of Sub-Saharan Africa. Gold Coast was independent from Great Britain in 1957.

The general survey on these two newspapers is summarized as follows. (Kawabata, 1990, 1994) Firstly in the first half of the 1950s, quite a few articles regarding African affairs appeared in the Japanese newspapers. However, in the latter half of the same decade, specifically after the Afro-Asian Conference in Bandung the quantity of articles increased and interpretative articles of specific issues were also reported.

Secondly as far as North Africa and Sudan are concerned, an outline of the process of political development to independence could be understood solely by reading the articles which appeared in the Japanese newspapers. However, the reports of the Japanese newspapers about West, Central, East and Southern Africa were too fragmentary for one to gain a systematic understanding of the problems that arose in each area.

Thirdly valuable information based on reports on the spot and interpretative reports by Japanese correspondents steadily increased and were offered to the ordinary people in Japan. Regrettably, by today's standard some of their reports contained inappropriate terms and expressions, primarily based on stereotyped imagination invented by the Europeans in early times.

Fourthly it had already become a well known fact in the late 1950s that on the "Dark Continent" there had appeared an awaking of nationalism and the rise of liberation struggles to pursue independence against colonial rule. It was particularly after the Afro-Asian Conference that the reports which clearly and precisely showed these developments to the Japanese people became remarkable.

To be added finally, it is thought that it is of decisive importance to ascertain what kind of relations defined the Japanese framework to recognize and approach Africa by conducting a minute investigation into what information and knowledge was brought or was not brought to Japan in order to understand Japanese perceptions of Africa in the context of global decolonization processes. (Kawabata, 1990; Kweku, 1997; Sono, 1993)

3 Japan's Official and Unofficial Mind to Africa : MITI, MOFA and Private Economic Organization

(1) The Ministry of Industry and Trade : *White Paper on International Trade*

In 1951 the Ministry of Industry and Trade published the first issue of a *White Paper* while the Minister Ryutaro Takahashi took office. Exports surplus to Asia and special procurement by the Korean War could not upset the unfavourable international payments owing to 50% of total imports from the United States and unfavourable invisible trade. In coping with this situation the MITI not only externally promoted exports to the dollar areas, exploitation of the new import market, and cooperation to industrialization and development in Asian countries, but also internally pursued its policies to encourage the heavy chemicals industry in order to facilitate the exports of capital goods. (MITI, 1951)

Looking through each volume of the *White Papers* from the mid 1950s to 1960, a significant proportion of Japan's trade with the Sub-Saharan Africa was accounted for by British West Africa, British East Africa and the Union of South Africa. In these years such ministers as Tanzan Ishibashi, Mikio Mizuta, Shigesaburo Maeo, Tatsunosuke Takasaki and Hayato Ikeda arrived at the office one after another. (MITI 1955, 1956, 1957, 1958, 1959, 1960) It is very interesting in the sense that the *White Paper* published under the Minister Etsusaburo Shiina expressed an expectation of an increase of exports to newly independent Africa. In 1960, 17 independent states were given birth in Africa and formed their influential spheres in world politics. Although these newly independent African countries had close economic connections with such former metropolitan countries as Great Britain and France and a significant proportion of their overseas trade depended upon those countries, each country tended to push forward their nationalist policy in order to build autonomous economies.

The *White Paper* in 1961 indicated like this. "Immediately after their independence the political situation in African countries is not stable and there are not fully stable markets for Japanese exports. However, when Japan makes more efforts to develop their markets, including generous economic assistance, these are changed into the promising markets in the long run." (MITI, 1961)

(2) The Ministry of Foreign Affairs : *Diplomatic Blue Book*

It was in 1957 when the first issue of the *Diplomatic Blue Book* was published and in the same year Ghana was born. In this issue such topics as economic assistance to West Africa and correction of Japan's one sided trade with Ghana and Nigeria were taken up and reported. The minister of Industry of Eastern Province and the minister of Development of Western Province visited Japan from Nigeria in 1955 and 1956 one after another. (MOFA, 1957)

The fourth volume of *Diplomatic Blue Book* in 1960 is particularly impressive precisely because in 1960 it reported that Africa was awakening politically, Britain's Prime Minister Macmillan traveled around Africa where he delivered his well known speech of "Wind of Change", and diplomatic exchange with Ghana and its friendly mission visiting Japan. In these events it is unfailingly recognized that an active diplomacy of Japanese government developed in this period. The administrative and investigative activities toward Africa were also strengthened in the Ministry of Foreign Affairs. Coordination among each section in the MOFA was promoted in order to adopt thoroughgoing measures to plan Japan's diplomacy and to prepare for the necessary information and sources to analyse the state of affairs on the African continent. In 1960 in Sub-Saharan Africa, a consulate general was newly founded in Salisbury, the capital of Federation of Rhodesia and Nyasaland. And Tokyo decided to raise the consulate of Nigeria to the status of the embassy after independence. Moreover the first meeting of the heads of Japanese diplomatic missions to Africa was held in London in order to establish a basic policy to judge Japan's relations with Africa. In this *Diplomatic Blue Book* such reports were found as Japan's economic cooperation with Africa, negotiation of trade agreements between Japan and the Federation of Rhodesia and Nyasaland, and a trade conference on the issue of cotton imports from Egypt. (MOFA, 1960)

(3) Kansai Economic Federation : *Monthly Keizaijin*

Keidanren (Federation of Economic Organizations) was born in August 1946, to help to reconstruct the war-devastated Japanese economy and Nikkeiren (Japan Federation of Employers' Association) was created in April 1948 as an umbrella organization of industrial and regional employers' associations to build a sound labour-management relationship in Japan.[1] (FOEO, 1966) This section takes up an interesting article which appeared in the *Monthly Keizaijin* (*Homo Economicus*) published by Kankeiren (Kansai Economic Federation) which was established in October 1946 (KEF, 1976) and suggests what areas Japanese business circles were concerned with and what kind of recognition it had shown about the economic, political and social development in those areas.

Economic organizations of Kansai (Western part of Japan) were very much involved in the trade with, interested in and concerned with East, Central and South Africa. A good example is the article on "Three African Problems – Central Africa, Union of South Africa and Kenya –" placed in the *Monthly Keizaijin* (July, August and September 1953). The discussions in this article written by Shotaro Miyano and Naoko Asada is summarized as below. (Miyano and Asada, 1953)

Anti-colonialism movement on the African continent has become an obviously established fact at last. In Tunisia, Morocco and Kenya indigenous people resorted to force. In Central Africa, African people disagreed with the building of the Central African Federation and the situation seemed to move from the stage of negotiation to the one of action. In these circumstances on the African continent the general election of the Union of South Africa was carried out on 15 April in 1952 and its curtain closed in the victory by the Nationalist Party under the leadership by Daniel Malan who campaigned the election by his slogan of strengthening racist policy. On the background of this extreme racist policy in South Africa, fear was sensed by the South African whites against the colored people living not only there but also the whole continent and its policy has been deeply connected with questions of

117

the labour market in which white industrialists and agriculturalists keenly longed to acquire stable and abundant black labour that formed an essential basis of the political economy of the Union. The rebelling by the colored people against the racist policy had already started in the moderate form to improve their political and economic life since the beginning of 20th century, but in 1952 this movement was organized on a nation wide scale and resorted to more positive action.

In the Central African Federation the direct and the most serious fear for indigenous peoples was loss of their land accompanied with the advance of industrialization by economic integration. The problem of this Federation became one big turning point not only to define the indigenous peoples' course of action but also to decide the fate of the historical process in this area.

In Kenya Mau Mau continued the battle against the British Army and lots of life, money and goodwill seemed to be lost in this area. It can never be thought that Mau Mau was suppressed by the armed forces. The Kikuyu peoples' fight meant not only an anti-British struggle but also all the coloured peoples' fight against white peoples. Although Britain viewed the position of this area in the world economy as relatively low compared with Central African Federation and the Union of South Africa and depended less upon it in terms of economic relations, this area was the only one where secondary industries developed relatively among the three British East African dependencies. Moreover this area was very important as a strategic base to secure the safe route to the Indian Ocean.

Japanese business circle paid much attention to the development in these areas as a trade market and Japanese advancement to this market primarily based upon the Anglo-Japanese economic and political relations. To be added at the same time the Japanese business world turned its attention to the change of indigenous peoples' lives simply because they were consumers of Japanese merchandize in both the pre-war and post-war period. (Kitagawa, 1994, 2001)

4 Japanese Intellectuals and Independent Africa

Japanese academics and journalist "discovered" Africa in the late 1950s and 1960s, when its colonial empires collapsed and more than forty new states were established. All at once intellectuals in Japan were faced with the challenge of investigating and interpreting the meaning of African nationalism and self-government. This section is an inquiry into the nature and causes of the different ways that Japanese opinion makers reacted to events in newly independent Africa.

In Japan many people were interested in Africa in the period of independence and tried to disseminate the knowledge of this movement. Three prominent intellectuals are taken among these and very briefly introduced in this section.

(1) **Terutaro Nishino** (1914 –1993)

Nishino was born in Tokushima and was a specialist of Asian and African

Studies. In 1937 he graduated from Kyoto University and worked at Hokoku Fire Insurance Company. After this Nishino served in the naval attaché office and became a special researcher in the State Library of the Japanese Parliament. He made an enormous effort in establishing African Studies in Japan. (JAAS, 1983) Nishino modified the image of Africa as the "Dark Continent" by publishing his book of *Africa Breaks the Chain* (1954) and introduced the African peoples fight against imperialism and colonialism. He also collected and classified works written about Africa by Japanese and traced the history of political, economic and cultural exchange between Japan and Africa. (Nishino 1963) Among many works written by Nishino, *Africa at Crossroad* (1967) and *Newly Emerging States and their Pains* (1968) were highly recommendable as valuable enlightening books. Additionally Japanese edition of *Awaking Africa* written by B. Davidson (*Ahurika no Mezame*, 1959) was translated by Nishino.

(2) **Kanjiro Noma** (1912 –1975)

Noma was born in Kobe and left many works as a prominent writer. While a student in the Medical Department of Keio University, he was arrested against violating the Peace Preservation Law and imprisoned for four years immediately before the World War II. Because in the pre-war period Noma worked as an editor in Kaizosha Publishing Company, which played a significant role to disseminate progressive ideology including Socialism and Marxism in the pre-war Japan. In the post-war period Noma worked as an editor in Iwanami Publishing Company. After these services he started writing and introduced the independence movement and state building in Africa to the ordinary people in Japan.

In *The Origin of Discrimination and Treason: Apartheid State* (1969), racial discrimination of South Africa was described in detail and cries by political offenders were included. In the 1970s Noma introduced to Japanese people the reality of armed struggle in Portuguese Angola, Guinea Bissau and Mozambique and organized supporting campaigns for the liberation struggle camps. Moreover a series of Noma's translations of Kwame Nkrumah's writings into Japanese should be added, including *Ghana : An Autobiography of Kwame Nkurumah* (1957) and Jomo Kenyatta's *Facing Mount Kenya (*1938). Noma was the Japan's anti-apartheid leader and described the origins of the formation of this group. Noma summarized like this.

"My first meeting with South Africans took place in 1963 in Moshi at the foot of Mt Kilimanjaro in East Africa. It was the third Asia-Africa Peoples' Solidarity Conference and the South African delegates asked for a special meeting with the Japanese delegation. The South African side was represented by seven men, including Oliver Tambo and Moses Kotane. The Japanese group included the Socialist Party Dietman Mineo Tanaka, his wife Sumiko, a member of House of Councillors, myself and five others. The South African delegation charged that

Japan, a non-white nation, ignored moves to cut off diplomatic relations with South Africa or to impose economic sanctions suggested in the UN resolutions and was in fact the only non-white nation to have diplomatic relations with South Africa. The atmosphere was not tense but the criticism was severe, and we felt it was a challenge to Japan's progressive forces. I had heard of apartheid but was not well aware of how terrible it was. On behalf of the group, Tanaka said that when we returned to Japan, we would make efforts to fulfill their expectations but it was an embarrassing moment for us. After this external appeal The South African Anti-Apartheid Planning Committee was set up under the auspices of the Asia-Africa Solidarity Committee of Japan but the Japanese anti-apartheid movement was soon faced with a serious internal crisis. Because the deep rift between China and the Soviet Union caused Japanese left-wing organizations either divide along pro-Soviet and pro-Chinese ideologies or to go independently". (Noma, 1969; Osawa, 1963) Then Noma managed to extricate the anti-apartheid movement to create his own independent group, called the South African Problem Discussion Group.

(3) **Koshiro Okakura** (1912 –2001)
Okakura was born in Tokyo and a specialist of international politics. In 1936 he graduated from Tokyo University and engaged in Indian studies at the Institute of East Asia Studies. Since 1947 he was very much involved in the study of the US world policy and the nationalist movement in Asia. Then Okakura taught at Doshisha University, Osaka University of Foreign Studies and Daito Bunka University. In 1961 he founded the Institute of Afro-Asian Studies. The purpose of this Institute is to advance Asia-Africa-Latin America Studies and bring up the promising specialists in Japan. He left a lot of academic works, and among them, *An Introduction of Asia-Africa Problems* (1962) and *An Introduction to the Study of Nonaligned Movement* (1961) were published and widely read in the early 1960s. (Afro Asian Institute of Japan, 1961)

In his introductory book to Asia and African problems, Okakura notified the Japanese people how the people of Asia and Africa and their leaders fought against imperialism and colonialism in order to hasten independence, construct peace and democracy, and promote social reform. Also in his articles such as "Asia, Africa and Japan" (1961) and "An approach to Asia and African Problems" (1962) Okakura warned that Japanese people who seriously learned the movement in Asia and Africa should watch the state of affairs in Japan in the same manner. (Okakura, 1961, 1962)

Although after opening the country to overseas in the mid nineteenth century, Japanese devoted themselves to imitate and import systems and cultures of advanced countries, they seldom showed their interests in the countries that achieved independence after the Meiji Restoration. Japanese intellectuals in the first half of Meiji period were very much concerned with the colonization process in Asia and Africa by the invasion of European Imperialist countries and warned the Japanese people in fear of the influence to Japan. However, they did not study the countries that newly emerged in the latter half of the 19th century.

If one put up an exceptional example, one cannot help paying attention to Nichinan Fukumoto (1857-1921) and his book on *New State Building* (*Shin Kenkoku* in 1900). This book is a highly admired one in the sense that it considered the economic weakness in which such new states as the Republic of South Africa (Transvaal) and the Orange Free State tried to exploit gold and diamond by depending upon foreign capital investment and to accomplish capitalist economic development in the late 19th century when Imperialist invasion was predominant. This book might be thought as the first one in which newly emerging states were discussed by Japanese. (Fukumoto, 1868)

As far as Japanese government and its ruling classes had always turned their eyes mainly to such advanced countries as Europe and the United States, prominent figures outside of government who wrote about newly emerging states tended to stand in critical manner against government. This tendency seemed to be sustained until the period immediately after the World War I but seemed to disappear under the suppressive measure taken by the authorities concerned.

After the World War II much attention was paid upon new countries in Asia and Africa. Many works were written in the mood of sympathy and praise to the liberation struggle against imperialism and colonialism. Those who stood in this manner attempted to express that Japan which was ruled under the United States occupation should try to acquire national independence by learning the liberation struggle against imperialism and colonialism and constructing solidarity with newly emerging states. However, it was concluded that all the domestic problems which new independent states had to solve were caused by the intervention of imperialist and colonialist. Therefore there emerged an optimistic view of liberation struggle in which the suffering of new independent states was solved by tightening their political solidarity and strengthening their voices in the international political arena. On the contrary the interests in new independent states by government and business world gave birth to another view of newly emerging countries. For government and business circles new independent states were the object of economic and technological assistance and trade and investment markets. (Nishino 1963) In this regard, a genealogy of the theory of newly emerging countries lacked the ability to analyse sufferings objectively.

Notes

1 Keidanren and Nikkeiren have maintained close contacts and performed their tasks. However, the times have changed during the half-century of postwar history. The economic agenda and labour issues have become inseparable and, coupled with the declining birthrate, aging of the population and diversifying interests among Japanese, emerging issues such as social security

reform, employment and labour issues, and educational reforms have become ever more important for Japan's business community. Against such a historical background, the two organizations amalgamated and the new Japan Business Federation (Nippon Keidanren) was born May 28, 2002.

References

Alden, C. and Hirano, K., (2003), *Japan and South Africa in a Globalizing World : A Distant Mirror*, Ashgate, Hampshire.

Ampiah, K., (1997), *The Dynamics of Japan's Relations with Africa : South Africa, Tanzania and Nigeria*, Routledge, London.

Afro-Asia Institute of Japan, (1996), *Monthly Bulletin*, No. 1, April.

Federations of Economic Organizations, (1996), *The Activities of Keidanren [Keidanren no Katsudo]*, Tokyo.

Fukumoto, N. (1990), *New State Building [Shin Kenkoku]*, Tokyo.

Hunt, M. H., (1987), *Ideology and U.S. Foreign Policy*, Yale University Press, New Haven.

Japan's Association for African Studies, (1983), "A 20 year History of Japan Association for African Studies" *[Nihon Ahurika Gakkai 20 nen Shoshi]*, *Journal of African Studies*, Special Issue for the 20th Anniversary, May, pp. 1-35.

Kansai Economic Federation, (1976), *The Three Decade History of Kankeiren [Kankeiren 30 nen no Ayumi]*, Osaka.

Kawabata, M., (1994), *Africa and Japan [Ahurika to Nihon]*, Keiso Shobo, Tokyo.

Kawabata, M., (1990 a), "Independence of Africa and Japanese Press (1)" [Ahurika no Dokuritsu to Nihon no Hodo], *Ryukoku Law Review*, Vol. 23, No. 2, September, pp. 486-452.

Kawabata, M., (1990 b), "How Independence of Africa was reported to Japan ?", *Quarterly Bulletin of Third World Studies [Ajia Ahurika Kenkyu]*, Vol. 30, No. 4, pp. 2-25.

Kitagawa, K., (1994), "Japan's Economic Relations with South Africa in the Post-War Period: Determinants of Japanese Perceptions and Policies towards South Africa", Shikoku Gakuin University, *Ronshu*, No. 86, July, pp. 87-100.

Kitagawa, K. and Hirata, M., (1999), *Anatomy of Imperialist Mind [Teikoku Ishiki no Kaibogaku]*, Sekai Shiso Sha, Kyoto.

Kitagawa, K., (2001), "Japan's Trade with East and South Africa in the Inter-War period: A Study of Japanese Consular Reports", *Kansai University Review of Economics*, No. 3, March, pp. 1-41.

Marshall, P.J., (1996), *The Cambridge Illustrated History of the British Empire*, Cambridge University Press, Cambridge.

Ministry of Foreign Affairs, (1957), *Diplomatic Blue Book [Gaiko Seisho]*, No. 1, Tokyo.

Ministry of Foreign Affairs, (1960), *Diplomatic Blue Book [Gaiko Seisho]*, No. 4, Tokyo.

Ministry of Industry and Trade, (1951), *White Paper on International Trade [Tsusho Hakusho]*, No. 1, Tokyo.

Ministry of Industry and Trade, (1956), *White Paper on International Trade [Tsusho Hakusho]*, No. 6, Tokyo.

Ministry of Industry and Trade, (1957), *White Paper on International Trade [Tsusho Hausho]*, No. 7, Tokyo.

Ministry of Industry and Trade, (1958), *White Paper on International Trade [Tsusho Hakusho]*, No. 8, Tokyo.

Ministry of Industry and Trade, (1959), *White Paper on International Trade [Tsusho Hakusho]*, No. 9, Tokyo.

Ministry of Industry and Trade, (1960), *White Paper on International Trade [Tsusho Hakusho]*, No. 10, Tokyo.

Ministry of Industry and Trade, (1961), *White Paper on International Trade [Tsusho Hakusho]*, No.

11, Tokyo.

Miyagi, D., (2001), *Bandung Conference and Japan's Return to Asia : Between the U.S. and Asia [Bandon Kaigi to Nihon no Ajia Fukki Amerika to Ajia no Hazama de]*, Soshisha, Tokyo.

Miyagi, D., (2003), "The Identity of Japan in the Post-War Asia", *Sobun*, January-February.

Miyano, S. and Asada, N., (1953), "The Three African Problems – Central Africa, Union of South Africa and Kenya – " [Mittsu no Ahurika Mondai : Chuo Ahurika, Minaim Ahurika Renpo oyobi Keniya] *Monthly Keizaizin*, July pp. 80-84, August pp. 69-74, September pp. 60-62.

Morikawa, J., (1997), *Japan and Africa: Big Business and Diplomacy, Hurst and Company,* London.

Moss, J. and Rvenhill, J., (1985), *Emerging Japanese Economic Influence in Africa : Implications for the United States,* University of California, Berkely.

Nishino, T., (1963), "On Economic Research in Africa between the Wars (part 1) – an Aspect of African Studies in Japan –" [Ryotaisenkan ni okeru Ahurika Keizai Chosa – Nihon ni okeru Ahurika Kenkyu no Hitokoma to shite], *African Studies [Ahurika Kenkyu]*, Vol. 1, No. 1, pp. 5-16.

Nishino, T., (1968), *Newly Emerging States and their Pains [Kuno suru Shinko Shokoku]*, Kinokuniya Shoten, Tokyo.

Noma, K., (1969), *The Origin of Discrimination and Treason: Apartheid State [Sabetsu to Hangyaku no Genten : Aparutoheito no Kuni]*, Riron Sha,Tokyo.

Okakura, K., (1986), *Bandung Conference and Asia in the 1950s [Bandon Kaigi to 50 nendai no Ajia]*, Institute of Eastern Culture Studies, Daito Bunka University, Tokyo.

Osawa, M., (1963), "Africa – Report on the Asia-Africa Solidarity Conference –" [Ahurika – Ajia-Ahurika Rentai Shokoku Kaigi kara Kaette] *Buraku*, No. 164, August, pp. 49-63.

Research Organization of Asian and African Studies, (1966), *The Present State and the Problems of Asian and African Studies in Japan [Nihon ni okeru Ajia Ahurika Kenkyu no Genjo to Kadai]*, Tokyo.

Sono, T., (1993), *Japan and Africa : The evolution and nature of political, economic and human bonds, 1543-1993*, HSRC Publisher, Pretoria.

Staniland, M., (1991), *American Intellectuals and African Nationalists, 1955-1970,* Yale University Press, New Haven.

Sugihara, K., (2003), *The Rise of Asia-Pacific Economy [Ajia Taiheiyo Keizai no koryu]*, Osaka University Press, Osaka.

Ch 10
Conclusion : Retrospectives on and Prospects for Japanese Policy on Africa

Today, the relationships between Africa and Japan, whether they are government-to-government or private sector, are truly wide ranging. This can be surmised by observing the number of embassies that Japan and the nations of Africa have opened in each other's countries. Just by looking at the number of agreements and treaties that have been entered into between the two, one can see that the diplomatic ties have deepened. The people of Africa live in an age of changing nation states and politics, and the political and diplomatic actors have become truly diverse.

What is contemporary Africa seeking by entering into relationships with Japan? How should Japan approach the ever-changing socio-political circumstances in Africa? What common goals should they set for building future relationships? This chapter attempts to answer these questions by examining the following topics: (1) charting the basic framework of Japanese diplomacy with the nations of Africa; (2) reviewing the changes in Japan's relationships with the nations of Africa during the Cold War Era; (3) examining relations between Africa and Japan in the post-Cold War period, specifically focusing on the Tokyo International Conference on African Development (TICAD) process until the beginning of the twenty-first century; and (4) considering what the common challenges are in building sustainable relationships between Africa and Japan in the new century.

1 Basic Framework of African-Japanese Relations
(1) Basic Framework of Newly Emerging African Nations' Relations with Japan

In the late 1950s and 1960s, many African nations, burning with the desire to build new nation states, became independent. For many, the process of independence continues today. Common challenges for African nations include forming a nation state, breaking away from colonial economies, restoring human dignity, and taking their due place in the international community. It can be said that African-Japanese relations have been formed under the political actions of African nations striving to overcome challenges such as these. In the course of doing so, there are a number of factors that have had an impact on relations between the two.

It goes without saying that the main players are the state governments.

Consequently, the basis of African diplomacy has been bilateral, taking place between the various nations within the African continent and countries outside the African continent. The nations of Africa share a common past in that they were colonized. Whether the previous colonial masters were good or bad, they served as a type of 'reference society' as the African countries built independent nation states and formed external relations. In the course of forming these relationships, some African nations did develop bilateral diplomacy individually. However, in the case of former French territories, a special relationship has been maintained, officially known as the Central African Franc (CFA) zone. The 14 nations of Central Africa, which historically have had deep ties with France, have also formed regional cooperative organizations: the West African Economic and Monetary Union (UEMOA) and the Economic and Monetary Community of Central Africa (CEMAC). Similarly, the nations that are former British territories have maintained relationships with the former colonial power Britain and conduct diplomacy in a forum called the Commonwealth Heads of Government Meeting (CHOGM). In addition, regional cooperative organisations such as the Economic Community of West African States (ECOWAS) and the Southern African Development Community (SADC) have been formed.

In contrast, under the Pan Africanism advocated by Kwame Nkrumah, independent African nations have cooperated on a continental level to build relationships with nations outside of Africa. For example, although there were differences between the radical Casablanca Group and the moderate Monrovia Group, the Organization of African Unity (OAU) was established in 1963, and the concept of 'One Continent, One Destiny' has been maintained to this day. This spirit has also been inherited by the African Union (AU). After independence and during the Cold War Period, the newly emerged nations of Africa adopted a clear stance that they did not belong to either the Eastern socialist camp or the Western liberal camp, joining the non-aligned movement. They also cooperated with each other and conducted diplomacy in international arenas, such as the United Nations Economic Commission for Africa (UNECA), which takes place at the United Nations (UN), to deal with and reform the existing international system. (Gordon and Gordon, 2013)

As described above, the political relationships between Africa and Japan were formed bilaterally, with continental organisations as well as with regional cooperatives; through international movements and organisations, and so on.

(2) Basic Framework of Post War Japanese Relations with Africa

In 1952, Japan had regained its sovereignty, but was still carrying the experience of defeat from the war. Thus, Japan's post-WWII diplomacy took the path of pacifism, antinationalism, and passive cooperation with the international environment, using the United States as a model 'reference society'. At the time, Japan's top priorities with regard to foreign policy were sustained economic growth, minimal defence spending, and the alliance with the US. Since the formation of the two-party system in 1955, in which the conservative parties merged, three cooperative principles became clear, advocating liberalism, Asia centrism, and UN centrism. Japan's Africa policy was defined by these interconnected elements, the specific aspects of which were: Japan's economic needs, a Japan-US Security Treaty, and political awareness about Japan's international standing and role. (Iokibe, 2006)

The fact that Japan emerged as an industrial nation after WWII and showed a strong interest in increasing exports and securing sources of raw materials hastened the establishment of diplomatic relations with African nations. However, the expansion of trade relations between Japan and Africa was hindered by the influence of the former colonial powers over the African nations and the invocation of trade restrictions in Article 35 of the General Agreement on Tariffs and Trade (GATT). In order to resolve such issues, the Japanese government made an effort to build friendly relations with Africa, largely through the use of development assistance. As Japan accumulated payment surpluses and the Japanese economy grew rapidly, Japan was able to start assistance programs, and contributed to the formation of the Development Assistance Committee (DAC) at the Organisation for Economic Co-operation and Development (OECD) in 1961. (Engel and Olsen, 2005)

The Japan-US Security Treaty was another reason Japan became involved in Africa. Japan's role of supplementing and reinforcing US strategic interests became an important element of its foreign policy. As a result, Japan's Africa policy during the Cold War took the form of following US initiatives in Africa. (Morikawa, 1997)

The final element that defined Japan's relationship with Africa was the fact that Japan, as an industrial nation, sought a commensurate role and standing in international society. Since joining the UN in December 1956, Japan had tried to use international organisations to resolve issues in a manner commensurate with its economic standing. In doing so, Japan made efforts to gain favour with African nations in order to gain recognition at the UN and other international forums. (Alger, Lyons and Trent, 1995)

2 Chronology of African-Japanese Relations during the Cold War Period
(1) Africa under the Development Plans and Japan Pursuing Trade and Investment Opportunities (1960 to 1973)

With the establishment of diplomatic relations with African nations, Japan expected to be able to expand trade and investment opportunities. For the African nations, there was the hope that securing markets for agricultural produce and raw materials, and the income that would be obtained as a result, would promote industrialisation and economic growth.

In the 1960s, Japan's industrial production grew in leaps and bounds and the market share of Japanese goods in international markets also increased. The Japanese government was seeking the possibility of securing sources of raw materials for industrial use from Africa as well. In 1965, imports of Zambian copper ore increased, and in 1967, Japan entered into a copper ore development agreement with Zaire, and with Uganda as well. Japan invested large amounts of money in the extraction industry, particularly in South Africa under the apartheid regime, in order to obtain strategic mineral resources such as coal, chrome, manganese, vanadium, and platinum.

There were two aspects to Japan's strategy for the newly independent African nations: to establish friendly relationships with Kenya and Tanzania—non-aligned nations who were influential on the pro-West side—and to strengthen ties with mineral resource supplier nations including Gabon, Nigeria, Zaire, and Zambia. When an African nation became independent, Japan quickly established diplomatic relations and, after negotiations, entered into long-term agreements for the supply of raw materials. These friendly relations were useful in opening up new markets for Japanese products in African nations, which were striving to stimulate economic growth. Although the value of exports of industrial goods to Africa continued to rise, the value of imports from Africa remained small, creating a trade imbalance. African nations, increasingly concerned about a blowout in the trade deficit, invoked Article 35 of GATT, which stipulates the non-application of the agreement between particular nations. Trade missions were dispatched from Japan to Africa to address the trade imbalance. (MOF, 1963, 1972)

(2) Japan's Pursuit of Resource Security and Africa's Criticism of Japan (1974 to 1979)

The oil shock of October 1973 had a serious impact on the world economy, and Africa was no exception. Economic growth rates fell and per capita income also stagnated. The cost of energy and raw materials went up, sparking inflation while simultaneously triggering recession. Demand for African-produced petroleum also ebbed and there was no growth in exports. African nations tried to pull through the current deficit using borrowings of private sector money and aid from foreign countries.

Meanwhile, the Japanese government changed its national security objectives to secure a stable supply of resources. Cheap petroleum was the wellhead of economic growth and fundamental to the Japanese economy. The cutback of oil supplies by Arab nations triggered the Tokyo stock market collapse and a state of emergency was declared. In December 1973, the Arab nations' oil supplies recovered, and Japan had learnt a difficult lesson. As a result, Japan sought alternative sources of supply for the strategic mineral resources and energy essential for its industrial production. Of the African nations, Japan focused particularly on crude oil from the Congo (Brazzaville), Niger, Nigeria, and Zaire, and uranium from Namibia. (MOF, 1977)

In January 1974, Prime Minister Kakuei Tanaka relaxed the conditions on Japanese aid and loans. As a result, the proportion of aid to Africa that was from Japan rose. In addition, a preferential tariff scheme was introduced and tariffs on African goods were lowered. As a result, African exports to Japan increased. By 1982, Japan had become South Africa's second most important trading partner. However, this drew heightened criticism of Japan by other African nations on account of South Africa's apartheid policy. But since South Africa had become such an indispensable source of mineral resources, Japan was not prepared to jeopardise its economic relationship with South Africa, even despite the fact that UN economic sanctions had been imposed.

In October 1974, Foreign Minister Toshio Kimura, in a bid to blunt such criticism, made a historic visit to Africa, the first by a Japanese Foreign Minister. In July 1979, Foreign Minister Sunao Sonoda visited the Ivory Coast, Kenya, Nigeria, Senegal, and Tanzania. These visits deepened Japan's understanding of Africa's process of independence from colonialism and the anti-apartheid struggle and demonstrated Japan's intent to promote friendly relationships with African nations. (Engel and Olsen, 2005; Mangala, 2011)

(3) African Poverty and Increasing Amounts of Aid from Japan (1980 to 1992)

Around 1980, African nations went into a serious economic slump recording negative growth. The second oil shock of 1978-79 and the US high-interest rate policy had triggered a global recession. African nations were hit hard by deteriorating terms of trade, falling exports, and rising interest rates on foreign debt. In 1984, there was also a drought across much of Africa, which took its toll on agricultural production. Moreover, in the early 1980s, the key donor nations, such as the UK and the US, cut their aid budgets. For the African nations, external assistance was essential to ride out their economic woes, so, in exchange for assistance, International Financial Institutions (IFIs) introduced Structural Adjustment Programs (SAPs). This was also the period in which the US was pressing Japan to reduce its trade surplus. While the US was pressing Japan to take its fair share of the Western collective security burden, it was simultaneously calling for the Japanese government to increase the amount of aid it extended to Africa to deal with the trade surplus and to alleviate the negative results of structural adjustment programs. (MOFA, 1981; Koppel and Orr, 1993)

Driven by the recommendations of its comprehensive security cabinet meeting to maintain the US-Japan relationship and to deal with IFIs' Africa projects, the Japanese government decided to increase the amount of aid it gave to Africa. In doing so, the formative principles for Japan's aid policy became the 'development of developing nations' and 'humanitarian assistance'. Policy ideals changed from 'pursuit of the national interest' to 'promoting socio-economic stability and global peace'. This indicated that Japan was on the verge of being able to be directly involved with Africa. This direction is evident in the fact that Japan was proactively involved in the debate that led to the adoption of the Declaration on the Critical Economic Situation in Africa at the 1984 UN General Assembly. In fact, Japan was the only country that extended a substantial amount of financial assistance for the structural adjustment programs and special loans to deal with Africa's economic crisis. In this way, from the mid-1980s, Japan's new policies towards Africa reflected the fact that Japan began to play a role in the international community commensurate with that of an 'economic superpower'. (MOFA, 1992; Stein, 1998, OECF, 1989)

3 Africa and Japan in the Post-Cold War Period : TICAD and NEPAD
(1) Africa's Economic Recovery and Japan's Active Involvement
For Japan, which had adopted a foreign policy that conformed to the post-WWII world order, the end of the Cold War and the aftermath of the first Gulf War meant that Japan had to review its policy goals and how they were pursued. Japan began to redefine the concept of comprehensive security. *The Official Development Assistance (ODA) Charter* was drafted in June of 1993. Japan's affirmations included observance of the principal of democracy and basic human needs, the promotion of economic development, and cutting military spending and arms transfers. International peace and stability were made the focal point for Japan's own wellbeing and international relations. (Engel and Olsen, 2005)

The end of the Cold War took away Africa's strategic importance and the nations of the West abandoned policies of intervening in the internal affairs of African nations. African nations were left to deal with the failure of the structural adjustment programmes and the political changes that occurred as a result. In the first half of the 1990s, new leaders came on the scene in Africa and nations began trying to achieve political stability, democracy, and economic recovery through their own efforts.

Amidst this situation, Japan emerged as the only nation state prepared to raise its level of aid to Africa and was therefore able to exert influence over political and economic changes. In addition, Japan tried to transform relations with Africa by developing a pro-active agenda. The most notable initiative in this process was the Partnership for Democratic Development (PDD). Under this initiative, institutional support is given to various sectors of African nations, such as law, administration, elections, and mass media.

It was necessary for Japan to participate in the UN's Peacekeeping Operations (PKO) in order to play an international role commensurate with its economic might and receive recognition. Japan began participating in the PKO by contributing personnel to the United Nations Operations in Mozambique (UNOMOZ) in May 1993. Following this, Japan sent personnel to the International Peace Cooperation Corps in Rwanda to assist with delimiting the border between Ethiopia and Eritrea, and contributed to disarmament in Sierra Leone. (Lehman, 2010)

One of Japan's contributions to Africa is the fact that through jointly holding high-level meetings it became involved in the prevention and resolution of African conflicts. Examples of this are the 1995 and 1996 conferences held in Tokyo: "Peace and Development—the Issues around Conflicts in Africa" and "Conflicts in Africa—the Road to Nation Building in the Post-Conflict Period", respectively. Japan has supported humanitarian activities and refugee relief activities through the Office of the United Nations High Commissioner for Refugees (UNHCR) and the United Nations International Children's Emergency Fund (UNICEF). In addition to providing material support and financial assistance to UN organisations, Japan also contributes to the eradication of HIV/AIDS, polio, and malaria through the US-Japan Common Agenda.

Since *The East Asia Miracle* was published in 1993, Japan, together with newly developing Asian nations, has tried to promote the Asian development model to reduce poverty through economic growth as a key strategy for African socio-economic development. Japan has driven this initiative by supporting workshops in various regions across Africa, encouraging economic development based on the experiences of Asia, and promoting Asia-Africa cooperation. It is hoped that such institutions will form the foundation for establishing South-South cooperation and will also bring the experiences of developing Asian nations to Africa, with Japan providing the necessary expertise, capital, and logistics, to make the transition process easier. (Engel and Olsen, 2005)

(2) Birth of the New Partnership for African Development (NEPAD)

In the 1990s, the new leaders who emerged as a result of democratic elections started to think about strategies for Africa to develop by its own hand. For example, South Africa's President Mbeki advocated an 'African Renaissance' to rejuvenate Africa for the purpose of economic recovery and democratization in Africa. This thinking took shape in the Millennium Africa Recovery Plan (MAP) in 2000. Similarly, in Senegal, at President Wade's initiative, the 'Omega Plan' was formulated to put in place and maintain an African economic development infrastructure.

The MAP and Omega Plan were integrated and, in July 2001, the New African Initiative (NAI) was adopted at the 37th session of the OAU Assembly of Heads of State and Government. NAI was renamed New Partnership for African Development (NEPAD) in October of that same year. At the G8 Genoa Summit in 2001, the African heads of state sought support from the international community in order to implement NEPAD. The G8 developed nations welcomed NEPAD's adoption of the Genoa Plan for Africa, and the Africa Action Plan was adopted at the Kananaskis Summit. These events verify the fact that NEPAD obtained the support of the international community.

The preconditions for African development, such as peace, democracy, human rights, and good governance, as well as the actions that African nations should aim for and the goals they should achieve, are clearly specified in NEPAD. NEPAD's action plan had the cooperation of the African Development Bank (AfDB) and the United Nations Economic Commission for Africa (UNECA) and was put together by a steering committee made up of the five nations that played a leading role: South Africa, Nigeria, Senegal, Algeria, and Egypt. What is worth noting in the implementation of NEPAD is the introduction of a peer review mechanism. The purpose of this was to promote the adoption of policies that would be useful in making progress with political stability, sustainable development, and economic integration and to improve governance by allowing African nations to monitor each other's implementation of NEPAD. (Obayashi, 1999, 2003)

The developed nations drafted the G8 Africa Action Plan in response to the voluntary actions and self-help efforts of African nations. 'Selective implementation of aid' was adopted in this action plan to enhance support for African nations achieving results based on the idea of 'enhanced partnerships'. Japan had already incorporated selective implementation of aid into its Africa policy based on the various principles of its ODA Guidelines. The development philosophy of *ownership* by the African nations and *partnership* with the international community is common to NEPAD, the G8 Action Plan, and the TICAD process promoted by Japan. (Lumumba-Kasongo, 2010; Kawabata, 2003, 2006, 2012)

(3) Tokyo International Conference on African Development (TICAD), 1993-2008

The TICAD process began when Western nations began to focus on incorporating Eastern countries into the post-Cold War market economy because it was gradually becoming apparent that aid to Africa was not getting results. TICAD I was held on 5-6 October 1993, and was attended by participants from 48 African nations, 13 donor nations, 10 international organizations, and more than 45 observer nations and organisations, including non-government organisations (NGOs). TICAD II was held from 19-21 October 1998. Representatives from 80 countries attended, including 13 heads of donor countries, accompanied by other senior government officials, representatives from 40 international organisations and private-sector organisations, and representatives from 22 NGOs. Five years later, TICAD III was held from 29 September to 1 October 2003, and was attended by 50 African nations, 47 regional and international organisations, and many NGOs. Then from 28-30 May 2008, TICAD IV was held in Yokohama and was attended by representatives of 51 African nations, including 41 heads of state, 34 development partner nations and Asian nations, and representatives of international organisations. A summary of each of the TICAD conferences is given below.

(a) TICAD I

The topics of debate at TICAD I were political and economic reform, development of the private sector, regional cooperation and integration, international cooperation, and the 'Asian experience and African development'. Of these five themes, the new topic was 'Asian experience and African development'. Foreign Minister Yoriko Kawaguchi said, 'In our thinking, we believe that Asian experiences and specialized knowledge regarding development are useful for African development in the 21st Century'.

The key messages that were conveyed at this conference were that the purpose of growth is to alleviate poverty and to promote African participation in the global economy. The *Tokyo Declaration on African Development* was adopted in order to achieve these goals. The *Declaration* is about embarking on political and economic reforms in the African region under the slogan of 'good governance'. Avenues for making use of Asian experiences in order to assist with African development were also pursued. The important factors that contributed to noteworthy performance of East Asian economies were cited in this declaration, including rational application of macroeconomic policies, maintaining political stability, long-term investments in education, and the development of human capital. The declaration was manifest in the first Asia-Africa Forum (AAF), organised in Indonesia in 1994, which sought to promote cooperation between Asia and Africa. (ACT 3003 Activity Report Writing Committee, 2004; ACT 2003 Activity Towards TICAD III, 2003)

The Asia-Africa Forum was started as part of the South-South cooperation and tried to encourage direct dialogue and cooperation between African and Asian policymakers. The intent was to jointly formulate specific sectors where African development could potentially benefit from Asian experiences. The Bandung Framework for Asia-Africa Co-operation, which incorporates ongoing interaction between leaders of these two regions, was adopted at the forum. Initiatives such as development of human capital and formation of systems for that purpose, improvement of productivity in the agricultural sector, and obtaining the required capital for the development process were recommended. Regional level workshops were also held. One such workshop was held in Harare, Zimbabwe, in July 1995, and another in Yamoussoukro of the Ivory Coast, in July 1996. These workshops were held to evaluate the results of TICAD I and verify the principles of the overall TICAD process. In addition, the Second Asia-Africa Forum in Bangkok, Thailand, was held in June 1997 in preparation for TICAD II, and was designed to confirm the points agreed on at the first forum. TICAD I was successful at least in that it made the international community aware that various African economic and social problems remained fundamentally unresolved. (Ampiah, 2007, 2011; Lee, 2010;

Miyagi, 2001, 2004)

(b) TICAD II

A preparatory meeting for TICAD II was held in Tokyo on 10-11 November 1997, and was attended by senior officials from 46 African nations, 9 Asian nations, 13 donor nations, 6 international organisations, and representatives of regional organisations. At this meeting, three main goals were discussed: verification of the initiatives since TICAD I, confirmation of the key themes of the Agenda for Action, and the establishment of an Agenda for Action Preparatory Committee to be proposed at TICAD II. Topics discussed at this Preparatory Committee meeting also included social issues (eradication of poverty, education, sanitation, gender, and population), farming and the environment, conflict resolution, development, and governance.

The Tokyo Agenda for Action was adopted at TICAD II in October 1998. The issues discussed included reducing poverty by speeding up economic growth and sustained development, and the integration of African nations into the global economy. More specifically, the Agenda for Action pertained to the following three areas: (1) Social development (education, sanitation and population, and other measures to assist people living in poverty), (2) Economic development (development of the private sector, industrial development, agricultural development, and foreign debt), and (3) Building the foundations for development (good governance, conflict prevention and post-conflict development). The goal was set to cut the proportion of the population living in extreme poverty to at least half of the current level by 2015 through implementation of the above measures.

The fact that education was the focus for 'human capital building' stood out in the Tokyo Agenda for Action. This was due to an awareness that education that had been the key to accelerating growth and delivering sustained poverty reduction in East Asian nations. The goal was to have at least 80% of children receive a complete primary education by 2005, and to have universal primary education by 2015. It was also hoped that by 2005, that the adult illiteracy rate (particularly for women) would be lowered to half its level in 1990. The Agenda emphasised leaving the initiative for development up to the African nations. A TICAD II review meeting was held in November 1999, and at the same time the Asia-Africa Investment and Technology Promotion Centre (AAITPC) (also known as the Hippalos Centre) was established in order to institutionalize the economic ties between the regions, and the Africa-Asia Business Forum (AABF) was held. The former is a project that is implemented through contributions to Japan's UN Industrial Development Organization (UNIDO) and this centre was established in Malaysia. The latter is supported by using the 'Human resources development fund', which Japan contributes to the United Nations Development Programme (UNDP). (ACT 3003 Activity Report Writing Committee, 2004; ACT 2003 Activity Towards TICAD

III, 2003)
(c) TICAD III

Two preparatory meetings were held in New York in June and September 2001 leading up to TICAD III. At these meetings, 'African ownership of development initiatives' was emphasised and senior government officials were invited to attend from the nations promoting NEPAD, namely, South Africa, Senegal, Nigeria, Algeria, and Egypt. The addition of NEPAD to the TICAD process gave legitimacy to Japan's initiatives.

In December 2001, a TICAD ministerial-level meeting was hosted by Japan, the UN, the Global Coalition for Africa (GCA), and the World Bank. At this meeting, an exchange of opinions was conducted on TICAD II and on the development plans drafted by the African nations. Specifically, there was discussion of putting foundations in place for development, investing in human capital, reducing poverty through economic growth, South-South cooperation, regional cooperation, and the principles for development. The Chair's statement emphasised collaboration between NEPAD and TICAD.

A TICAD preparatory meeting was also held in New York, in July 2002, in Japan's representative office in the UN. At a senior government officials' meeting in Ethiopia, in March 2003, the high priority themes were identified. From May to June, a meeting regarding Southern African issues was held in Pretoria, South Africa, a meeting regarding the East African and North African issues was held in Nairobi, Kenya, and a meeting regarding West African issues was held in Yaoundé, Cameroon. The purpose of these meetings was to deepen understanding of region-specific issues and to proceed with work in various sectors according to the priorities in line with regional circumstances. This series of regional summits indicated Japan's resolution to respect African ownership of the development process. In July, an Organisers' Steering Committee Meeting was held in London and, in August, an international symposium of NGOs was held at the United Nations University.

TICAD III was held in Tokyo from 29 September to 1 October 2003. At the conference, international community support for NEPAD was mobilised, and a broad-ranging debate was conducted over the initiatives of both Africa and the donor nations towards African development. One objective that emerged was the specific aim of forming new partnerships with Asian nations. On the first day of the conference, the previous TICAD process was examined and a comprehensive approach regarding the pressing issues was explored. On the second day, the most serious problems, HIV/AIDS and unemployment, were discussed. The importance of Asian-African regional cooperation was emphasised, including technical assistance from Asian nations to African nations, as well as the importance of trade and investment. There was also a call for cooperation to prevent reoccurring conflicts.

Since the start of the TICAD process, Japan had contributed 12 billion dollars in economic aid to Africa and conducted training in various fields for 10,000 African people. In addition, Japan sent 7,000 experts to Sub-Saharan Africa for the purpose of development assistance. Prime Minister Junichiro Koizumi announced that Japan would provide Africa with a total of one billion dollars in grant aid over five years. These grants were intended for education, supplying clean water, and humanitarian aid for victims of HIV/AIDS.

Finally, the 'TICAD Tenth Anniversary Declaration' was announced, delineating the direction for the TICAD process. At this time, the 'TICAD III Chair's Summary' was released, which summarised the specific priorities. The philosophy of 'human security' pursued by Japan was incorporated into the 'TICAD Tenth Anniversary Declaration' confirming its importance in African development. (Inoguchi, 2005; ACT 3003 Activity Report Writing Committee, 2004; ACT 2003 Activity Towards TICAD III, 2003)

(d) TICAD IV

A TICAD IV regional preparatory conference for Southeast African nations was held in Lusaka, Zambia, in October of 2007, and a regional preparatory conference for Northwest African nations was held in Tunis, Tunisia, in November 2007. During this time, the TICAD IV Secretariat was set up within the Ministry of Foreign Affairs of Japan. In addition, in early January 2008, Foreign Minister Masahiko Komura visited Tanzania and gave a speech entitled 'Partnership to Create a "Happy and Healthy Africa"' and Former Prime Minister Yoshiro Mori gave a speech at the 10th AU General Assembly on the significance of TICAD IV.

TICAD IV was held 28 - 30 May 2008, in Yokohama. Its basic message was 'Aiming for a Happy and Healthy Africa - The Continent of Hope and Opportunity'. Under this banner, direction for African development was discussed with a focus on accelerating economic growth, establishing human security, and dealing with environmental and climate change issues. In attendance, there were 41 heads of government, including Prime Ministers, representatives from 51 African nations, 34 development partners and Asian nations, and 74 international organisations and regional organisations, as well as representatives from the private sector and civil society. There were over 3,000 attendees making this the largest international conference in Japan's diplomatic history.

Japanese Prime Minister Yasuo Fukuda, who served as overall Chair of the conference, announced Japan's aid strategy to Africa: to double Japanese ODA and to support the doubling of private investment as well. Former Prime Minister Mori, who had served as the Chair of TICAD III, served as MC of the conference.

The conference drafted three documents. The 'Yokohama Declaration', indicated political will regarding the initiatives and direction for future African development. Based on this declaration, the 'Yokohama Agenda for Action', indicated specific initiatives for the future TICAD process. Finally, the 'TICAD Follow-up Mechanism', intended to verify the status of implementation of the TICAD process. Details of the discussions conducted at TICAD IV were compiled into the 'TICAD Chair's Summary'. (Obayashi, 2006, 2009)

TICAD IV acknowledge that political and economic progress that had been achieved in Africa since TICAD III while also confirming the need to intensify initiatives by the international community toward further African development. The recent self-help efforts in Africa were acknowledged and the direction of strengthening the cooperative relationship between the AU and TICAD was indicated. However, Africa was (and is) faced with a mountain of issues such as rapid population growth, unemployment problems in farming villages and cities alike, infectious diseases, and soaring food prices, necessitating a renewed call for continued focus. TICAD IV confirmed that in order to solve problems such as these, economic growth needed to be accelerated by promoting industrial and agricultural development, trade and investment, and human resource development. Additionally, the conference recognized the need to address the Millennium Development Goals (MDGs) relating to the socio-economic aspects of human security, the entrenchment of peace and establishment of good governance, and issues relating to the environment and climate change. Partnerships needed to be further broadened, collaboration with existing initiatives attempted, and proactive participation in civil society would be required. (Lumumba-Kasongo, 2010; Mangala, 2010; Yamada, 2011)

4 Prospects for African-Japanese Relations in the New Century
(1) Africa as the Front Line of Japanese Diplomacy
One of the elements that make up the historical background of the relationship between Japan and the nations of sub-Saharan Africa is the spirit of the 1955 Asia-Africa (Bandung) Conference. This conference covered the desire to pursue independence from colonialism, to be neutral during the Cold War period (non-aligned movement), and to develop economic cooperation and technical assistance between the attending nations. Japan, as the only industrial nation present, was eager to provide the necessary technology for the economic development of the newly emerging nations of Southeast Asia and in exchange obtain the rights to access their raw materials and markets. This might also mean open access to African materials and markets, as Africa was beginning to show signs of independence. Japanese initiatives through TICAD can probably be seen as an extension of the commitments made at the Bandung Conference in 1955.

Japan's attitude toward Africa during the Cold War period was one of caution. In a period of international political and economic change, the wisdom of dealing with Africa at all was called into question. For example, after the 1973 Oil Shock, Foreign Minister Toshio Kimura chose to visit the African continent, urging Japan to establish politically friendly relations for economic reasons. Although it was dangerous diplomatically, Japan was then able to weather the impact of expanded trade relations with South Africa through negotiations.

New developments in international politics, such as the demise of the apartheid regime in South Africa, followed by the collapse of the Soviet Union, added a new dimension to Japan's relationships with African nations. At TICAD I, Prime Minister Morihiro Hosokawa declared, 'Japan will continue to proactively support Africa's political and economic reforms' and, 'Since the end of WWII, Japan has benefited greatly from the generous support extended by the international community. Now is the time for Japan to repay that goodwill by playing a proactive role in assisting Africa'. TICAD marked the start of a new phase in African-Japanese relations and indicated a change in Japan's attitude to the 'Africa problem'.

Prime Minister Mori's visit to sub-Saharan African nations in January 2001 marked a turning point in African-Japanese relations. During his visit to Africa, Prime Minister Mori gave a speech entitled 'Africa and Japan in the New Century' and declared that finding solutions to Africa's problems was a high priority on the Japanese foreign policy agenda. Not only did Prime Minister Koizumi announce 'Collaboration between Japan and Africa - Specific Actions' to the African diplomatic corps stationed in Tokyo in June 2002, he also made the keynote speech at TICAD III in 2003. When he visited Addis Ababa in May 2006, Prime Minister Koizumi, in a speech entitled 'Africa becoming the Birthplace of Self-help Efforts', outlined Japan's diplomacy with Africa. He announced specific assistance measures and detailed the areas in which Japan should cooperate with Africa for achieving international peace and stability. It was envisaged that the relationship between Japan and the African continent required either the Prime Minister or the Foreign Minister to visit at least once a year. Africa became the 'front line' of Japanese diplomacy.

TICAD IV was held in Yokohama in May 2008. The conference was covered by 1,300 journalists of whom 1,000 were domestic and 300 were international. Despite the fact that this conference drew so much attention, it seems that, since 2006, Japanese diplomacy with Africa has lacked something of its previous vigour. That is because, since 2006, the conditions that made TICAD diplomacy possible in the past have been gradually diminishing.

One such condition is Japan's economic position in the world. At the turn of the 21st Century, Japan was no longer an economic super power, and in some aspects had also ceased to be the dominant economy in Asia. As of 2001, Japan's ODA had lost its standing as the top source of aid to Africa. Japan was no longer a key creditor either. Consequently, it became impossible to mention the 'Pax Nipponica' with a straight face anymore. This was symbolized by the article titled, 'Japan is Fading', which ran in the 24 August 2009 edition of *Newsweek*.

Japan's diminishing role in Africa is also suggested by the fact that not one of the Prime Ministers who have taken over from Prime Minister Koizumi in 2005 has visited Africa. Even Prime Minister Taro Aso, who has experience working in Africa in the past, did not have enough time to visit Africa. Given that Prime Minister Aso and those who succeeded him had such short terms in office, this is understandable. Even so, it seems that Japan's African diplomacy is moving into a post-TICAD stage and losing its dynamism as a result.

(2) TICAD IV Follow Up and Looking Toward TICAD V

TICAD IV compiled specific assistance measures for Africa into the Yokohama Agenda for Action. At the same time, the TICAD Follow-up Mechanism was established to monitor the status of the assistance measures announced through the TICAD process. This mechanism consists of three layers. The first is the Secretariat, which was established under the Director General, African Affairs Department, Ministry of Foreign Affairs of Japan. The purpose of the Secretariat is to gather and analyse information in conjunction with the related government organisations regarding the status of TICAD priority areas, as well as carrying out PR activities. The second is the Joint Monitoring Committee of the TICAD Process. This committee puts together an annual progress report and a committee meeting is held once a year. Third is the TICAD Follow-up Meeting. This ministerial-level meeting is held once a year to verify and evaluate TICAD-related activities based on the annual progress report.

A meeting of the Joint Monitoring Committee of the TICAD Process was held on 9 February 2009. The meeting was chaired by Yoshitaka Akimoto, Director-General, African Affairs Department, Ministry of Foreign Affairs of Japan. Participants included relevant government agencies and organisations, TICAD organisers (UN, UNDP, World Bank), the AU Committee, the African diplomatic corps stationed in Tokyo, and the donor nations. The meeting verified the state of progress regarding assistance measures to Africa. On 11 March that same year, the 'TICAD Follow-up Symposium - Japan's Efforts to Promote Peace and Stability in Africa: the Case of Sudan and Beyond' was held at the United Nations University. This symposium commenced with Luka Biong Deng, Minister of Presidential Affairs in the Office of the President, Government of Southern Sudan (GOSS) reading the speech of the First Vice President. This was followed by an exchange of opinions between experts from home and abroad on the topics of 'The current state of the peace process between North and South Sudan and Japan's assistance in Sudan' and 'The importance of enhancing the peacekeeping capabilities of African countries and Japan's assistance'.

Additionally, the inaugural TICAD Ministerial Follow-up Meeting was held in Botswana on 21-22 March 2009. At this meeting, Foreign Minister Hirofumi Nakasone announced assistance to progress the Yokohama Agenda for Action (two billion dollars in grant aid/technical cooperation, three-hundred million dollars in food/humanitarian assistance, and two-hundred million dollars to fight infectious diseases) and to implement the commitments made at TICAD IV. The second meeting was held in Arusha, Tanzania, on 2-3 May 2010. At this meeting, Foreign Minister Katsuya Okada served as co-chair together with the Tanzanian Finance and Economic Affairs Minister Mustafa Mkulo. Foreign Minister Okada declared the new government's resolve to implement the TICAD IV commitments and indicated that Japan would work on certain initiatives in the future. These included extending assistance with three projects designed to enhance cooperation with Africa: two billion dollars in loans over two years for infrastructure projects designed to boost African recovery from the economic crisis, one billion dollars in support of maternal and child health in order to achieve the MDGs, and support based on the 'Hatoyama Initiative' to deal with climate change. The third meeting was held in Dakar, Senegal, on 1-2 May 2011. The meeting was attended by Japanese Foreign Minister Takeaki Matsumoto and State Secretary for Foreign Affairs Chiaki Takahashi. Foreign Minister Matsumoto co-chaired the meeting with Minister of Foreign Affairs Madické Niang. Foreign Minister Matsumoto expressed Japan's appreciation for all of the support that had been rendered to Japan by African nations and the international community in the wake of the Great East Japan Earthquake. He declared Japan's determination to faithfully implement the TICAD IV commitments in order to actively promote peace and stability in the international community. The Foreign Minister also announced that in order to contribute to African economic growth, the sectors and countries eligible for loan projects would be handled flexibly and that the granting of new loans would be sped up. State Secretary for Foreign Affairs Takahashi proposed that TICAD deal with the changes occurring in Africa and the Middle East from a 'human security' perspective, calling for cooperation between Japan and the nations of Africa in promoting UN Security Council (UNSC) reforms. This would include striving for close cooperation towards COP17, convening in South Africa, and formulating a strategy for low-carbon growth and sustainable development in Africa.

At TICAD IV, Prime Minister Fukuda had announced the formation of joint missions to promote trade and investments in Africa. The joint missions, made up of representatives from the Japanese business community, political circles, relevant government ministries, and agencies, would be put together to visit the Southern, Eastern, and Western regions of Africa. Their purpose would be gathering information, networking, and unearthing potential trade and investment projects. They would achieve this by having meetings with key leading figures in each country, exchanging opinions with the local chambers of commerce and industry as well as corporate representatives, visiting various facilities, etc. It was expected that dispatching these missions would further expand trade and investment between Japan and Africa, contribute to accelerating economic growth in Africa, and be useful in promoting Japan's resource diplomacy. Since 2008, several joint missions have been sent to various nations across Africa. In September 2008, the Joint Mission for Promoting Trade and Investment in East Africa was led by Parliamentary Vice-Minister for Foreign Affairs Nobuhide Minorikawa. This was followed by a string of missions led by Parliamentary Vice-Minister for Foreign Affairs Yasutoshi Nishimura: the Joint Mission for Promoting Trade and Investment in Central and West Africa, the Joint Mission for Promoting Trade and Investment in Southern Africa, and the Joint Mission for Promoting Trade and Investment in East Africa. In October 2008, the Joint Mission for Promoting Trade and Investment in Central and West Africa was dispatched. In September 2010, the Joint Government-Private Sector Southern African Trade and Investment Mission was dispatched, and in October 2011, the Joint Government-Private Sector African Trade and Investment Mission visited Sudan, South Sudan, and Kenya.

The fourth TICAD Ministerial Follow-up Meeting was held in Marrakesh, Morocco, on 5-6 May 2012. At this meeting, the state of progress on the Yokohama Agenda for Action was examined, and discussions were held in preparation for TICAD V, which is scheduled for 1-3 June 2013. The attendees outlined the current state of African development and discussed the key themes for TICAD V, as well as the format and approach. The attendees recognized that TICAD V should work towards achieving comprehensive and sustainable growth as well as towards building strong societies in Africa. A senior working group level meeting was scheduled for autumn 2012, to be held in Burkina Faso, and a ministerial level preparatory meeting was proposed for the first quarter of 2013, to be held in Ethiopia. Prior to this, a meeting of African Ambassadors was held from 14-15 December 2011, at which opinions were exchanged regarding TICAD V and regional situations in Africa. On 21 March 2012, the TICAD V Secretariat was set up within the organization under the Director General, African Affairs Department, in the Ministry of Foreign Affairs of Japan. The secretariat had begun the overall work of setting up and running TICAD V to be held in Yokohama. Moreover, on 12 June the Ministry of Foreign Affairs of Japan and NGOs held their first meeting to exchange ideas regarding TICAD V, and on 2 August, the first government-private sector cooperative conference on the promotion of TICAD V was held. At this conference, there was joint recognition that, while there were business opportunities for Japanese companies in Africa, it would be necessary to invest in industries that would increase in value and add to human resource development in order to promote African business.

Since December 2008, Japan, China, and South Korea have held annual, trilateral consultations on African policy. The fourth consultation fell on 7 December 2011, and took place in Tokyo. At this meeting, the three nations exchanged opinions on their general and economic policies in Africa, as well as political information on Sudan and the Horn of Africa. They discussed initiatives designed to enhance political and economic relationships with Africa as well as cooperation with the AU and with African regional organisations, as well as each of the three countries' frameworks for cooperation with Africa (TICAD V, 2013, the fifth Forum for China-Africa Cooperation (FOCAC), 2012, and the Third South Korea-Africa Forum (KAFs), 2012, respectively). Japan explained its policy of proactively supporting Africa in expanding development aid, trade, and investment; contributing to peace and stability; and dealing with global issues.

(3) Japan and China in Africa

Japan's African diplomacy has been conducted recently amidst a backdrop of heightened Chinese activity on the African continent. In 2005, China overtook Japan and became the second largest importer of African-produced oil. In 2007, Chinese trade with Africa reached roughly three times that of Japan. China has become one of the major trading partners of many countries in Africa, from Angola to Burundi, from Cameroon to the Central African Republic and Chad.

Compared to Japan, China has few restrictions on its actions in Africa. For instance, China will buy what it intends to, heedless of potential consequences or whether their actions antagonise Western nations. Of course, Japan and China are not rivals in the same sense that China and the United States are rivals. What's more, Japan and China are not as yet equal with each other in terms of economic strength. From an economic perspective, for China and Japan, the relationship with Africa may not be as important as the relationship with the neighbouring countries of the United States and Europe. (Raine, 2009)

China is attracting a lot of attention from African politicians. This is not surprising when one considers that China, compared to Japan, is expressing the intention to strengthen all political and economic ties with African nations. Moreover, Africa-China relations have a deeper history compared to Africa-Japan relations. China's major involvement in Africa has given new stimulus to Japan's diplomacy in Africa. A number of aspects of Japan's diplomacy in Africa may be, in part, in response to China's heightened presence in Africa. The Japanese government was relieved that TICAD IV held in Yokohama, in May 2008, had a comparable number of African leader attendees to that of FOCAC, held two years prior in Shanghai. (Taylor, 2009, 2011)

Japan's *ODA White Paper* (2007 edition) states the following in relation to Africa: 'Japan is considering plans to advance infrastructure development in Africa and these include, for example, construction of extensive road networks'. The same message was also present in the 2008 edition: 'Development of regional infrastructure focused on roads and power networks is vital in order to stimulate the acceleration of growth in Africa'. As a result of increased Chinese activity on the African continent, the Japanese government expects a range of business communities to become even more proactive in various sectors. (JICA, 2007)

However, the differences in Japan and China's foreign policy approaches to Africa should not be exaggerated. If anything, Japan has created African development plans with a focus on cooperation with international organisations and with other developed nations. Specifically, in regards to TICAD IV, Japan has consulted not just with multilateral organisations, but also donor nations and aid agencies in order to achieve the results of the Yokohama Declaration. Even the TICAD II declaration of 1998 stated that African nations would probably agree to and implement economic reforms or structural reform programs supported by the Bretton Woods system. The fact that the United Nations Development Programme (UNDP) and the World Bank were key organizers of TICAD I is broadly remembered.

It is worth pointing out that Japan and China's diplomatic approaches on Africa differ on the following points. First, China does not view the Bretton Woods system as having much legitimacy. That is because China has doubts about the process by which the system was made - by whom and for whom it was made. This is not the case for Japan. Japanese activity in Africa has been constrained by the national interest and by its intention to remain an important member of the so-called Western block. In spite of these facts, or because of these facts, two aspects have appeared in Japan's foreign policy on Africa: the ongoing aspects and the changing aspects.

As the only non-European nation that has succeeded in industrialising, and as a sympathetic supporter that pro-actively participated from the outset in the Africa-Asia group, it is natural that Japan has been regarded by the post-Colonial nations of Africa not only as a reference country but also as a development partner. However, at times, Japan's motives in seeking economic security and international legitimacy in an US-Europe centric world, have, by necessity, taken a different course from that desired by many African nations. Until recently, Japan was not only the first non-European nation to successfully industrialise, but also the first non-European economic superpower. The fact that Japan has had a close alliance with the West in the post-WWII period is also reflected in its policy on Africa.

While the rise of China has added a new member to the non-European nations who have successfully industrialised, in some aspects, its ideology is out of sync with those of Japan and the West. Whether this fact should be welcomed or denigrated depends on each party's perspective according to where they stand.

Controversy is also arising in Africa regarding China's emergence. This is because opinion is divided amongst the African nations as to whether China is starting to emerge as a new colonial power, or whether it is a true partner for African development. While the degree differs, similar doubts arose in the past regarding the relationship between Africa and Japan. By observing this retrospective on the past half century of Japanese foreign policy on Africa, one might infer that what preordains the results of interrelationships between countries is not so much the intentions of the nations, but rather the degree to which their interests coincide. (Adem, 2006; Harneit-Sievers, Axel and Naido, 2010; Cornelissen, Chru and Shaw, 2012)

References

ACT2003 Activities Report Writing Committee ed., (2004), *A Decade of TICAD from a Citizen's Perspective - Citizens' Actions Towards TICAD III (ACT2003) Activities Report.*

ACT2003 (Activities Towards TICAD III) ed., (2003), *Collection of Declarations and Other Documents Issued by International Conferences on African Development 1993 – 2003.*

Adem, S., ed., (2006), *Japan: A Model and Partner: Views and Issues in African Development,* Leiden, Brill.

Alger, C. F., G. M. Lyons and J. E. Trent, eds., (1995), *The United Nations System : The Policy of Member States,* Tokyo, United Nations University Press.

Ampiah, Kweku, (2007), *The Political and Moral Imperatives of the Bandung Conference of 1955: The Reactions of the US, UK and Japan,* Kent, Global Oriental.

Ampiah, Kweku, (2001), 'Anglo-Japanese Collaboration about Africa in Early 1960s: The Search for 'Complimentarity' in the Middle of Decolonization', *The Journal of Imperial and Commonwealth History,* Vol. 39, No. 2, June, pp. 269-295.

Cornellisen, Scarlett, Fantu Cheru and Timothy M. Shaw eds., (2012), *African and International Relations in the 21st Century,* London, Palgrave.

Engel, Ulf and Gorm Rye Olsen eds., (2005), *Africa and the North : Between Globalization and Marginalization,* London, Routledge.

Gordon, A.A. and Gordon, D.L., (2013), *Understanding Contemporary Africa,* fifth edition, Boulder, Lynne Rienner.

Harneit-Sievers, Axel, Stephen Marks and Sanusha Naido eds., (2010), *Chinese and African Perspectives on China in Africa,* Cape Town, Pambazuka Press.

Inoguchi, Takashi, (2005), *Views on International Politics - Japanese Diplomacy after 9/11 [Kokusai Seiji no Mikata - 9.11 go no Nihon Gaiko],* Chikumashobo.

Iokibe, Makoto ed., (2010), *Japan's Post War Diplomatic History [Sengo Nihon no Gaikoshi],* Third Edition, Yuhikaku.

Ito, Osamu, (2007), *The Japanese Economy - Historic and Contemporary Points of Contention [Nihon no Keizai-Rekishi, Genjo, Ronten],* Chuokoron.

Japan Bank for International Cooperation (JBIC) website https://www.jbic.go.jp/

Japan International Cooperation Agency (JICA), *ODA White Paper* (various editions)

Japan International Cooperation Agency (JICA), (2005), *For a Better Tomorrow for the World - Report on JICA's Initiatives Towards the Millennium Development Goals (MDGs).*

Japan International Cooperation Agency (JICA) website https://www.jica.go.jp/

Kawabata, Masahisa ed., (1994), *Africa and Japan [Ahurika to Nihon],* Keiso Shobo.

Kawabata, Masahisa ed., (2003), *African Renaissance - 21st Century Course [Ahurika Runessansu - 21 Seiki no Shinro],* Horitsu Bunka Sha.

Kawabata, Masahisa and Takehiko Ochiai eds., (2006), *Reconsidering African States [Ahurika Kokka o Saiko suru],* Koyo Shobo.

Kawabata, Masahisa and Takehiko Ochiai eds., (2012), *Africa and the World [Ahurika to Sekai]*, Koyo Shobo.

Kitagawa, Katsuhiko and Motoki Takahashi eds., (2016), *Contemporary African Economics : A Changing Continent under Globalization*, African Development Bank.

Koppel, B. M. and Orr, R.M. ed., (1993), *Japan's Foreign Aid : Power and Policy in a New Era*, Boulder, Westview Press.

Lee, Christopher J. ed., (2010), *Making a World After Empire: The Bandung Moment and its Political Afterlives*, Athens, Ohio University Press.

Lehman, F.P. ed. (2010), *Japan and Africa: Globalization and Foreign Aid in the 21st Century*, London, Routledge.

Lumumba-Kasongo, T. (2010), *Japan-Africa Relations*, London, Palgrave.

Mangara, J. ed., (2010), *Africa and the New World Era : From Humanitarianism to a Strategic View,* London Palgrave.

Ministry of Finance (MOF), *Annual Report of Customs and Tariff* (various editions), Tokyo, MOF.

Ministry of Foreign Affairs (MOFA), *Diplomatic Bluebook [Gaiko Seisho]* (various editions), Tokyo, MOFA.

Ministry of Foreign Affairs (MOFA), website https://www/mofa.go.jp/

Miyagi, Taizo, (2001), *The Bandung Conference and Japan's Return to Asia - Between the U.S. and Asia [Bandon Kaigi to Nihon no Ajia Fukki - Amerika to Ajia no Hazama de]*, Soshisha.

Miyagi, Taizo, (2004), *The Pursuit of Post War Asian Order and Japan - Post War History of 'The Sea of Asia' 1957-1966' [Sengo Ajia Chitsujo no Mosaku to Nihon - Umino Ajia no Sengoshi]*, Sobunsha.

Morikawa, Jun, (1997), *Japan and Africa : Big Business and Diplomacy*, London, Hurst.

Obayashi, Minoru, ed., (2003), *Africa's Challenges - NEPAD (New Partnership for African Development) [Ahurika no Chosen],* Showado.

Obayashi, Minoru ed., (1999), *Africa - The Third Metamorphosis [Ahurika - Dai San no Henyo]*, Showado.

Obayashi, Minoru and Yoko Ishida eds., (2005), *African Policy Citizens White Paper 2005 - Beyond Poverty and Inequality [Hinkon to Hubyodo o Koete],* Koyo Shobo.

Obayashi, Minoru and Yoko Ishida eds., (2006), *African Policy Citizens White Paper 2005 - African Development and Civil Society [Ahurika no Kaihatsu to Shimin Shakai]*, Koyo Shobo.

Overseas Economic Cooperation Fund (OECF), *Annual Reports*, (various edition) Tokyo, OECF.

Raine, Sarah, (2009), *China's African Challenges*, London, Routledge.

Shiba, Yoichiro, (2011), *Introduction to African Business - The Real Picture of the Last Enormous Market on Earth [Ahurika Bijinesu Nyumon - Chikyujo Saigo no Kyodai Shijo no Jitsujo]*, Toyo Keizai Shinposha.

Stein, H. (1998), "Japanese Aid to Africa : Patterns, Motivations and the Role of Structural Adjustment", *The Journal of Development Studies*, 35 (2), pp. 27-53.

Taylor, Ian, (2009), *China's New Role in Africa*, Boulder, Lynne Rienner.

Taylor, Ian, (2011), *The Forum on China-Africa Cooperation (FOCAC)*, London, Routledge.

Wada, Haruki et. al. eds., (2011), *Iwanami Lecture Series, Complete Modern History of East Asia 7 - The Asian Wars Era 1945-1960 [Iwanami Kaze, Higashi Ajia Kingendai Tsushi 7 - Ajia Shosenso no Jidai, 1945-1960 nen]*, Iwanami Shoten.

Yamada, S, (2011), 'The Discourse on Japanese Commitment to Africa: The Planning Process of the Fourth Tokyo International Conference on African Development (TICAD IV)', *Journal of Contemporary African Studies*, Vol. 29, No. 3, pp. 315-330.

Index

Index